THOMAS KINSELLA

A.B

THOMAS KINSELLA
Designing for the Exact Needs

Maurice Harmon
University College Dublin

IRISH ACADEMIC PRESS
DUBLIN • PORTLAND, OR

First published in 2008 by
IRISH ACADEMIC PRESS
44 Northumberland Road   Suite 300
Dublin 4   920 NE 58th Avenue
Ireland   Portland, Oregon 97213-3786

www.iap.ie

British Library Cataloguing in Publication Data
An entry can be found on request

ISBN 978 0 7165 2951 4 (cloth)
ISBN 978 0 7165 2952 1 (paper)

Library of Congress Cataloging-in-Publication Data
An entry can be found on request

Typeset in 11/12.5pt Ehrhardt by FiSH Books, Enfield, Middx.
Printed by Biddles Ltd., King's Lynn, Norfolk

The Glimmer Man

for TK

He has known this half-light
half a century
its blank space
its emptiness

Sitting together in his kitchen
his face soft as when in 86
we argued Thomas or MacNeice

He uses fewer words now
As I lean close I hear him mention
'the harried self'

As we touch stems
a pale light
hisses around us
like gas

CONTENTS

ACKNOWLEDGEMENTS

I wish to thank Thomas Kinsella for his kind permission to quote from his published and unpublished work and to thank the staff of the Robert W. Woodruff Library, Special Collections, at Emory University, Georgia, for their help. Tom and Eleanor Kinsella have been generous and supportive throughout the years when I have been preparing this book. Michael Hayden and Barbara Brown have once again been of great assistance in the preparation of the manuscript.

GENERAL INTRODUCTION

Six years after the founding of the Irish State in 1922, Thomas Kinsella was born and raised in the Inchicore-Kilmainham area west of Dublin. Separated geographically and socially from the city itself, life there was self-contained and intimate, with much visiting between homes of the extended family. There is little direct reference to the childhood world or the locality in his early collections, *Another September* (1958) and *Downstream* (1962). It is only in *Notes from the Land of the Dead* (1972)[1] that he records particulars of family life and family members. That exploration continued in *One* (1974), *The Messenger* (1978), *Songs of the Psyche* (1985), *St Catherine's Clock* (1987), and *The Pen Shop* (1997), so that the locality and family members, previously ignored, become a substantial part of his imaginative world. Apart from one or two poems about specific figures outside the family, the early collections avoid an identifiable reality of place and person. It is as though the issues he deals with – the processes of erosion, change and death – do not manifest themselves at home or at school. Nevertheless, the awareness of mutability was acquired within the rough-and-ready intimacies of a cramped, working-class home. They included the early experience of death when his baby sister, Agnes, died, the terrifying experience of having to face his grandmother on her death-bed, both recalled in 'From the Land of the Dead', and the unforgettable memory of looking into the doomed face of a cousin dying from tuberculosis. Although initially he does not write directly about these matters, they left their mark on his sensibility. Experience helped to keep his feet on the ground with the result that he was closer in spirit to James Joyce's unromantic portrayal of life in *Dubliners* than to W.B. Yeats's commemoration of the patriotic dead or the world of the Big House.

In an interview, John Haffenden asked Kinsella if he had been born in Dublin:

> Yes, born in Dublin in 1928, and raised in a little village near Chapelizod. My father and mother were both from the Liberties area of Dublin, and my grandparents were there, so I grew up knowing a very central part of Dublin – Bow Lane, Basin Lane, the end of the Canal – and aware also of where my

grandparents had come from: in one case, south Wicklow, in the other, near Mullingar. I have a fairly complicated sense of Irish origins mixed up with my own first memories of life on a fringe of Dublin, an almost rural village. My father and his father before him worked in Guinness's: my grandfather ran one of the barges from the brewery jetty to the sea-going vessels in the harbour; my father worked in the cooperage.[2]

By bringing together many of the poems set in the city together with illustrations and a prose commentary, *A Dublin Documentary* (2006) confirms the city's importance in the poet's general development. The chronological order presents the poems as a series of discoveries, expanding radii in which the interaction between the growing child's consciousness and family members is a matter of primary contact. The poet's trust in the given data, including atmosphere and what is merely sensed, is absolute, their importance never in doubt.

Two places are central: the Inchicore-Kilmainham area where he grew up and Percy Place where he lived with his family in the 1970s. Each stage of the documentary is a *via dolorosa* of the psyche, an encounter with an exterior or interior darkness. In his growing years, much of Dublin 'seemed threatening and strange'.[3] When the poet moves to Baggot Street as a young man, it is to 'a dark and unhealthy single room'.[4] In keeping with this atmosphere of the dark unknown, the illustrations are also drained of light.

The anthology introduces the shaping contexts of Kinsella's world. Here are the spots of time, the incidents, places, people and encounters that he identifies as important in his growth. His radiating perception, instinctive at first, then backed by reading, opened his imagination to the possibilities of an interfacing account by which poems about individual family members are fused with echoes and parallels from the past, from mythology and from archetypal patterns. *A Dublin Documentary* describes the start of the poet's journey, its first stations, central figures and significant stops along the way.

While his mother receives little specific attention at any time, apart from general references in *Personal Places* (1990), he paid considerable attention to his father, who was interested in literature, Irish myth and story, politics of the Left and classical music. An admirer of James Larkin, the Labour leader, he was active in unionising workers at Guinness's Brewery. His varied reading is suggested in *The Messenger*: *A Midsummer Night's Dream*, *Sartor Resartus*, *The Divine Comedy*, Moore's *Melodies*. He also read the defining texts of the Left by Marx and Engels and surrounded his two sons, Thomas and John, with books and music. The elder became a poet, the younger a composer. 'It would certainly be impossible', Kinsella told Haffenden, 'to miss what was going on, that a world war was developing and that social issues of various calibres were involved.'[5] The example of his father's espousal of social issues left a permanent mark on his elder son.

Kinsella's reaction to Irish politics is clear. As a young man he was not disposed to glorify nationalists and that included exaggerated accounts of their achievements. He questioned the myths that had developed about participants in the Easter Rising of 1916 and the Anglo-Irish War of 1919–21. He was, for example, critical of the cult that grew around Kevin Barry, whose actual engagement was minimal, and was sceptical about Eamon de Valera's role in the defence of Bolands Mills. The generation of Seán O'Faoláin and Austin Clarke had to recover from their youthful attraction to romantic nationalism and had to deal with the realities of life in a post-Independence Ireland. With his working–class background and more hard-headed outlook, Kinsella was less vulnerable to the seductions of Kathleen Ní Houlihan, although these had been acclaimed at his primary school, St Canice's. O'Faoláin and his fellow rebels responded enthusiastically to Yeats's celebration of nationalists; Kinsella did not, as he makes clear in 'A Country Walk' (*Downstream*, 1962) and 'Nightwalker' (*Nightwalker and Other Poems*, 1968).

The period from 1928 to 1958 was affected by occasional Republican violence and various economic ills. The suppression of the IRA, who disputed the legitimacy of the State, was a continuing test of the new government's resolves to bring peace to the country, but unemployment and emigration were a constant problem. In 1932 the Fianna Fáil government led by Eamon de Valera brought more stability; and although the Economic War, which that administration conducted with Britain, hindered economic development, the government's policy of self-reliance succeeded in pulling the country back from economic ruin. During the Second World War it dealt firmly with Republican dissidents but the romantic nationalism the de Valera government espoused when mated to a conservative Catholicism produced a situation throughout the 1930s and 1940s in which illiberal values, conservative policies, obscurantism and literary censorship were dominant. This was the Ireland that Seán O'Faoláin engaged with through historical biography and editorials in *The Bell* magazine. It was an Ireland that chose isolationism in preference to internationalism and an uncritical glorification of all things Irish, including language, history and culture, instead of refreshing reappraisal. The policy of neutrality during the Second World War compounded the sense of isolation as official policy enshrined the ideal of a Catholic, Gaelic Ireland. The two decades after the war were dispiriting. The economy suffered, national confidence was low and emigration increased to a massive 60,000 in 1958. Kinsella's 'Handclasp at Euston' (*Moralities*,

1960) is a single, representative portrait, but the first thirty years of Kinsella's life took place in an uncertain world where unemployment, economic stagnation, indifference to the needs of the workers and indifference to cultural interests were endemic. Kinsella's view of the 1950s in poems like 'Nightwalker', the collections, *One Fond Embrace* (1988), and *Open Court* (1991) is shaped by this general sense of frustration. It is not a case of rejecting an unpalatable past, but rather one of resigned identification with a neglected generation whose potential was denied.

In an unlucky miscalculation his father moved the family to Manchester just as war started and remained there for three years. Kinsella had immediate evidence of the destructive power of man's capacity for violence. He experienced the air raids and remembers being brought with gas masks into cold cement shelters where people were urged to encourage one another and to 'sing along'. When the family returned to Ireland, they settled into Basin Lane after living in a number of 'primitive places'. There Kinsella followed the movements of the war on a large wall-map. On the day the Germans attacked the Soviet Union his father said, referring to Hitler, 'He's finished.' The war confirmed Kinsella's sense of man's capacity for destruction. It was, he noted later, 'no news that the human mind was an abyss, and that the will, just as much as the imagination, was capable of every evil. But it was something new that in Nazi Germany creatures out of Hieronymus Bosch should have materialised into the world...'.[6] This cracking apart of innocence was fundamental. The discovery of evil is the central preoccupation of 'Downstream' (*Downstream*). It is the issue behind the unleashing of atomic destruction in 'Old Harry' in the same collection. It shapes the disappointment of 'Nightwalker'. In 'Phoenix Park' his wife, Eleanor, asks why he no longer writes love songs for her. He had done so in *Poems* (1956), in fact had come to writing through the urge to find words to express the experience of love, but what he had discovered about man's inhumanity had destroyed that innocence. He dwells on the trauma of this discovery and its effects on the imagination.

University College Dublin, which he entered in 1946, then located at Earlsfort Terrace, not far from St Stephen's Green, released him from the coercive pressures that had marred his years at secondary school. He attended lectures in a variety of subjects – science, economics, English, German – but opted for a position in the Civil Service when he passed the Junior Executive Examination. This was a period of intellectual, imaginative and emotional liberation and growth. He read widely, published poems and stories in the college magazine, *St Stephen's*, and in *Comhar* (an Irish language publication), met people who became important to him – Eleanor Walsh, Liam Miller, and Seán Ó Riada – and moved to a flat in Baggot Street, a short distance from his Civil Service office and from the university to which he returned as a night student.

Eleanor Walsh was a radiology student but had developed tuberculosis and was in St Mary's Hospital, Phoenix Park, across the River Liffey from his first home in Phoenix Street. Love poems in *Another September*, reprinted from *Poems*, commemorate their relationship; throughout his work the flat in Baggot Street is associated with Eleanor, whom he married in December 1955, and with Seán Ó Riada, who extended his knowledge of music. His significance is well attested in several poems, but particularly in *A Selected Life* (1972) and *Vertical Man* (1973). The flat became the setting for 'Baggot Street Deserta', his first major self-examination, and for many subsequent poems. Eleanor's role varies from the beloved in *Poems* to the dramatic partner in 'Wormwood', to the Muse figure in 'Phoenix Park', to the goddess of *Madonna and Other Poems* (1991). In effect she becomes a multiple woman whose importance as an enduring and reliable partner – wife, companion, Muse – is successively affirmed. Her background was very different from his: on her mother's side it included auctioneering and farming in the north of County Wexford; on the father's politics and business based in New Ross. Her parents retired to Enniscorthy in the late 1940s about the time Eleanor moved to Dublin as a student. It is central to the narrative of the relationship between Tom and Eleanor that they learned to recognize and respect each other's differences.

By the mid-1950s the bleak economic situation had produced a profound national despondency. Four out of every five children born between 1931 and 1941 emigrated in the 1950s and in the 1953–58 period there was zero growth in GNP. The transformation of the economy in the late 1950s and early 1960s was a decisive turning point in the history of the Irish State. Since Kinsella worked under T.K. Whitaker, Secretary to the Department of Finance and architect of the First Economic Programme, he had direct experience of these changes. Published on 12 November 1958, the white paper, *Programme for Economic Expansion*, marked a movement from protectionism towards free trade, from 'social' to 'productive' investment. It ushered in a revolutionary official policy by which outside investors were encouraged to become involved in the Irish economy, with the result that emigration figures fell significantly and continued to fall between 1956 and 1971. Economic growth accelerated, living standards improved, and defeatist gloom was banished, temporarily.

Written when Ireland was commemorating the fiftieth anniversary of the Easter Rising of 1916, 'Nightwalker' personifies 'Productive Investment' as a prostitute who lures investors into the country. Like much of the poem the incident is symptomatic of what was happening and the consequences for the following decades. In the 1960s aggressive capitalists emerged who used political contacts to become affluent. There were demoralizing rumours of an unhealthy alliance between Fianna Fáil, the government party, and the construction industry. Speculators bought vacant properties for new office developments; planners and city councillors allowed parts of Georgian Dublin to be demolished and approved the erection of high-rise flats in Ballymun. No institution was immune to the virus of corruption – the government, banks, insurance companies, financial institutions. In the late 1990s money and the abuse of power in its pursuit dominated the news. It emerged that Charles Haughey, 'Foxhunter' in the poem and the new political leader, had benefited through the years from large donations from businessmen and had some of his debts written off by the banks. Illegal offshore accounts arranged by his accountant benefited an inner circle of businessmen. 'Productive Investment' was another name for greed. What 'Nightwalker' associated with 'The Wakeful Twins' became a reality. What it presaged in 'Foxhunter' became increasingly visible. The consequences appear in *Personal Places* and *Poems from Centre City* (1990) when Irish life has become pitted with corruption and failed aesthetic values. 'Nightwalker' marks the beginning of that decline.

The sense of shock experienced by the walker leads him to examine the education he had received. In the first place its uniformity and rigidity assumed that individual talents should be fitted into the prescribed curriculum, no matter what their background, urban or rural, or their particular aptitudes. It discriminated against the economically deprived who could not afford second or third-level education. Kinsella received a modest scholarship that enabled him to go to primary school at St Canice's, which was part of the O'Connell Schools system and where subjects were taught through Irish. His parents denied themselves the financial advantages of sending him out to work at an early age. The Department of Education expected that the teaching of history should underline examples of patriotism in order to rebut the calumnies of Ireland's enemies. The Christian Brothers schools were breeding grounds for nationalism and O'Connell's had a particular success in this regard. Many of those who participated in the Easter Rising were former pupils. In 'Nightwalker' Kinsella makes the point that this simplistic approach to history did not prepare him for what life was really like. It demonstrates the strength of his reaction to a narrowly nationalistic form of education and may be seen as part of his personal recovery from a restrictive education and cultural climate. He is thinking his way out of the entanglement.

The Catholic Church was a powerful and autonomous power. It had a controlling position in Irish education where, in denominational schools, religion had a primary place in the curriculum. It sought to control much of the intellectual and emotional life of the country and its grip only weakened late in the century. In 'Nightwalker' Kinsella associates the statue of the Blessed Virgin in the classroom with the young Queen Victoria to suggest the prolongation of Victorian values in the country. The association with sexual morality recalls the Church's obsession with sins of the flesh.

'Nightwalker' touches all the chords as it echoes the voices of teachers extolling the virtues of the native language, reminding students that the English had tried to exterminate it, that past-pupils had participated in the fight for freedom, and impressing on them the possibility that they in turn would be called upon to work for the language and their country. Kinsella's generation absorbed this Catholic, Gaelic nationalistic spirit. His satire is all embracing, taking in the political rigidity, the intellectual passivity, the coercive education, the absurd sexual morality and the debasement of the Irish language. A controlling metaphor of violence identifies the revolutionary violence through which the State was born, the nature of the economic drive and the hypocritical policy towards the Irish language. The poem directly evaluates the consequences of the new economic programme – its effects on moral values, culture and the directions of Irish life. Once commercial interests were given primary status, everything was devalued. It is an angry and bitter poem.

Meanwhile the Troubles in Northern Ireland were like a bad dream made up of sectarianism, Civil Rights marches, republican violence, the introduction of the British army, the emergence of the Civil Rights movement, the fall of Stormont, internment in August 1971, and the catastrophe of Bloody Sunday when on 30 January 1972 British para-troopers killed thirteen unarmed civilians at the end of a Civil Rights march in Derry. The British government set up the Lord Widgery Inquiry to determine responsibility for what had happened, but from the beginning the inquiry was skewed. Widgery ignored the evidence from 700 eyewitnesses that shots had been fired over the walls of the city down at the marchers. He also ignored medical evidence, which sug-gested that some of the victims had been shot from above. His report maintained that shots had been fired at ground level only and asserted that there was no reason for the paratroopers to shoot unless they themselves had been fired at. Nail bombs had been secreted in one victim's pockets and this was the only 'evidence' that the protesters had planned aggression. The report, scandalously unjust and unreliable, exonerated the soldiers. For many in the south the shootings in Derry were the last straw. Anger, resentment and frustration led to the burning of the British Embassy in Dublin.

The publication of Lord Widgery's report spurred Kinsella into instant action. 'Butcher's Dozen: A Lesson for the Octave of Widgery', published in pamphlet form in 1972, is an angry, measured indictment of the injustice of the report. He is his father's son, enraged by what has happened, by the suffering of people in the North, the cruel killings, the sense of helplessness at a system that discriminated against Catholics in housing, health, education and employment. In 1967 the newly formed Northern Ireland Civil Rights Association had formulated a programme that included one man, one vote in local elections; no gerrymandering of constituency boundaries; fair distribution of local authority housing and a formal complaints procedure against local authorities. They organized several marches. Kinsella took part in the one in Newry that may have connected in his imagination with the Civil Rights march in Derry. Through these years the Troubles in Northern Ireland reminded him of the injustice that operated there, with the tired acceptance that things were not going to change except through the workings of time.

At the time when Thomas Kinsella was writing his first poems and making his first translations from early Irish literature, Irish poetry was in decline. Only two poets of significance were visible – Patrick Kavanagh and Austin Clarke. The former's concentration on his rural origins, with occasional forays into Dublin settings, had little attraction for Kinsella as he looked about for models, but the publication of *A Soul for Sale* (1947) was a revelation. It gave a stunningly accurate depiction of rural life in 'The Great Hunger' and the lyrics, with their freshness of imagery and imaginative delight, would secure Kavanagh's status in Irish poetry. In Kinsella's work, specifically in *Open Court*, Kavanagh appears as the 'ruined anonymous' who is caught between affection for the beauty and integrity of life in the countryside and disdain for the urban surroundings in which he lives. Kinsella saw the strength of Kavanagh's concentration on the local, a quality he also admired in Clarke.

Austin Clarke had more appeal for Kinsella. He appears in 'Thinking of Mr. D.' (*Another September*) as a sly, reticent figure and in 'Brothers in the Craft' (*Personal Places*) as an exemplary 'elder'. The two poets had much in common, a shared experience of city life and a realistic assessment of the ills of modern society – social injustice, discrimination against workers and illiberal values. Clarke's relationship with the Catholic Church had been intense whereas Kinsella loosened the Church's hold with less of a struggle. Clarke's disgruntlement fitted easily with Kinsella's own feeling of dissatisfaction with Irish society. He recognized too that Clarke had worked hard to deepen the tradition of Irish writing which he had inherited from W.B. Yeats by drawing also upon Irish myth and history. In addition, Clarke made creative use of the Hiberno-Romanesque period to reflect his own spiritual problems in an Ireland that was controlled by a repressive and puritanical Catholic Church. He was a committed craftsman whose work at times had a chiselled objectivity and restraint. But at the time when Kinsella first knew him Clarke was not writing poetry.

The late 1940s and early 1950s always appear in Kinsella's poetry as an inhibiting context from which a few adventurous spirits wriggle free, while others are locked into a depressive miasma in which people, as in James Joyce's *Dubliners*, do not have the intellectual strength or power of will to escape. The decision of Liam Miller to start Dolmen Press (1951) gave valuable opportunity to aspiring poets. From the mid-1950s onwards there was a gradual and growing sense that Irish writing was experiencing a second renaissance after the depressed years. For the first time the centre of poetry publication was Dublin, not London. Then, just as the new generation of poets – Thomas Kinsella, Richard Murphy, John Montague and others – began to publish their first collections, Clarke, in a fresh release of energy, began to write poetry that was directly engaged with contemporary Irish life. He could be satirical, angry, humorous or personal and wrote intense, carefully worked lyrics as well as capacious autobiographical poems. His work sometimes had a density and allusiveness that made it hard to comprehend; but Kinsella, who liked intellectual challenge, did not object, since the poetry yielded its meaning to the seriously attentive reader. When Clarke had experienced public neglect and indifference, he had not complained; and when he reinvented himself in the 1950s, he was fully responsive to the world about him, capable of writing at the highest level but also badly at times, a man who confessed private pain and projected his dissatisfactions with Church and State. His example was not lost on Kinsella, who edited Clarke's *Selected Poems* after his death in 1974. While not blind to Clarke's failings as a poet, he was aware of his courage, craft and integrity.

In his generous Introduction he says that Clarke's work constitutes one of the notable modern careers. The lack of recognition outside of Ireland he attributes to the unevenness of the work, which requires that readers have patience and discrimination. In addition, the poems reflect only the 'immediate milieu'; some are virtually private, or so particular in their comments that it would be helpful to have the relevant newspaper handy, but they accumulate. 'They illuminate each other and establish relationships among themselves so that a microcosm of the human scene is formed, small in scope but complete. Raising the question of obscurity, these poems, by their authority and integrity, lay the question to rest.'[7] Acknowledging the poetry's verbal idiosyncrasy, narrowness of reference, economy of means and lack of superficial glamour that present a real problem to the casual reader, Kinsella concludes that it is, however, 'the energetic and attentive reader, meeting the poetry's demands', who will find that it meets his.[8] The defence, although this is not its intention, may be read as an *apologia* for Kinsella's own work, which has some of the same strengths and difficulties that he identifies in Clarke's poetry.

Essentially, Kinsella's survey of his predecessors concludes that there was only one major poet from whom he might be able to learn his trade and that was W.B. Yeats. Since Yeats's time there was no one he could mention. The omission of Clarke from this investigation of useable predecessors may seem strange, but in fact Kinsella saw him as a contemporary. Before Yeats, there were only the minor poets of the nineteenth century who wrote a few poems worth remembering. Although they had no living tradition to sustain them, they had, he said, provided the morning of a truly great, imaginative literature that would come.[9]

Kinsella's assessment is based not only on the presence of 'competence' in the work of any particular poet but on the evidence of a career. Many Irish poets had gapped careers, whereas he valued a lifetime's work. That intention indicates the direction and commitment Kinsella had, almost from the beginning. He read systematically in English and Irish literature. His early poems show the effects of some of this reading in influences from W.B. Yeats and W.H. Auden, William Blake, John Keats, the poets of the English Renaissance and Villon. Not only is he educating himself but he is finding a poetic identity, situating himself in relation to what had gone before. It is, in fact, an example of an emerging poet taking the measure of his predecessors, discovering what may be helpful to him as he tries to write his own poetry. His work also shows the influence of Goethe, Thomas Mann, Dante, Joyce and Pound. Unlike a literary historian or scholar, he was not trying to assess or to place the work of individual poets within historical or literary contexts. He was concerned with his own needs. 'Who are those', he asked himself, 'whose lives in some sense belong to me, and whose force is there for me to use if I can, if I am good enough, as I try to write my own poetry?'[10]

That sense of division and its complementary sense of a great heritage within the other language led Kinsella into a deep-rooted involvement with the Irish heritage. It was evident in the enormous amount of translation from Modern Irish, a language he had learnt at school, and from Early Irish, a language he had to teach himself. Later he modified the idea of a major disruption in Irish tradition in the recognition that it was not necessary to abandon one aspect of the country's literature in order to deal with another. 'We have a dead language with a powerful literature and a colonial language with a powerful literature. The combination is an extremely rich one.'[11]

He could learn little, he said, from his contemporaries, whose 'scattered' lives only showed his own isolation, and here he makes a distinction between his own position and that of Yeats. In the first place,

Yeats felt isolated from Irish-speaking people in the west of Ireland whose language he did not share and whose lives he therefore could not reach. In the second place Yeats, he argued, chose his isolation by deciding not to deal with the unpleasant actualities of modern Irish life, whereas Joyce had done precisely that. Joyce was an ongoing and exemplary influence on Kinsella, who had read *Dubliners* as a young man and who appreciated its relevance to his own experience of city life. Joyce's presence is evident in the use of the stream of consciousness technique in parts of 'Nightwalker', in specific references in *Songs of the Psyche*, *Poems from Centre City*, and *The Pen Shop*, and above all in the trust in detail that characterizes Kinsella's work at all times.

Despite the regret for what has been lost, he refuses to be defeated by the circumstances in which he finds himself. Yeats, he points out, who was similarly isolated, was not preoccupied by discontinuity. He was concerned instead with the work of the imagination, which makes historical events that are not part of his imagining self of no account. James Joyce sensibly accepted the world as he found it and Kinsella makes clear that he himself does not function exclusively within an Irish tradition. 'The continuity or the mutilation of tradition becomes, in itself, irrelevant...as the artist steps back from his entire world, mutilations and all, and absorbs it.'[12] Relationship to tradition is only part of the picture. There is also the relationship with other literatures, with the present, with the 'human predicament, with the self'.[13] The writer, Kinsella maintains, finds his identity in relation to all literary traditions. He shares more with all men than he does with any class of men: 'he may lack the sense of tradition and still share most of human experience'. There is, Kinsella declares, no virtue for literature or poetry in the mere continuity of a tradition. Every writer has to make his own imaginative grasp at identify and 'if he can find no means in his inheritance to suit him, he will have to start from scratch'. Being part of a discontinuous, polyglot tradition is the common experience of modern writers. If the function of tradition is to link them with a significant past, even a broken tradition will do. 'I am certain that a great part of the significance of my own past, as I try to write my poetry, is that the past *is* mutilated.'[14]

The publication of *The Dolmen Miscellany of Irish Writing* in September 1962 declares that a new generation of writers had emerged. The editorial, written by John Montague and Thomas Kinsella, was careful to say that while they did not form any sort of movement, they did reflect a change of sensibility. Emerging from the long shadows of W.B. Yeats and James Joyce, Irish writers were expressing a different Ireland from that found in the work of Austin Clarke and Seán O'Faoláin. 'They were part not only of a post-Civil War mentality but of a post-World War II consciousness and did not want to be identified

on the basis of "Irishisms".' They looked outwards, whereas the generation that preceded them tended to look inward. As time passed, they
manifested a dual vision, outward-looking for ideas, for awareness of
literary developments, inward-looking for a deeper exploration of their
cultural and linguistic origins.[15]

Although Kinsella's essay on the Irish writer concentrates on self-
definition in relation to the Irish literary tradition in both languages, his
interests and ambitions were not limited to them. His understanding of
modern poets from Auden and Eliot to Ezra Pound, William Carlos
Williams, Robert Lowell and others enabled him to escape from the
restrictions of traditional forms. 'My poems', he declared, 'have a form
which ought to be felt as a whole, rather than in, e.g., stanzaic expectations. Each poem has a unique shape, contents and development.'[16] He
may have been released from the requirements governing rhyme, metre
and given forms, but the freedom and flexibility gained as a result were
replaced by a different kind of accountability. Now all the particulars –
of language, imagery, line length, tone, space, positioning and development – had to be deployed judiciously. Each poem must find its own
exact shape, all its elements measured accordingly. The abandonment of
those aspects that had distinguished his early poetry – fluency, ornamentation, and euphony for its own sake – had to be compensated for. Not
that the resources of language are totally set aside. After 1973 there is a
remarkable strength and subtlety in the poetry and, when required, a
linguistic power and a dramatic presence.

He noted how Pound introduces himself as a character in the work,
as the artist in the act of discovery. This accorded well with Kinsella's
tendency to portray himself within the poem in an act of emotional
growth, while at the same time showing himself as its observer. His poem
'Worker in Mirror at his Bench' (*New Poems*, 1973) is a pertinent
example. He noted, more generally, that the meaning in Pound's *Cantos*
is derived from the manner in which material moves about in a kind of
whirling motion within which we may discern what the poet has in
mind. 'Everything is dramatic and immediate, concerned with ideas only
in so far as they manifest themselves in action.'[17] The same might be said
particularly of individual poems and collections in the Peppercanister
publications. It became his practice after 1973 to plan poetic sequences
with the result that a number of the Peppercanister publications are
integrated through subject matter, situation, character, incident and
imagery. Some of these are single poems, such as the Seán Ó Riada
elegies, *The Messenger* and *The Pen Shop*. The poetic sequences are
personal and dramatic, offering a wide variety of approaches, sometimes
fragmentary, integrated through the recurrence of themes and situations.
The poems associate with one another and accumulate into a complex

and integrated whole, which has to be discovered by the reader. Kinsella provides the data and develops the materials in a meaningful fashion.

Kinsella's sense of the individual poem is primary. *Readings in Poetry* (Peppercanister 25, 2006) is based on the principle that poems need to be read closely. His exemplary readings of Yeats's 'The Tower' and Eliot's 'The Love Song of J. Alfred Prufrock' are what he calls 'primary': each reading enacts a response that takes into account the poem's textual detail of content, method and structure, and notes the data as they are given and accumulate. 'The text of the poem is taken as initiating an act of communication, and the reading is offered as a completion of the act, the poem read at its own pace.'[18] This task, he argues, should be completed before one considers other matters, such as the poem's relationships with other poems, its place in a poet's career, in literary or other contexts, or in tradition.

That central idea informs much of this book whose aim is to introduce the reader to Kinsella's work, to suggest ways of reading it, and to provide as much contextual discussion as seems useful. This approach is possible because several valuable studies of his work have appeared: Derval Tubridy, *Thomas Kinsella: The Peppercanister Poems* (2001); Thomas H. Jackson, *The Whole Matter: The Poetic Evolution of Thomas Kinsella* (1995); Brian John, *Reading the Ground. The Poetry of Thomas Kinsella* (1996); and Donatella Abbate Badin, *Thomas Kinsella* (1996). When my first book on Kinsella – *The Poetry of Thomas Kinsella: With Darkness for a Nest* (1974) – appeared, it was the only book available, so that it was necessary to provide detailed and basic analysis of the work as it had developed. That restriction is no longer necessary, except in Part IV, which deals with recent collections.

This book is divided into four parts. Part I: 'Poet of Many Voices', dealing with collections published between 1958 and 1973, reveals dominant themes and the use of different voices. It charts Kinsella's progress from traditional forms to the use of modern techniques of organization, from the use of objective personae to the psychological enactments of *New Poems*. Part II: 'Style and Substance', dealing with collections published between 1972 and 1987, focuses on a time of major achievement that included the two Seán Ó Riada elegies, *Her Vertical Smile*, and various interpretations of human behaviours in the present and in the past. At the heart of Kinsella's engagement with the past is a fascination with the ways in which things develop – a country's past, language and culture, the creative process itself. *One* commemorates man's instinctive hunger for discovery. *A Technical Supplement* demonstrates the need for a dynamic interaction between the poet and his subject matter, whether in the natural, mythic or personal worlds.

The dominant method is that of contrasting voices. *The Good Fight* works through interactive portrayals of individual wills and values, and their interpretations of human nature. In *Her Vertical Smile* and *Out of Ireland* the meaning is revealed through distinct voices, each enunciating a particular point of view, none expressing the entire meaning of the poem. Many of the issues that permeate the work at this period – the nature of existence, the relevance of the Divine, the role of the artist – are encapsulated and orchestrated in the dramatic interplay of *Her Vertical Smile*. *Songs of the Psyche* also uses dramatic voices as Kinsella moves again into the dark, nutrient waters of the unconscious.

Part III: 'Translations: From Paganism to Christianity' considers Kinsella's translations from the Irish in three works – *The Táin* (1969), *An Duanaire. 1600–1900: Poems of the Dispossessed* (1981), and *The New Oxford Book of Irish Verse* (1986). These reflect another aspect of his engagement with the past. His translations proceed from his initial involvement with the Old Irish epic, the *Táin Bó Cuailnge*, to his work on the lyric poetry of the same period, in all its variety, to his attention to the equally varied poetry of the medieval period. He followed the course of Irish poetry from the early modern period to the modern and came to understand the historical, cultural and personal issues involved. In the end he provided access to the whole range of Irish Literature.

Part IV: 'Tales of the Dispossessed' examines collections published between 1988 and 2007. As Kinsella turns his attention again to contemporary Ireland, he selects officials, speculators and others who, in the interests of commercial gain, have destroyed some of the city's heritage and disfigured the cityscape with ugly buildings. A haunting, mysterious 'Stranger' embodies threatening forces, one of a number of ominous presences culminating in the figure of Aogán Ó Rathaille standing at the ocean's edge contemplating meaninglessness. It is a state towards which Kinsella has been travelling, a radically reduced and exposed place where there are no compensations to be derived from the past and no expectation of a change for the better in the future. Furthermore, Kinsella's feeling of isolation is now felt in relation to all contemporaries. In the absence of communication, he speaks through projections of himself in Aogán Ó Rathaille, Oliver Goldsmith, Marcus Aurelius and others. Given his isolation, how the artist manages is crucial. He must, in Kinsella's view, have moral courage, must condemn the wrongdoer and praise the good man, and must always search for aesthetic beauty. As always in Kinsella the woman companion is the indispensable source of strength. Once again Eleanor appears in *Madonna and Other Poems* and in *The Familiar* (1999). Their moment of first encounter back in the early 1950s is worthy of reaffirmation, their companionship worthy of celebration. The warmth between them is totally absent from the relationship between the poet and the Almighty in *Godhead* (1999). In the incompleteness of His creation, God merely reflects the human condition.

In a stark existence the poet also has to cope with public indifference to his work, a state voiced through Oliver Goldsmith and James Boswell; but his job, exemplified in *The Pen Shop*, is to deal with what he observes. In its calm allegories *Marginal Economy* (2006) embodies Kinsella's philosophy: mankind lives in soiled survival, expecting little, doing the best he can, while he can. Mankind's capacity for self-destruction drives the argument in *Man of War* (2007), whereas the poems in *Belief and Unbelief* (2007) illuminate modes of discovery and understanding. Kinsella explains:

> I see poetry as a form of responsible reaction to the predica-
> ment one finds oneself in. If a person has an impulse to record
> the situation, I believe that is necessary, but I have no idea
> what use it is. It has something to do with continuity, with
> trying to compensate for the limited life span of the individual.
> But it's essential to get the matter recorded before one disa-
> ppears... the experience of an individual *can* be significant and,
> if the impulse is there, it is a responsible thing to record the
> particularities of that experience... accompanying the record of
> the experience with a record of the response.[19]

Notes

1 Subsequently all references, unless specifically noted, are to the edition of Thomas Kinsella's *Collected Poems 1956–2001* (Manchester: Carcanet Press, 2001) in which *Notes from the Land of the Dead*, 1972, is incorporated in *New Poems*, 1973, as 'From the Land of the Dead' with some omissions.
2 John Haffenden, 'Thomas Kinsella', in *Viewpoints: Poets in Conversation with John Haffenden* (London: Faber and Faber, 1981), p.108.
3 *A Dublin Documentary* (Dublin: The O'Brien Press, 2006), p.68.
4 Ibid., p.70.
5 Haffenden, p.101.
6 *Directions* (Springfield, IL: Illinois Art Education Association, 1966–67).
7 Austin Clarke, *Selected Poems*, ed. Thomas Kinsella (Dublin: Dolmen Press; Winston Salem, NC: Wake Forest University Press, 1976), p.x.
8 Ibid., p.xi.
9 W.B. Yeats and Thomas Kinsella, *Davis, Mangan, Ferguson? Tradition and The Irish Writer* (Dublin: Dolmen Press, 1970), p.70.
10 Ibid., p.57.
11 Donatella Abbate Badin, *Thomas Kinsella* (New York: Twayne Publishers, 1996), p.193.
12 Ibid., p.13.

13 Ibid., pp.14–15.

14 Ibid., p.15.

15 See Harmon, 'The Dolmen Miscellany' in *The Dolmen Press: A Celebration* (Dublin: Lilliput Press, 2001), pp.96–7.

16 Haffenden, *Viewpoints*, p.108.

17 'So That', rev. of *The Cantos of Ezra Pound*, *Hibernia*, 4 June 1976, p.23.

18 Peppercanister 25, 2006, p.16.

19 Badin, 'Excerpts from 14–15 August 1993 Interview', in *Thomas Kinsella*, pp.199–200.

Part I
POET OF MANY VOICES

Another September, 1958
Moralities, 1960
Downstream, 1962
Nightwalker and Other Poems, 1968
New Poems, 1973

INTRODUCTION

It did not take Thomas Kinsella long to recognize and explore the issues that were expressing themselves in his work. While *Poems* (1956) is a book of love poems, the preoccupations in *Another September* (1958), which gives a fuller and a more complex picture of his sensibility, are love, death and the artistic act. *Another September* absorbs *Poems*, a wedding gift to his wife, Eleanor, whom he married in December 1955. He has experienced the transforming power of love and celebrates it in several lyrics, but mutability and death emerge as a constant threat. Writing itself, he has discovered, is an instinct and while not immune to erosion together with love it is a positive power that can counter life's destructive forces. In Kinsella's outlook, change and impermanence are not merely something discovered through personal experience; they belong to the world's processes of growth, maturity and extinction. In his mental and poetic universe death is constant, disappointment a fact, and writing a strain. Out of the tension between creativity and destruction he finds a voice and an idiom through which he encapsulates his sense of conflict and absorbs the destructive propensities of the world. The unpalatable is ingested and processed. The result is poetry that makes the paradoxical marriage of menace and creativity both theme and texture.

The formal shape of the poems, their even length of line, regular rhyme schemes and objectivity of manner point to enjoyment in their making. They reveal a love of language, a pleasure in its possibilities and an attractive vigour. They may be enjoyed for their rhyme, rhythm and beauty; but when Kinsella changes his style later, he regards these as unnecessary, a pointless elegance. Writing permits a degree of performance. However rawly he may be exposed to negative factors, including some dissatisfaction with inherited forms and with language itself, he writes in two poetic modes, one meditative and focused on particular incidents, the other a construct of self-delighting images. In short lyrics and through longer forms, he explores the connection between menace and survival and seeks to identify and to adjust to the presence of evil in the world.

By the time he completed *Downstream* (1962), he was fully alive to the issues that had surfaced in his work. He was, he wrote, increasingly concerned, in longer poems,

> With questions of value and order, seeing the human function
> (in so far as it is not simply to survive the ignominies of exist-
> ence) as the eliciting of order from experience – the detection
> of the significant substance of our individual and common pasts
> and its translation imaginatively, scientifically, bodily, into an
> increasingly coherent and capacious entity; or the attempt to do
> this to the point of failure.[1]

The discovery of a personal voice with which to explore the experience of evil is present in each of the long poems – 'A Country Walk',
'Downstream', 'Nightwalker', 'Phoenix Park' and the innovative
sequence 'From the Land of the Dead'. Through their dramatic
narratives of a self and its discoveries we are drawn into the narrator's
intellectual and emotional worlds. We understand the nature of the self
through the disclosure of its preoccupations and the changing incidents
of its responses. The biographical elements round out the enactment.
While the full reasons for Kinsella's tragic sensibility remain hidden, the
political and social elements become clear in references to Irish historical
events and to the Second World War in 'A Country Walk'. That personal
dimension is increased in the harrowing psychodrama that is 'Nightwalker' where the depressive sensibility is more fully realized. The long
poems enact the drama of an individual's encounter with the evil that is
outside in 'A Country Walk' and 'Downstream', the drama of his
confessional response to internal chaos in 'Nightwalker', and his
philosophical assessment in 'Phoenix Park'. The first three are archetypal
journeys into the underworld of death and suffering leading to ultimate
clarification.

At the same time Kinsella was developing as a poet, moving from the
ornamental style and morose manner of some early lyrics to the simpler
style of 'The Laundress' (*Downstream*). The final poem in that collection,
'Mirror in February', foreshadows a spare diction. The 'Wormwood'
sequence of seven poems in varying stanzaic forms in *Nightwalker and
Other Poems* (1968), introduces an ethic of suffering and a philosophy of
endurance and transmutation expressed by means of a painful marriage
relationship. Stripped to the minimal, language is a visible sign of hard-
won survival. The tension between partners who are clamped together is
now the compact illustration of the clash between inescapable forces,
both creative and destructive, which has been a marked feature of his
work from the beginning. To live is to suffer or, as Kinsella phrased it
in his notes, 'Time = Hope & Disappointment'.[2] The landscape of
depression in 'Nightwalker' externalizes through several voices and
changing tones the spiritual state of the alienated and disaffected persona,
now grievously exposed to the stunting effects of Irish life. The poem

shows what has been removed: a culture has been lost, coarse commercial values have become primary, and in the educational system his generation was not prepared for the realities of modern life. In a poetry that has been notably without references to particular Irish events, the change is dramatic. This is his 'Sea of Disappointment' where the pervasive metaphor of violence threatens from all sides. But if the poem is unshirking in its depiction of menace and if the self is understandably depressed, suffering 'the brute necessities', undergoing the existential ordeals, and registering the components of failure, he will not turn away from what he sees. He is the product of this world, of these specific social, political, religious and cultural realities, and out of its ingredients will make his poetry, much as James Joyce made dear, dirty Dublin the material for his fiction. Here, for the first time, Kinsella directs his anger and disappointment at the Ireland that made him.

His own assessment of *Nightwalker and Other Poems* says that their subject in general is a developing view of life as an 'ordeal'.

> The first two sections of the book begin with certain private experiences under the ordeal, and follow with celebrations of the countermoves – love, the artistic act – which mitigate the ordeal and make it fruitful, and even promise a bare possibility of order. The poems in the third section are about a few poets, and the function of poetry. In the last section the feeling reaches out to the Irish historical landscape and the 'new' Ireland, and inward to the imaginative hunger that (I believe) gives to existence whatever significance it may have. These poems are trying (as the whole book is) to find a balance in the violent zone, between the outer and inner storms, where human life takes place.[3]

In his eyes men are all finally helpless in the service of a general brutality. His defining terms are 'brutal', 'squalid', 'ordeal', 'ignominies', 'failure' and 'horror', countered by positive terms – 'order', 'honesty', 'acceptance', 'maturity', 'renewal', 'understanding' and 'love'. Existence takes place in a threatening zone.

The many voices used in *Nightwalker and Other Poems* to render despair within its historical and personal contexts show the use of dramatic personae. Much later he will articulate views and feelings through historical figures, such as Denis Diderot, Oliver Goldsmith or Marcus Aurelius, but now experience is close-up and subjective. 'Nightwalker' itself is a search for structure in the chaos of the violating quotidian; 'Phoenix Park' is a formulation of the results of that search. It is a measured and objective restatement of values, made in a convent-

ional stanzaic structure, in which he reaffirms the necessary presence of
the Beloved in his ability to produce poetry through the 'laws of
suffering and increase' to which he adheres. This is less a choice than a
tactic through which to manage the kind of person he is and to release
personal feelings and ideas into poetry. More simply, it is a poem about
leaving, about assessment of what has been achieved, and about the
courage required to move forward. They will accept the ordeal cup.
They will investigate the darkness that lies ahead which includes the
unconscious with all its Jungian associations.

Kinsella started as a love poet, but soon began to register the forces
of mutilation and mutability that threatened the love relationship.
'Wormwood' put that relationship under the microscope to identify its
inherent fragility and inner strength. Without external supports, he turns
to the one vital and transformative experience he has known. Only in
love has he known a force strong enough to offset his sense of destruction
and loss. Therefore only in love and through the imagery of an intense
and nurturing relationship can he express his belief in the possibilities of
creativity. He thrusts the idea upon her, unasked, and in an almost
desperate gamble offers her the bitter cup of survival on his terms. At
that point he becomes for her the figure of Death, asks her to imbibe
the full infection, 'Night's carnality'. Standing back from the investigation, 'Phoenix Park' presents the conclusion as evidence of creative
possibilities. It was a long-term commitment. In his many subsequent
returns to the past, the moment at which Eleanor entered his life is the
most significant.

The inward-turning nature of Kinsella's imagination becomes
dominant in *New Poems* (1973). In the complex, integrated theories of
Carl Jung, whose exploration of the individual make-up and the ways in
which primordial images coalesce corresponded to Kinsella's understanding of the workings of his imagination, he finds an alternative for
the deprivation he has known and he articulates it here. This is a
substantial advance in Kinsella's career. It validates personal experiences
by relating them to archetypal actions so that particular incidents become
part of a universal tapestry of events. It was accompanied by a break-
through to a fragmentary style, adapted to the abrupt and dramatic
expression of experience, however deep-seated or momentary, in which
individual poems have, as he said, a 'form which ought to be felt as a
whole, rather than in, e.g., stanzaic expectations'.[4] It is connected with
the Gestalt theory, also found in Jung, that makes what has been
included in, or accomplished through, a particular poem or fragment of
a poem an open-ended aesthetic. The brooding persona in individual
poems, such as 'Hen Woman' or 'From the Land of the Dead', itself is
the voice of an individual sunk in his own psyche, involved in experience

below the consciousness, a truth-teller of exceptional insight. Through encountering the poetry of William Carlos Williams in the early 1960s, Kinsella has begun to understand what he called 'a kind of creative relaxation in the face of complex reality' and of remaining '"prehensile", not rigidly committed'.[5] Again, 'Hen Woman' is an example of both an alertness to what is happening, an ability to seize upon its significance, and to brood upon it, like a hen covering a clutch of eggs from which new life will emerge. He has been rigidly insistent on the ethic of suffering. Now, buoyed up and strengthened by his reading of Jung and by his liberating technique, he enjoys a more relaxed approach and, when this is joined with the fluidity and range of Jung's archetypal patterns, the result is a poetry that connects poem with poem and collection with collection. Kinsella follows a structuring, numerological system, ranging from O to the Quincunx, the meeting place of Heaven and Earth. Even in the 1960s he remarked on the risks involved in working to a predetermined system. Inevitably, the unpredictable could not be excluded. In any case the method flew in the face of what he had always maintained – that poetry consists in the eliciting of order from experience, not in the imposition of order upon it.

'From the Land of the Dead' pursues the Jungian path of individuation. More than Teilhard de Chardin's evolutionary thin line that Kinsella found significant earlier, this has depth and complexity; it joins time present with time past. It entails a combination of the dramatic methods of characterization and voice-identification used in 'Nightwalker'. Now the persona resembles the figure in Goethe's *Faust* who enters the depths, falls out of consciousness to be reborn and to return to a state of enlightenment. Goethe had been part of Kinsella's consciousness from the bicentenary of his birth in 1949. His was the last of the universal minds able to encompass all domains of human activity and knowledge. The Faust legend itself was the product of orthodox Protestantism and its moral, the inevitable doom that follows the individual revolt of the intellect against divine authority, accorded with Kinsella's ethic of suffering. Goethe's trope of the unsatisfied yearning of the human mind appealed to Kinsella because the other side of the coin stamped by his personality is an intellectual curiosity.

As the walker turns for home, he expresses Kinsella's belief in the value of domestic love, in persistence and the understanding that may be gained. Behind the three-part structure of 'Nightwalker' is Dante's *Divine Comedy*. The poem begins in an atmosphere of death, in the necropolis, but it is in this return to home that the fuller correspondence comes through. Dante is the poet of intellectualized love, love being the inevitable consequence of knowledge. Kinsella's notes emphasize this aspect of the *Comedy*. Dante, he explains, looks on the

Eternal Light and it consumes his sight. Within its depths he saw ingathered, bound by love in one volume, the scattered beams of the entire universe (box 5, folder 18). In the walker's return, Dante's Virgin Mary fuses with the Moon and with the image of Queen Victoria, who presides over the country. The book imagery of this passage echoes the lines in Dante's description of the Eternal Light. There is a connection with *Faust*, which also ends with prayers to the Virgin Mother. The significance of the Victoria–Virgin association may be seen in further notes.

> Today the *positiveness* of the Victorian mind survives in Ireland (in me...) after the catastrophes of W.W.II & Hiroshima. And who will say this is not an *enrichment* rather than an impoverishment? To be able to face the contemporary world, with the positiveness (marginal, yet there) of commitment to structure, meaning, purpose, giving, maybe, a means of dealing with a monster of formlessness & malignity. In this light, one can look back & see the *formalism* of Yeats & Joyce is important, & not unconnected. (box 71, folder 13)

In the final tableau the walker is transmitted to the surface of the moon where he sees in stark terms the reality of life's barrenness and sterility and the Sea of Disappointment. In the Joycean line that ends the poem in *Collected Poems* (2001) – 'Hesitant, cogitating, exit.' – Kinsella salutes the watcher in the tower at Sandycove towards which the walker had moved and in a note remarks that exile is the true condition of the modern writer – 'the post atomic chaos where everyone is lonely/exiled, not only you, watcher in the Tower' (box 5, folder 18).

In *From the Land of the Dead* Kinsella combines Celtic and classical myth in the stories of the arrival of peoples in Ireland in prehistoric times and the story of Persephone's descent into Hades and return to the upper world. Both express the paradigm of death and rebirth. Their fusion is instinctive with the scheme of primordial images. The integrating narrative of the collection is the path of individuation; it concludes in a return that is implicit in the images of living particles and creative appetite. Life takes hold.

Notes

1   *Contemporary Authors: A Bio-Bibliographical Guide to Current Authors and Their Works*, ed. James Vinson, vols. 17–18 (Detroit, MI: Gale Research Co., 1976), p.263.
2   Thomas Kinsella's papers and materials, both prose notes and poetry, are in Special Collections at Emory University, Atlanta, Georgia. The Kinsella Papers are

identified here and subsequently by box and folder number: (box 4, folder 10).
3   'Statement', *Poetry Book Society Bulletin* 55 (December 1967).
4   Haffenden, *Viewpoints*, p.108.
5   Ibid., p.106.

1

THE FULL INFECTION

At the beginning of his literary career Thomas Kinsella wrote poems in celebration of love, but could not ignore forces that threatened it, such as mutability, mutilation, violence and death. In 'Test Case', 'The famous towering Death [is] already avalanching'. 'King John's Castle' makes a powerful statement about 'the man-rot of passages' and 'great collapsed ruins'. When Death seeks him out in 'Dead on Arrival', he treasures 'The full infection, Night's carnality'. In short poems Kinsella frequently uses oxymoron to encapsulate these oppositions. In longer poems he subjects his sense of conflict between good and evil to detailed investigation. He has an affinity with death and destruction and finds analogies in loss and disappointment for how he feels. By making dissolution and death ever-present and powerful, he creates a force against which he can create versions of beauty. In 'Lead' he is a Vulcan of the quotidian, compelled to emphasize the principle of destructive opposition.

> Flame-breathing Vulcan in a maker's rage
> Smelted and hammered on his smoking ledge
> A bit to bridle Chaos. Hoof by hoof
> The red smith snared and shod. Life reared its roof
> Over the brilliant back.
> Space locked a door. Time set a rock on edge.
> I held a stallion's eyes, a stuff
> That glared so wild its elements went black.[1]

The poem thrives on energy, on dynamic engagement between the maker and his material. The energy is felt in the emphatic rhythms and the powerful verbs – 'Smelted', 'hammered', 'snared', 'shod', 'reared', 'locked', 'set', 'held', 'glared' – in the full rhymes and in the powerful personification of Vulcan. The smith works strenuously, creating something to control Chaos. The rock on the edge is menacing but within time and space the poet creates the 'stallion' whose eyes blackened by time, have survived.

In *Another September* he creates the artist/maker who constructs powerful artefacts in the face of Time's processes, even as he understands that the art-product also has to succumb to ruin. Kinsella writes with self-conscious, self-delighting artistry, but is aware of artificiality and transience. It is fundamental in the early work that the erosion he contemplates and the death that is its inevitable ending constantly undermine the work of art, which in itself is arrested from the Lucretian flux. All achievements of beauty and of love are doomed. Nevertheless, the way to deal with destructive forces is to become their master, to counter the world of erosion with a new world verified by the imagination and shaped with consummate artistry.

In 'Baggot Street Deserta', the key poem in *Another September*, disappointment is central. Its mood of self-scrutiny comes in a lull after writing. 'The breaking-cry, the strain of the rack,/Yield, are at peace.' He has worked hard and now, recovering from the 'attack', puts the 'will to work' aside. The Past is a kind of nightmare, the Muse a frightening marsh bird. Nevertheless, driven by an 'obsessed honesty', he will persist. Risks and confusions attend the examination of the past, but he will not be deterred. 'I nonetheless inflict, endure.' Possessed by an 'alien/Garrison' of urges and instincts, the imagination reaches out to the frontiers of understanding in search of 'the Real'. Poetry-making is in part a virtuoso performance; the basic requirement is to *'Endure and let the present punish.'* Despite its decorative artistry and linguistic flair, the poem is close to emotional aridity, but its dramatization of complex feeling is fluently managed in four-stressed lines, alternate rhymes, a changing rhythm and concrete language. He writes an accomplished poem while ironically highlighting the strain of doing so. He experiences uncertainty, confusion and isolation and in the lull registers a sense of 'common loss'. Despite the poem's formal elegance, the sense of threat undermines his feeling of achievement. The risks deny him satisfaction in the work. But 'doctored recollections', his term for what he does, is too harsh.

Its self-deprecating manner is replicated in *Downstream*, where the introductory poem is a mocking portrait of what might be expected of a poet: an account of dull routine, the 'pain' of suburban life, 'the weekly trance at Mass', and his 'bored menagerie', Energy, Laziness, Discipline, Jaws-of-Death, Routine.

> *...Energy,*
> *Blinking, only half-awake,*
> *Gives its tiny frame a shake;*
> *Fouling itself, a giantess,*
> *The bloodshot bulk of Laziness*
> *Obscures the vision; Discipline*
> *Limps after them with jutting chin,*
> *Bleeding badly from the calf;*

> *Old Jaws-of-Death gives laugh for laugh*
> *With Error as they amble past;*
> *And there as usual, lying last,*
> *Helped along by blind Routine,*
> *Futility flogs a tambourine....* (30)

The self-criticism is undeserved. The poet is not given to laziness or indiscipline. Death is an ever-present reality, Error occurs, Routine may prove futile, but the dissatisfaction and masochism are unmerited. Kinsella is known to be a hard, disciplined worker.

While in the first two collections he emerges as a dedicated poet concerned with fragility in the nature of things, the epigrammatic poems in *Moralities* (1960), medieval in nature, define his outlook more sharply. 'An Old Atheist Pauses by the Sea' declares a shocked response to erosion – 'I choose', 'I confess', 'I know'.

> I choose at random, knowing less and less.
> The shambles of the seashore at my feet
> Yield a weathered spiral: I confess
> – Appalled at how the waves have polished it –
> I know that shores are eaten, rocks are split,
> Shells ghosted. Something hates unevenness.
> The skin turns porcelain, the nerves retreat,
> And then the will, and then the consciousness. (24)

Something wears objects away – 'eaten', 'split', 'ghosted'. 'Something hates unevenness.' Lacking certainty, he yields to signs of weathering, has to recognize not that the process makes something beautiful, but that it takes the entire self into oblivion.

In powerful monosyllables 'A Garden on the Point' declares that 'great ebb tides lift to the light of day/The sea-bed's briny chambers of decay'. In expressive strong verbs – 'smelled', 'Loomed', 'Limped', 'chose', 'moaned', 'begged' – the grey devourer is also present in 'Dead on Arrival'.

> It smelled our laughter, then, in vivid shroud,
> Loomed with averted face (*Dont think, dont think*),
> Limped with its poison through the noisy crowd
> And chose my glass. It moaned and begged me: 'Drink.'
>
> I woke in mortal terror, every vein
> A-flood with my destroyer; then fought free.
> I lie in darkness, treasuring in my brain
> The full infection, Night's carnality. (27)

Not only is this an acceptance of death's poisoned glass, but of the condition of death-in-life. It is recognition through nightmare of human circumstances and a 'treasuring' of that knowledge. The driving force, as 'At the Heart' affirms, is appetite; images of jaws and feeding, including devouring and consumption, make their presence felt. The sacred tree stands for creativity, the ability to absorb and to be absorbed, positive and negative energy, deepening sources, increased discipline, maturing, improvement and appetite.

> Heraldic, hatched in gold, a sacred tree
> Stands absorbed, tinkering with the slight
> Thrumming of birds, the flicker of energy
> Thrown and caught, the blows and burdens of flight.
> Roots deepen; disciplines proliferate
> And wings more fragile are brought into play.
> Timber matures, the game grows nobler, yet
> Not one has sped direct as appetite. (28)

The declarative, emblematizing manner animates the lines so that the entire stanza is alive with movement – tinkering, flickering, thrumming. The playful language attests a developing maturity, ennobling in the process, but all lead to the affirmation in the final line – 'Not one has sped direct as appetite' – appetite being the capacity of the creative being to absorb and use experience. The lines are in effect a manifesto of artistic faith.

The joining together of apparently contradictory terms is found throughout *Downstream* and *Nightwalker and Other Poems*. Even a random list shows the frequency with which oxymoron is used: 'with darkness for a nest'; 'a rack of leaves', 'a skull of light', 'both to horrify and instruct', 'crumbling place of growth', 'tender offals', 'the slithering pit, the shapelessly/Adjusting matter of the rubbish heap', 'grim composure', 'a jewel made of pain', 'a pale unmarriage', 'Ephemeral, perpetual'. When this technique is joined to the high incidence of 'unattractive' images, it creates a characteristic style that verifies the perception of threatening forces. By *Downstream* the unpalatable is an established part of the poetry. In the adjectival 'Cover Her Face' the first two stanzas have 'Haunts the chilly landing', 'Shabby with sudden tears', 'drab walls'. In 'Tyrant Dying', 'Fat hands...rest their talons', 'His wasted legs lie cauterised...'. In 'Brothers', man and hound move 'Over high ridges of rock, through tempest of salt and sun/And pounding wind'; the dog catches his breath 'with tongue and maddened ribs,/Paws a slant stone' and by the end has become an image for the man, 'his gasping eagerness/Islanded in storm, his coat shivering-on-end'. In 'Office for the

Dead' mourners are 'grief-chewers', the thurible is 'A silver pot' that 'tosses in its chains', voices 'grind across her body', 'Church/Latin chews our different losses into one'. The language is transformative, not towards comfort, beauty or glorification but towards dissonance, threat and disappointment.

The transformative style is seen in many instances. In 'Brothers' not only do man and dog coalesce, but both are blended with seascape/landscape and weather. In 'Mirror in February' the pollarded trees are exemplars for the adult to suffer and survive like them. 'Office for the Dead' is a major example of the transformation towards harshness and obliteration as a secularizing mind records its perceptions of a religious service. In 'The Shoals Returning' the wave is made human, men are sea creatures, and the motions of the ocean and the actions and feelings of the men reflect one another. In the ghostly world of 'Nightwalker', figures appear and disappear.

These early collections show Kinsella's skills and sensibility, but it is in *Downstream* that his poetic qualities are clearly established. Some poems embody values that he finds attractive. In beautifully crafted and musical lines, fusing the pregnant woman with the natural world and its seasonal cycles, 'The Laundress' portrays one who finds fulfilment in what she is.

> As a fish disturbs the pond
> And sinks without a stain
> The heels of ripeness fluttered
> Under her apron. Then
> Her heart grew strained and light
> As the shell that shields the grain.
>
> Bluntly through the doorway
> She stared at shed and farm,
> At yellow fields unstitching
> About the hoarded germ,
> At land that would spread white
> When she had reached her term. (31)

The acceptance that underlies that relationship with herself and her surroundings is also present in poems that examine less pleasing circumstances or events, as many poems in *Downstream* do. 'Cover Her Face', while following the structure of the elegy in its movement from grief towards consolation, achieves this progression not by means of consolatory language, literary or mythological allusion but through a merciless exposure of loss, ugliness and numbing grief. Virtually everything in the

poem creates estrangement – people are uncertain of what they should
do, the poet-narrator 'gropes for function', no one is able to cope with
the basic question: 'Who understands the sheet pulled tight/And
Maura's locked blue hands?' Failing to find an answer, the poem fills the
void of incomprehension with images of bad weather, parents at a loss,
and fragile memories of the dead girl.

Drama is inherent in the linked oppositions of oxymoron. It is a
unifying factor in the accounts of journeys into a widening understanding of the interaction of good and evil. In those explorations, voice
and tone, both part of the characterization of the central consciousness,
are adapted to reflect the evolving drama of his changing perceptions. In
the first long poem, 'A Country Walk', Kinsella finds a personal voice
and employs the language of everyday use. The opening lines create an
immediate characterization.

> Sick of the piercing company of women,
> I swung the gate shut with a furious sigh,
> Rammed trembling hands in pockets and drew in
> A breath of river air. (44)

The bluntly assertive 'Sick of' and a succession of active verbs – 'swung',
'Rammed', 'drew in' – all in dominant positions – and strong adjectives
– 'piercing', 'furious', 'trembling' – leave no doubt as to the poet's
emotional state.

The persona is realized in these opening lines – emotional, and
responsive to the natural world. Active verbs bring him alive: 'I clapped
my gloves…I knelt, baring my hand, and scooped and drank'. The
direction is not towards descriptions of nature, although these are exact
and evocative, but through the graph of emotional change. The personal
becomes linked with the impersonal as he responds to immediate
surroundings.

> On either hand, dead trunks in drapes of creeper.
> I walked their hushed stations, passion dying,
> Each slow footfall a drop of peace returning. (44)

The lines move with deliberate slowness through varying stresses, a
changing caesura and an additional stress; 'peace' comes step by step, the
pace mimicking the emotional movement. In addition, the imagery is
comforting – fragrant cattle, their liquid passage, beaded grass, the holy
stillness of the well from which he drinks in a natural communion in the
context of these images where the sensuous language conveys his
feelings. The poem's enjoyment comes not only from what is said but

from the ways in which language is used; imagery, rhythm and sound create the meaning.

Farther on, in a calming mood, the walker observes the roofs of the town. The steady pace, an outward sign of growing composure, enables Kinsella to take in the mythical and historical events associated with the place. The mythical include the Cú Cuchulain–Ferdia combat at a ford and the death of Conchobar Mac Nessa on the day Christ died. The historical include more recent events. 'There' the Normans slaughtered his 'fathers'. That cross commemorates the Anglo-Irish War, followed by Civil War, followed by independence when 'our watchful elders' exchanged 'A trenchcoat playground for a gombeen jungle'. The tone is explicitly judgemental, as is the sarcasm in the anti-nationalistic 'MacDonagh and McBride/Merchants, Connolly's Commercial Arms'.

In the concluding section the walker passes the Christian Brothers School where the words 'silent', 'never looked on lover', 'frosted glass', 'turned away' intimate a loveless isolation. Descending to its conclusion in suggestions of the underworld, the poem ends positively with images of activity, river waters – 'Kissing, dismembering', accepting and giving – and the appearance of the evening star, *'Venit Hesperus'*. The peace that comes has been arrived at through the assuagement of place and the moral distancing, feeling and mind both affected, bringing the walker to a condition in which he can resume his writing. The poem is directed towards bringing him into focus. His character issues in his reactions to the changing scene. He is a particular kind of walker. He speaks bluntly, identifying place and event. The violence of the past goes with him. Things happened at 'that shallow ford', 'There' and 'there' and 'twice more', and on the day 'Christ hung dying', 'twin' brothers fought. The 'day darkened', there was 'a full eclipse'. Irish saga and biblical narrative fuse. He also connects the Norman massacre of his 'fathers' and Oliver Cromwell's butcheries to the place. In the references to the Anglo-Irish War and the Civil War the tone changes. Kinsella's sarcastic account anticipates one of the voices that will emerge later in *Nightwalker and Other Poems*.

These references to Irish revolution and commerce are reminiscent of Yeats's observations on the Paudeens at their greasy tills. But Kinsella keeps his distance. His voice will not be lost in the language of the Celtic Revival or the attitudes of romantic nationalism. The way he describes the countryside is also different from the imprecise and delicate depiction of landscape in Yeats's early poetry. Unlike Yeats, Kinsella deals with an actual landscape. The difference from Yeats is more sharply marked in the tone he uses to recall nationalistic figures.

Yeats celebrated those who had brought about the terrible beauty of the 1916 Rising.

> I write it out in a verse –
> MacDonagh and MacBride
> And Connolly and Pearse
> Now and in time to be,
> Wherever green is worn,
> Are changed, changed utterly:
> A terrible beauty is born.[2]

Kinsella's voice is deflating,

> I came upon the sombre monuments
> That bear their names: MacDonagh and McBride,
> Merchants; Connolly's Commercial Arms...(46)

Yeats raises his nationalists to heroic status; Kinsella, who will not uphold a heroic agenda, lowers them to a mercenary reality. Yeats's energy and passion are countered by Kinsella's levelling speech in which there is no tolerance for nationalist violence and no trace of admiration.

The first person narrator in 'Downstream', the second long poem in *Downstream*, has a more muted voice, interacting at a diminished rate with the natural world into which he brings a narrower and more burdened sense of historical violence. The connection between the two poems is that Kinsella's voice is again literary and historical and that the issue of violence is central, a matter of terrifying reality, not of romantic glorification. To an even greater degree than 'A Country Walk', 'Downstream' affirms a sense of historical catastrophe not within the comforting cycle of Yeats's *A Vision*, but within a disturbing evolutionary progression. The 'I' figure is not as vividly present as the figure in 'A Country Walk'. He and his companion are literary travellers who talk of poetry as they set out. The narrator reads out a page from Ezra Pound's *Cantos* and then, as he takes the oars, names 'old signs' above the Central Plain. As in Dante's *Inferno* this, too, is a journey into the abyss, the voyagers resemble Dante and Virgil, the *terza rima* in which much of the poem is written being a further attempt to relate this journey to the previous one.

Those self-conscious literary allusions, however, give way to a sense of dread: the 'black cage' closes in, 'furred night-brutes' stop and listen. At once the narrator remembers the frightening story of the man who died among these bushes, the shell of his body half-eaten before it was found. That revived memory has an instant effect: the 'cold of hell', 'a terror in the glands' stop his blood. He associates that 'terror' with the

immense evil of the Second World War in which 'swinish men'
replicated what 'furred night brutes' did in the woods. He experiences
war by day and at night in hellish, metaphorical dreams.

> ...Each night a fall
> Back to the evil dream where rodents ply,
> Man-rumped, sow-headed, busy with whip and maul
>
> Among nude herds of the damned.

This perception of moral evil is all the more traumatic because the poet
had been 'impervious to calamity' before he heard as a child the story of
the dead man in the woods, 'Imagining a formal drift of the
dead/Stretched calm as effigies...', but the story of the dead man

> ...thrust
> Pungent horror and an actual mess
> Into my very face, and taste I must. (49)

That shocked confrontation with the fact of evil and death is one
discovery he wants to emphasize. The end of the poem will replace it
with a more positive one.

Now, as he journeys into the 'alleys of the wood', he remembers the
body 'Spreadeagled on a rack of leaves'. Now, however, the horror is
transmuted to a calm encounter between the dead man and the stars. At
the heart of the journey as the boat trembles across the 'abyss' the poet
has a radiant insight, signalled by the movement of the swan, 'A soul of
white with darkness for a nest'. In the heart of darkness this creature 'bore
the night so tranquilly': the narrator raises his eyes to see the pattern of
order in which the stars descend to the starlit eye of the dead man.

> The slow, downstreaming dead, it seemed, were blended
>
> One with those silver hordes, and briefly shared
> Their order, glittering. (50)

The slow-moving stream carries a slow-moving poem that is freighted
with significance, past and present joined, all the memories determining
the consciousness of the speaker. He is burdened by the past, by the
experience of evil, by the shock of its discovery, but the plot of that past
is summarized, its mystery plucked from the stream of existence and
vividly realized. The voice is earnest and purposeful, a witness to a truth
arising from blackness. What is new is the perception of order, the

countering of brutish evil with the swan's serenity. The movement is internal as well as external, from dread to tranquillity.

Thomas Kinsella looks into situations, enters into them imaginatively, and out of the engagement reaches insight, a momentary understanding before the next encounter. This process of ever-deepening engagement, a growing capacity to absorb over an expanding radius, is the basic movement in his work. The tranquillity embodied in the swan becomes representative of a newly perceived order, a confirmation of something ultimately reassuring and positive. It contrasts with the account of his terrifying discoveries of death, the 'evil dream' and man's capacity for rat-like behaviour. That shock is calmed by the vision of peace and harmony. The accomplished, varied rhythms of this poem are one of its main achievements, moving it through its successive engagements with horror and its mingling of past and present dread. The adventurer, Dante-like in his descent into the depths towards the discovery of the evil that men do, moves through and towards insight. But the 'barrier of rock' that brings the poem to its 'landing place' qualifies the vision of peace at the end.

These explorations and discoveries, extended journeys through personal clarifications, require a sharper style. 'Mirror in February', the last poem in *Downstream*, a self-examination, is a farewell to youth and a declaration of a change in diction. Spring is imminent, but he will not be made whole again in 'this untiring, crumbling place of growth'. The pollarded trees have 'suffered their brute necessities'; their mutilation corresponds to his, but he is stoically ready. 'I fold my towel with what grace I can,/Not young and not renewable, but man.' To be 'Riveted' by an awareness of ageing at 30 seems excessive, but there is no reason to doubt the mood in which the self-scrutiny is conducted. It is in keeping with the melancholy that dogs Kinsella's life. Just as the trees have been 'hacked clean for better bearing', he will endure and be fruitful in a sparer diction.

That linguistic change is evident in the *Nightwalker* collection. The allegorical 'Ballydavid Pier' has a simpler style and 'Folk Wisdom', which is similarly reduced, is a palpable expression of death's impending horror. But the pictorial 'Landscape and Figure', a compact philosophical poem, written in a direct and unemotional manner, indicates Kinsella's new-found ability to compress meaning in simple, unadorned language and at the same time to enrich it with dual significance. It acknowledges Pierre Teilhard de Chardin's concept of the omega point towards which all processes move. Many of the short poems are versions of the same lessons of confusions, uncertainties or loss of direction. Together they form a comprehensive statement of Kinsella's philosophy of endurance and his sense of recurrent, temporary reward. Occasionally, as in 'Charlie', he will derive wry comedy from the 'traps' in which the self survives or, as in the introduction to *Downstream*, will run a self-deprecatory slide rule over his ordinary life. In 'Old Harry' he allows himself the luxury of unforgiving judgement on a monstrous evil. More usually he will juggle good against evil just as the bull-dancers of Knossos, whom he admires, will execute demanding acts of survival, one at a time, before going on to the next encounter, the next leap into risk, the next countering of the threat of the deadly beast.

Notes

1   *Collected Poems 1956–2001* (Manchester: Carcanet Press, 2001), p.21. Subsequent references are given in the text and, unless specifically noted, are to this edition.
2   W.B. Yeats, *The Poems: A New Edition*, ed. Richard J. Finneran (Dublin: Gill and Macmillan, 1983), p.182.

2

ORDEAL AFTER ORDEAL

If Kinsella's voice in these poems has been serious in manner, the persona in 'Wormwood' is even more earnest, as he addresses the '*Beloved*', and then interprets their relationship to illustrate his theory of redemptive endurance.

> It is certain that maturity and peace are to be sought through ordeal after ordeal, and it seems that the search continues until we fail. We reach out after each new beginning, penetrating our context to know ourselves, and our knowledge increases until we recognise again (more profoundly each time) our pain, indignity and triviality. This bitter cup is offered, heaped with curses, and we must drink or die. And even though we may drink we may also die, if every drop of bitterness – that rots the flesh – is not transmuted. (Certainly the individual plight is hideous, each torturing each, but we are guilty, seeing this, to believe that our common plight is only hideous. Believing so, we make it so: pigs in a slaughter-yard that turn and savage each other in common desperation and disorder.) Death, either way, is guilt and failure. But if we drink the bitterness and can transmute it and continue, we resume in candour and doubt the only individual joy – the restored necessity to learn. Sensing a wider scope, a more penetrating harmony, we begin again in a higher innocence to grow toward the next ordeal.
>
> Love also, it seems, will continue until we fail: in the sensing of the wider scope, in the growth toward it, in the swallowing and absorption of bitterness, in the resumed innocence. (62)

His is a serious, forthright and measured voice that assesses personal experience and lays out the evidence, confident that his conclusions are incontrovertible. He argues that the only way to handle life's ordeals successfully is to absorb and transmute bitterness. That belief depends on the sustaining force of the couple's love, on the Beloved's continuing support. It is an ethic of suffering similar to that found in Christian teaching, whose images of cup, ordeal, communion and purification through suffering it adapts.

This sequence of seven marriage poems matches images and vignettes of suffering and endurance against those of love and mutual support. The emblematic tree, obsessively undergoing self-punishment, stripping itself of leaves, demonstrates the state of the marriage partners. The metaphor of intertwined trees dramatizes the self as victim of nightmare and suffering. Yeats used the image to represent the continuance of love after death; Kinsella uses it to represent death-in-life: life itself, love itself, marriage, each a living death that must be endured.

> I have dreamt it again: standing suddenly still
> In a thicket, among wet trees, stunned, minutely
> Shuddering, hearing a wooden echo escape.
>
> A mossy floor, almost colourless, disappears
> In depths of rain among the tree shapes.
> I am straining, tasting that echo a second longer.
>
> If I can hold it...familiar if I can hold it.
> A black tree with a double trunk – two trees
> Grown into one – throws up its blurred branches. (63)

The speaker is trapped in nightmare, straining to hold on to the 'echo', possessed and in agony: 'I have dreamt it again'...'I am straining'...'I recognise'...'I will dream it again'. The intertwined trees stand for a love that assimilates and transmutes the ordeal into a dance of growth. Pain and love thus combined result in durable scar tissue. 'Iron sinks in the gasping core./I will dream it again.'

In 'Mask of Love' the poet stresses the need to 'Remember', to keep steadily in mind what they have achieved – 'climbed/the peaks of stress' and faced each other 'Wearily' across the 'narrow abyss'. His is a moral narrative. 'Remember', he insists again, 'That our very bodies lack peace'. It is as though he fears their situation might be misrepresented, or minimized, its value not understood and therefore not made available to absorption and transmutation. They exist in pain, the skin 'flames angrily', but 'Nerves grope for muscle' across the 'silent abyss' between them. Stanza 3 again calls attention to their 'nocturnal/Suicidal dance' and once again the oxymoron clinches the complex relationship. That which gives evidence of 'lack of peace' also shows movement towards connection. But there is no peace. As in tragicomedy the speaker clasps his paunch in laughter at the absurdity of the situation, but in grief at their predicament. 'Mask of Love' voices the feelings of a man doomed to utter his vision of the tragic nature of existence. He, who has seen the darkness and understands both its destructive nature and its potential, calls upon her to grasp the interlocking truth of their doomed fruitful relationship.

'The Secret Garden' provides a more balanced picture. Destruction and beauty coexist – bramble and dewdrop, father and child, death and birth, the 'sour encounter' and procreation. In a tentative and tender voice he accepts the conditions of life, appreciates beauty, of nature, of childhood, even as he knows both are subject to the all-encompassing withering. He is more human and more likeable in this poignant, gentle elegy.

> A child stands an instant at my knee.
> His mouth smells of energy, light as light.
> I touch my hand to his pearl flesh, taking strength.
> He stands still, absorbing in return
> The first taint. Immaculate, the waiting
> Kernel of his brain.
> How set him free, a son, toward the sour encounter? (65)

'The Secret Garden' portrays this truth, with dew as an image of fragile beauty in a threatening world. 'Tiny worlds, drop by drop, tremble/On thorns and leaves; they will melt away.' The withering is everywhere. The child is full of energy, 'light as light', but destined to absorb the necessary, inevitable 'first taint'. The wise father, in possession of insight, appreciates his son's 'pearl flesh', but knows he must release him 'towards the sour encounter'.

> Children's voices somewhere call his name.
> He runs glittering into the sun, and is gone
> ...I cultivate my garden for the dew:
> A rasping boredom funnels into death!
> The sun climbs, a creature of one day,
> And the dew dries to dust.
> My hand strays out and picks off one sick leaf. (65)

In these elegiac lines Kinsella voices his sadness at how things are – impermanence, suffering, death-in-life. The biblical echoes project the speaker as a witness to horror and beauty, raving and weeping over the human condition.

The linguistic texture in 'First Light' is bleak: the couple 'prone', light 'a pale gas', the garden 'dark', the grass 'soaking with grey dew'. The empty kitchen is 'Blank with marriage', 'shrill' lover and beloved 'have kept/Another vigil far/Into the night, and raved and wept.' Upstairs 'a whimper or sigh' lengthens into 'an ugly wail'.

> – A child enduring a dream
> That grows, at the first touch of day,
> Unendurable. (65)

'Unendurable' sums up the situation, but the next poem, 'Remembering Old Wars', takes up the 'Remember' motif from 'Mask of Love' with the opening question, 'What clamped us together?' The 'clamped' underlines the principle of firm bonding – tough and resilient. They lie in the smell of decomposition, their bodies leaking, 'Limp as the dead', and breathing in the odour of decay. Sleep is a simulacrum of death. To awaken is to be 'prodded' towards rediscovery of 'adversity', without hope of 'change or peace'. But they do not despair. 'Each dawn, like lovers recollecting their purpose,/We would renew each other with a savage smile.' Again the contradiction in 'a savage smile' sums up the paradox. The concluding four-line poem with its ironically affectionate title, mockingly true, '*Je t'adore*', summarizes the sequence.

> The other props are gone.
> Sighing in one another's
> Iron arms, propped above nothing,
> We praise Love the limiter. (66)

Despite the difficulties love sustains, enabling them to survive and to continue their suicidal dance, the beauty made of pain.

In the 'Wormwood' poems life is an ongoing conflict and, paradoxically, of fruitful tension. What was experienced in descriptive narratives is compressed in a psychodrama of almost unbearable stress between total collapse and steadfast support. The poems are allegories of intense engagement with life itself, with survival in which the ability to stay alive, that is to remain engaged, is earned at the point of maximum suffering, in the deepest part of the pit.

The depressive speaker is also at the heart of 'Nightwalker', a poem in many voices that ranges out from the self to encompass an environment that both reflects the observer and demonstrates why he suffers. Descriptions of place reflect his consciousness. The tone varies from weary to mocking, sarcastic to reflective and philosophical. Kinsella is the worn commuter – 'Mindful of the shambles of the day' – who has to endure the daily journey from the depressing surroundings of suburban Sandycove, the city of the dead, to the dispiriting routines of the Civil Service. He reacts with scorn and anger to the First Economic Programme by which the Government encouraged and subsidized outside investors. His disappointment is interfaced with the inscription

on New York's Statue of Liberty welcoming the huddled masses.
Kathleen Ní Houlihan, her opposite, has become a debased figure identified as Productive Investment. The tone is shaped by the clichés of the
business world and the meretricious seductions of the new programme.

> Robed in spattered iron she stands
> At the harbour mouth, Productive Investment,
> And beckons the nations through our gold half-door:
> Lend me your wealth, your cunning and your drive,
> Your arrogant refuse. Let my people serve them
> Holy water in our new hotels,
> While native businessmen and managers
> Drift with them chatting over to the window
> To show them our growing city, give them a feeling
> Of what is possible; our labour pool,
> The tax concessions to foreign capital,
> How to get a nice estate though German.
> Even collect some of our better young artists. (78)

The lines are bitterly sarcastic. Violence has been done to his country's
values.

The metaphor of violence permeates the poem. He sees it in the
metaphorical birth of the Moon, which was a sundering from the
earth. He sees it in the shift in values by which commercial interests
take priority over cultural and moral ones, in the debasement of education, in the cynical misuse of the Irish language, in the reduction
of religion to pious platitudes, in the educational failure to prepare the
young for the realities of the modern world. If the traveller in
'Downstream' once lived in a dream, the walker here has been shocked
wide awake and the many topics in the poem are a catalogue of events
and issues that have jolted him into clear-eyed assessment and into
the fundamental conviction that he must be vigilant. A local watchfulness is imperative.

His tale bristles at times with detail, as in the political fable of the
Wedding Group, which tells of a friendship that turned to enmity.
The Groom, Best Man, the Fox, and their three ladies form the
Wedding Group. Their sundering into violence and slaughter sum-
marizes what happened when former friends – Kevin O'Higgins, Rory
O'Connor, and Eamon de Valera, who had been at the wedding of
Kevin O'Higgins – took opposing sides in the Civil War and the first
two were killed.

                              There: The Wedding Group...
        The Groom, the Best Man, the Fox, and their three ladies.
        A tragic tale.
                              Soon, the story tells,
        Enmity sprang up between them, and the Fox
        Took to the wilds. Then, to the Groom's sorrow,
        His dear friend left him also, vowing hatred.
        So they began destroying the Groom's substance
        And he sent out to hunt the Fox, but trapped
        His friend instead; mourning he slaughtered him.
        Shortly in his turn the Groom was savaged
        No one knows by whom. Though it's known the Fox
        Is a friend of Death, and rues nothing. (78–9)

Significantly, as the walker approaches Sandycove, he appeals to James Joyce, the prose master, rather than to W.B. Yeats, the master poet, the Martello tower at Sandycove rather than the Norman tower at Thoor Ballylee. He is signalling the stance he has taken as an artist. On the one hand some sections of the poem resemble the stream-of-consciousness technique used in certain parts of *Ulysses*. They have the same fluidity of movement through incidents, memories, ideas and images. On the other hand, in invoking James Joyce, Kinsella declares an allegiance to a writer who made his work out of the gritty and often unattractive reality of life in twentieth-century Dublin rather than to a writer who preferred to commemorate the fallen majesty of the Ascendancy and distanced himself from the Paudeens at their greasy tills. Drawing from experience, Kinsella writes a loosely structured, rapidly evolving poem in which the registering consciousness seeks 'structure'.

The walker is angry, sorrowful and depressed but he is also positive, concluding with a clear metaphor of how arid life is when on the moon's barren surface he faces the Sea of Disappointment where 'massed human wills' grope for structure. That seems conclusive, but it is not the full picture. In itself the creative imagination is a positive force countering the negative forces in the poem – the primary violence, the widespread damage done to society, politics, language, culture and people. The changing tones – indignation, sarcasm, anger, mockery, affection, reflection, affirmation – and the variety of rhetorical responses – fable, injunction, address, elegy, drama, political allegory, symbolic narrative, historical and literary allusion – produce a dynamic response to the dismaying circumstances. The more devastating the portrayal of harmful events, the more positive the imaginative achievement; the darkness of its social and moral contexts are a foil for its satisfying aesthetic. Art itself, as Kinsella will affirm later in a succession of exemplary figures, such as

Seán Ó Riada and Gustav Mahler, brings order to the fragmentation of life and belief, provides an imaginative coherence, makes sense of the irrational ('the madness without,/The madness within'), seeks and at times attains that order which appears so repeatedly even in these earlier poems.

In 'Nightwalker' the transition towards a psychological landscape is complete. The idea of a violent era, indeed of a world created in a violent sundering, is described in language more surreal than real. The figures that enter the work, from the German siblings to political leaders like Eamon de Valera and Kevin O'Higgins, to the teacher Brother Burke are absorbed into a phantasmagoric texture that resembles the phantasmagory found in Goethe's *Faust*, Part II. If constellations seethe to the surface of the walker's consciousness, rising and falling, so the changing scenes, changing figures and changing voices appear and disappear, coalescing, present all together and separate in the mind of the walker. The poem acknowledges Joyce, the master, but goes beyond the fluidity of *Ulysses to* the more universal dream world of *Finnegans Wake*. More than ever before moving away from traditional forms, Kinsella has found a structure, a technique and a language that conjoins his philosophy and his belief in the sustaining force of love. Despite endemic violation, deprivation and betrayal, the poem is superbly creative as it gathers and transforms fragmentary elements into a coherent imaginative statement. That it concludes in a vision of barrenness that metaphorically confirms the cultural–political–educational failures makes its aesthetic vitality all the more admirable.

In blunter terms the poem attacks not only the vulgar, gombeen commercialism of the new Ireland embodied by Charles Haughey, the emergent leader, but the sentimental, superficially nationalistic education provided by the Christian Brothers, including the uncritical glorification of the Irish language that both Kinsella and Haughey experienced in the same school. The Cain and Abel implications of this association and of the Civil War he explores later. Haughey's emergence like a figure in medieval Irish narratives indicates, as Kinsella notes in a list that underlines the significance of their imaginal presence in the poem, the debased standards of modern Ireland, its gombeen culture, new hotels, land sold to Germans, and the coarse dynastic struggles engaged in by the new political leader (box 5, folder 18). Haughey is his dark Jungian brother. That education should have been presided over by the Catholic Church made a link between commercialism and Catholicism which Kinsella also examines later, in *Personal Places* (1990) and other collections. There was, he knew, a kind of brainless innocence about the situation, but it damaged an entire generation. That failure fuses with the poem's theme of disappointment.

If the 'Wormwood' sequence is realized in a straitjacket, the voice
of the persona in 'Nightwalker' is freer. Here the Tiresian consciousness in a sea of transient and changing circumstances seeks for
structure and in the end finds it within. In its shifting scenes and
changing voices, the poet's anger at what has been done to a generation is palpable – the debasement of cultural values, the nationalistic
pleading, all adumbrated in 'a dish of scalding tears.... The food of
dragons/And my own dragon self'. Juxtaposed with this angry summary is the elegiac voice of Amergin, the Old Irish poet, as a seamew
lamenting what has happened to the country in a style that imitates
voices in some early plays at the Abbey Theatre: '*Eire,/Eire. Is there
none to hear? Is all lost?/Alas, I think I will dash myself at the stones.*'
(82) Then in a dramatic change of mood and rhythm the speaker
makes an imaginary flight to the Moon whose barren surface gives an
unrestricted view of the depressive conditions he has seen. The poem
concludes:

> If I stoop down and touch the dust
> It has a human taste:
> > massed human wills.
>
> I believe
> > I have heard of this place. I think
> This is the Sea of Disappointment. (84)

'Disappointment' is the appropriate word for a generation that was fed
on the pap of false nationalism, for whom growing up meant being thrust
into a reality for which they had not been prepared. Kinsella projects
himself as a product and a victim of this Ireland. He may detest many
of its features, he may deeply regret and resent what has been done to
Irish culture and life, but as a writer he will not turn away from them.
From this position he will transmute its negative aspects into something
positive in the life of the poem. He belongs to the generation of the
1950s, something he has never forgotten. He understood and sym-
pathized with those who never escaped its stultifying atmosphere, even
as he knew that he himself had to wriggle free.

W.B. Yeats stepped out of the shadows of the Celtic Revival in his
collection *Responsibilities* (1914)[1] and mounted an attack on his contemporaries – the Paudeens at their greasy tills, the pious and cautious
people who would be incapable of understanding what patriots had
done in the past – his voice layered with sarcasm.

> What need you, being come to sense,
> But fumble in a greasy till
> And add the halfpence to the pence
> And prayer to shivering prayer, until
> You have dried the marrow from the bone?
> For men were born to pray and save:
> Romantic Ireland's dead and gone,
> It's with O'Leary in the grave.

Yeats's heightened litany of the names of those known as the 'wild geese' because so many went down the river Shannon into exile after the Siege of Limerick memorializes those who had died for what they believed, who did not pause to count the cost, who were capable of the admirable 'delirium of the brave', true forbears of the indomitable Fenian patriot John O'Leary.

> Was it for this the wild geese spread
> The grey wing upon every tide;
> For this that all that blood was shed,
> For this Edward Fitzgerald died,
> And Robert Emmet and Wolfe Tone,
> All that delirium of the brave?
> Romantic Ireland's dead and gone,
> It's with O'Leary in the grave.[2]

Kinsella's political attack is also unexpected. Until now the issues in his poetry have been traditional – love, mutability, creativity, death. Very little required an understanding of specific Irish contexts. Nor had he dealt directly with politics or social matters. *Nightwalker and Other Poems* deals specifically with them, his own time, place and generation, and with withering honesty.

In 'Nightwalker', an anguished self whose expectations have been cruelly disappointed and who can find no supportive values outside himself, searches for structure on his own. This accords with what Kinsella believes about the plight of the individual.

> The most sensitive individuals have been shaken loose from society into disorder, conscious of a numbness and dullness in themselves, a pain of dislocation and loss.... Everywhere in modern writing the stress is on personal versions of the world.... The detailed explorations of private miseries is an expedition into the interior to find out what may guide us in the future. It is out of ourselves and our wills that the chaos

came, and out of ourselves that some order must be con-
structed.[3]

Key terms – 'numbness', 'pain', 'loss', 'miseries', 'chaos', as well as
'exploration', 'guide' and 'order' – summarize the preoccupation of work
focused on the self. A credibility gap exists between appearance and
reality, 'I only know things seem and are not good'. In its examination
and ordering, 'Nightwalker' identifies issues that have created this
deceiving division. The perception goes beyond particular instances to
the realization that the human mind itself is an abyss, that the will is
capable of every evil. The Second World War accelerated the process of
disappointment and Kinsella's terminology is darkened with a peppering
of associated terms – 'brutal', 'squalid', 'ordeal', 'ignominies', 'failure',
'horror'. Life is a 'sour ordeal', one suffers its 'brute necessities'; history
is a treadmill, a nightmare of returning disappointments.

In 'Phoenix Park' the rational imagination is supreme, the objective
narrator organizes the poem into sections. Objectivity is natural in a
poem that is philosophical in the manner of some of Yeats's later work,
devoted to propounding and illustrating beliefs. On the one hand, it articulates where Kinsella stands, on the other it declares his wife's supreme
importance to him. As a love poem it is different from those in *Poems*
but closer to the 'Wormwood' poems in how it sees the couple's struggle;
but the language, while describing that ordeal and the cup that must be
drunk, is more lyrical, more fluent, exhibiting a greater variety of
rhythm. Ultimately, it is an *apologia* for the kind of poet he is and for
the beliefs that underpin his work.

In the poem those beliefs are expressed in a variety of mirroring
images and allusions – 'opposite within opposite', 'living surfaces/
Mirror each other', 'Figure echoes/Figure'. They also appear in statements about the ordeal, in acceptance of change, in laws of order.

> Laws of order I find I have discovered
> Mainly at your hands. Of failure and increase.
> The stagger and recovery of spirit:
> That life is hunger, hunger is for order,
> And hunger satisfied brings on new hunger
>
> Till there's nothing to come; – let the crystal crack
> On some insoluble matter, then its heart
> Shudders and accepts the flaw, adjusts on it
> Taking new strength – given the positive dream;
> Given, with your permission, undying love. (90)

This passage incorporates values that have been expressed before, including the process of adjustment to what is flawed, but the language clarifies what earlier poems had sometimes expressed less directly. Freed of their usual texture, words like 'stare', 'failure', 'cup', 'ordeal', 'bitterness', 'orders of stars', 'darkness', 'fever', 'one positive dream', 'tasting', 'tearing' have an accumulated richness and strength. But what is particularly significant, and indicative of the directions Kinsella's poetry will take, is the ways in which the poem incorporates the sense of fading and coalescence. Scenes and figures, particularly those of women, recur and change, as they will in later poetry.

> ...A few ancient faces
> Detach and begin to circle. Deeper still,
> Delicate distinct tissue begins to form, (94)

The comma invites us to read on, in the next collection.

'Phoenix Park' contains some of Kinsella's basic ideas, in particular the one he has had from the beginning: poetry should not impose order but elicit it, discover it in the process of writing. On the verge of departure from Ireland he and Eleanor visit the Phoenix Park, where a few years before she had been a patient in St Mary's Hospital and where he used to visit her. Those visits resulted in some of his earliest poems. Her fever there is now related to a more general force 'that eats everything'. How to counter that hunger is one of the quests in the poem, which searches for an order glimpsed in the movements of stars. It is based on the knowledge of opposition at the heart of a fruitful relationship. He interprets lessons of change and loss, of love and destruction, for her benefit.

For him the prospect of leaving, with its sense of a new beginning, are not as disquieting as they are for her. Life being an ordeal, or rather a series of ordeals, it does not matter, he argues, where they endure them. What matters is their readiness to absorb them. Within the cup are signs of order – mirror images of resemblances and correspondences....

> ...Figure echoes
> Figure faintly in the saturated depths;
>
> Revealed by faint flash of each other
> They light the whole confines: a fitful garden...(89)

Within the bitterness of existence lies a harmonious pattern. The poem becomes an intense acknowledgement of her importance to him as he lives through his profoundly threatened existence. Life, he believes, is a form of hunger, hunger for order, and there is no point of satiation. Defeat or failure can be adjusted to, but the processes of acceptance and renewal rest on 'the positive dream', on 'undying love'. As long as the positive dream continues, the spirit, on the brink of living, reaches out into the 'void', until everything that can be absorbed has been assimilated. Life is consumed; the process brings the cup to fulfilment: 'this live world is emptied of its hunger/While the crystal world, undying, crowds with light/Filling the cup.' (90) The tone of the poem is both intimate and tender as he explains his philosophy with fiercely realistic honesty. Now his intellectual rigour recapitulates the lessons of 'Wormwood'. Life is destructive; to live it fully is to be afflicted by its destructive aspects.

> ... Giving without tearing
>
> Is not possible; to give totality
> Is to be torn totally, a nothingness
> Reaching out in stasis a pure nothingness. (90)

The poem becomes a hymn of praise to the Beloved, to her fragility and her instinctive ability to assimilate suffering. She is the physically weaker partner, yet essential to him. Failure, death will come, when the self-enriching forward movement is inhibited by some refusal of the cup. Although he does not write love poems for her, he can offer her 'something for singing', something that rises above the sour realities of these reflections in an autumnal setting.

> *Fragility echoing fragilities*
> *From whom I have had every distinctness*
> *Accommodate me still, where – folded in peace*
> *And undergoing with ghostly gaiety*
> *Inner immolation, shallowly breathing –*
>
> *You approach the centre by its own sweet light.*
> *I consign my designing will stonily*
> *To your flames. Wrapped in that rosy fleece, two lives*
> *Burn down around one love, one flickering-eyed*
> *Stone self becomes more patient than its own stone.* (92)

Instead of 'Wormwood's' agony of scarred trunks, we have the Yeatsian–Swedenborgian union of flames. Joined in 'that rosy fleece' they endure the reduction of the flesh; they are not defeated by bitterness, but resigned and triumphant. In a final section they are attended by images of beauty, memories of love and sexual consummation, and intimations of creativity to come.

Notes

1   W.B. Yeats, *Responsibilities: Poems and A Play* (Churchtown, Dundrum: The Cuala Press, 1914).
2   Yeats, *The Poems: A New Edition*, p.108.
3   See Kinsella, 'Poetry and Man', *Directions*, 1966–67, pp.7–8.

IN THE YOLK OF ONE'S BEING

While taking part in a panel discussion held at McGill University in March 1973 on the subject of 'Ancient Myth and Poetry', Kinsella explained his understanding of the poetic process. It begins, he argued, with experience being ingested and then sieved by the imagination for its significance. It spends some time in the depths of the mind where it forms relationships with other material already absorbed. It lies ready, in a kind of ever-saturating solution, to be 'crystallized out' at the moment of inspiration. At this point a significant cluster – a structure of imaginatively processed reality – responds to a particular impulse and a poem may result.[1] The archetype, he had recorded in his notes, pre-exists and is immanent in the human psyche. It has been there in the 'darkness' ever since the typical and fundamental experience it reflects took place and became part of 'the psychic treasure house of mankind'. He goes on to say, quoting Jolande Jacobi, that 'as the image rises to consciousness, it is irradiated with increasing light, sharpens and clarifies its contours until it is visible in every detail in the process of illumination'.[2]

Jung's ideas of the primordial image and of the human psyche provided Kinsella with a system that validated his perception of the world, and in its shifting complexities and fluid accommodations accorded well with his understanding of his own psychic make-up and with his sense of how the creative unconscious works. Jungian concepts make sense of the dark forces within the psyche. They interpret familiar myths as archetypes in which man's inner terrors are externalized. They explore the significance of the dark brother or shadow as a manifestation of man's deepest fears and preoccupations and identify the anima as the personification of feminine psychological tendencies in man and his capacity to be receptive to the irrational. Above all, Jung's theories posit the influx of the unconscious into the consciousness and argue that when one accepts these darker forces a new balance may be achieved. He viewed the unconscious and its archetypal forms as symbolic images of the union of opposites: for him that union is a state of strength. The aim of psychic exploration, Kinsella notes, accepting Jung's theory of individuation, is psychic totality, in which at least three of the four functions of the mind – thinking, feeling, sensation and intuition – and both attitudes, the introvert and the extrovert, are made as conscious and available as possible for what he calls 'life's evening (making even)' (box 10, folder 21).

During the panel discussion he said that, as the poet comes to terms with something that is vital to him, he will find himself undergoing for the nth time the primary mythical experience of death and rebirth, imaginatively understood; the sea-journey in the dark; Persephone's season in Hades; encounters with the Snake; the breaking open of the egg, the hatching of things. All of these, he declares, 'can be aids in the muscular, imaginative struggle for understanding'. If they help the poet to understand, they also help towards communication since they are shared by mankind. The reader will complete the act of communication, because he will undergo in turn a primary mythical experience ('Ancient Myth', 10). As Jung argues, primordial image patterns evoke similar feelings in both reader and author. The value of the archetype for the writer is that it enriches the particular figure or incident by evoking similar figures or incidents. It provides a foundation of values for both writer and reader. Groundwork is provided, for communication and for understanding, 'for the poet's understanding of reality, of what his own life, his ordeal, is about' ('Ancient Myth', 9).

In Kinsella's view, the poet opens his psyche to 'the vast store of ancestral knowledge about the profound relations between God, man, and cosmos represented by the archetype'. The opening, he maintains, can save the individual from isolation and gather him into the eternal cosmic process, that is, to a way of life (box 10, folder 21). In Kinsella's notes, the tone of exhilaration is palpable. The Jungian system gave him ideological support and alleviated his feeling of existential disappointment. If the self feels isolated as a result of a breakdown in beliefs, feels alienated from society, has a frightening sense of evil, has entered into a process of investigation into its own make-up, then the Jungian world offers a possibility of understanding and support. By deliberately exploring the unconscious, he allowed the archetypes to irrupt, just as Jung had given free expression to the irrational side of his nature. The process of individuation could result in a fuller understanding of the self; Jungian psychotherapy may lead to the knowledge and fulfilment of personality. In reading Jacobi and Jung, Kinsella discovered a means by which he could absorb and transmute life's ordeals and disappointments. At the beginning of every coming to consciousness, as he cryptically notes, is the differentiation of the ego from the mother: 'Creation of awareness, formulation of ideas = logos = father: struggling out of the wombworld, e.g., "Let there be light" = logosfatherdifferentiating from original dark mother; then both continue differentiating to the end of the world' (box 10, folder 21).

The period may be said to begin with *New Poems* (1973), which absorbs the poems in *Notes from the Land of the Dead* (1972), subsequently referred to in the *Collected Poems* as 'From the Land of the Dead'. The psychological directions taken by the narrator in 'Nightwalker' is deepened in 'From the Land of the Dead', which Kinsella planned as a simple plot of individuation. The use of dramatic methods continues. Kinsella now imagines himself as a Faustian adventurer prepared to face abnormal states, one who has 'turned to things not right nor [*sic*] reasonable', as Faust did when he made his compact with the devil. In an exclamatory style the 'appalled' self remembers and recreates the extreme experience. To be appalled, in Kinsella's view, is the greatest gift of man, the active acceptance of the negative is a source of strength (box 10, folder 16).

> Dear God, if I had known how far and deep,
> how long and cruel, I think my being
> would have blanched: appalled. (95)

The poem's method bears witness for us, and once again acts out what was private and traumatic. Now we have the self as magician with his implements, preparing to go out of his mind into the depths of the unconscious, to fall out of this world into the abyss – 'So far from the world and earth' – where there is

> No bliss, no pain; dullness after pain.
> A cistern hiss...A thick tunnel stench
> rose to meet me. Frightful. Dark nutrient waves.
> And I knew no more. (96)

The loss of consciousness is followed by an embryonic state in which he drifts, seeking an empty shell in which to grow. The narrator remembers the ordeal, the fall, and the search for a way back to the upper world. This emblematic account prefigures what happens elsewhere in the collection, in particular in several poems that concentrate on the significance of scenes that use the dramatic trope of a child's encounter with his grandmother.

Goethe's *Faust* is an immediate source of the collection. The plot, as Kinsella cites, follows the story of Mephisto, who received the glowing key, descended to the Mothers, was appalled, but sees this as a gift, enters the realm of forms where there are drifting clouds of energy, and comes to the glowing tripod. The Mothers are shrouded in vapours; he touches the tripod with the key and returns with his prize to the Hall in the upper world (box 10, folder 15). The archetypal journey is ultimately redemptive. In the poem, the 'pit' to which he falls is a place of becoming. The 'naked ancient women' he meets prefigure later encounters with female figures, owls, birds of prey, taloned creatures. Above him is the grill through which he must return with his 'prize'.

In these poems the 'I' narrator is a witness. In 'Hen Woman' the tone is one of serious attention – alert, detailed, perceptive, reading the small event, the trivial scene, packing it with significance. He gives the details of place, time and the atmosphere surrounding the event. The objectivity of his narrative freezes the moment, the figures and the event into a diagram. 'Nothing moved', 'time stood still' – bird, woman, and child 'locked there...gaping'. Then the dung beetle, bearer of life, advances, the egg falls, thunder sounds. This searching into the substance for significance is presented as the way in which the imagination seizes experience and takes it in to be processed. 'I feed upon it still', he tells us:

> ...there is no end to that which, not understood,
> may yet be hoarded in the imagination,
> in the yolk of one's being, so to speak,
> there to undergo its (quite animal) growth,
>
> dividing blindly, twitching, packed with will,
> searching in its own tissue
> for the structure in which it may wake.
> Something that had – clenched in its cave –
> not been now was: an egg of being. (99)

The underworld setting, the movement from darkness to light, from the land of the dead to the land of the living, allusions to the rape of Persephone, the references to eating pip-filled fruit all suggest a primordial mythological level. The Persephone story is a vegetation myth, a story of death and rebirth, as is the story, also included, of the arrival of early peoples in Ireland in the synchronistic and unreliably edited *Book of Invasions*.[3] The purpose of the descent into the abyss is to complete the personality and to release creativity by facing up to inner darkness. According to Jung, the unconscious is the creative mother of consciousness. It wells up from unknown depths. To follow the Jungian path of individuation is to seek understanding and thereby find order. The artist, Kinsella believes, can take a positive attitude towards the figures of the vision (images, symbols and visions that rise up from the depths): this can lead to artistic achievement. The great artist, he notes, 'faces the figures actively – assimilates and integrates, humanly *experiences* and *understands* the images and symbols that rise up. The very greatest *can broaden* and *deepen their personality and their work in equal degree: all a function of consciousness*' (box 10, folder 21).

Kinsella's initial impulse to write a poem about one of his grand-mothers becomes an exploration of the contrasts implicit in that encounter, the one setting out on the road of life, innocent and untested, the other at the end of that road, aged, dying, shrivelling into death; the images associated with her are blackness, decay, smells and fear. To the little boy she is a figure of dread, witchlike, predatory, mysterious, someone he is urged to visit, to kiss, to encounter. She is based on a real person:

> ...a tyrannical old woman hawk faced who sold sweets ill-temperedly to the children of the neighbourhood: she drank behind the counter Power's whiskey from small bottles & Guinness's stout from a milk can and, when she was ready for bed, moved the length of the counter, threatening and black in her many aprons, & vanished behind plush red hangings into the darkness of her room and her husband. (box 61a, folder 11)

And from 'Ancestor':

> I was going up to say something,
> and stopped. Her profile against the curtains
> was old, and dark like a hunting bird's.
>
> It was the way she perched on the high stool,
> staring into herself, with one fist
> gripping the side of the barrier around her desk
> – or her head held by something, from inside.
> And not caring for anything around her
> Or anyone there by the shelves.
> I caught a faint smell, musky and queer.
>
> I may have made some sound – she stopped rocking
> and pressed her fist in her lap; then she stood up
> and shut down the lid of the desk, and turned the key.
> She shoved a small bottle under her aprons
> and came toward me, darkening the passageway.
>
> Ancestor... among sweet- and fruit-boxes.
> Her black heart...
>   Was that a sigh?
> – brushing by me in the shadows,
> with her heaped aprons, through the red hangings
> to the scullery, and down to the back room. (104)

The meeting is allegorical, a terrifying conjunction of youth and age, innocence and experience, the pristine consciousness and the consciousness burdened with life's ordeals.

The associations of these old women are consistent – darkness, a sour smell, an abyss, a back room, talons, a resemblance to a flesh-eating bird, such as an owl. 'Ancestor' is a portrait of this kind of woman. She carries a key and moves in darkness. In 'Tear' he goes to see his grandmother on her deathbed, carried 'to unfathomable depths'. He transfers his farewell kiss to her black aprons and is carried to a 'derelict place/ smelling of ash'. But what he tastes is her compassionate heart.

These poems dramatize the chasm between the boy and the grandmother. Exploring the chasm in mythical terms, they provide an understanding of what is involved in the encounter. In 'A Hand of Solo' the grandmother is a three-headed Hecate figure, offering him the pomegranate, the fruit of life and death, full of seed and blood. In 'The High Road' the boy throws away the sweet she gives him and experiences a feeling of sin even as he relishes the independence of his action. In 'Survivor' the persona may be identified with Fintan, one of the three men who came to Ireland with the prediluvial Cessair and her company of women. When they threatened him he took refuge in a cave and there survived the Flood. Still in the cavern 'Curled in selfhate', masochistically so, he is shown to be in deep distress, although not defeated. As the one who lived to recall the event, he resembles the persona in the prefatory poem who has also survived his descent into the abyss. The poem touches on these and other elements from the *Book of Invasions* such as references to the East, the search for an earthly paradise, the sickness that comes upon those who arrived, the Hag Rock, and the ambiguous nature of the place. In Celtic mythology, Munster, where they landed, is both the land of the dead and the place of origins. It corresponds to the abyss to which the persona falls, since it was also a place where the primordial liquid produced new life. The cave or cavern is the place of life and a rock from which the narrator's voice emerges. The poem moves from promise to failure, the earthly paradise becomes a place of 'gloom', the sinless land turns into a place of violence, promise turns to despair. The conditions – sickness, twilight, the great rock, the Hag – are images of barrenness, suffering and decay, but the speaker, the mythical survivor, endures, determined to 'remember' and 'to explain'.

In 'From the Land of the Dead' each poem gains in significance from its relationship with other poems. Just as the female figures are demonstrably the same figure, defined by recurrent associations, so basic objects, images and incidents that interact permeate the book as a whole. Some of the primary incidents are those of boy with grandmother,

Endymion with the moon figure, owls with their victims, the speaker with his environment. Closely allied with this encounter is the fall to another kind of world, out of normal surroundings towards a new experience. The book itself is situated in darkness, in the void or abyss so that one of its primary concerns is with beginnings. The idea of a place or state of potential is implied in references to pit, abyss, cavern, cave, orifice, shore and their associated images. Closely related to these are indications of potential, a musical sound, a tear, a drop of moisture, an echo, all of which signal release or the possibility of change. Most visible are the female figures: grandmothers, owls, Hecate, Persephone, the dreamlike woman in 'Nuchal', the ecstatic victim in 'Sacrifice', the predatory creatures.

Some poems take place in the land of the dead. In 'At the Crossroads' the triple threat is associated with Hecate, who is the moon/owl 'with blackness at her heart'. As Kinsella explains in his notes, she is a complex figure: the terrible Mother, Lamia, who devours men: the Moon, the evil side of the feminine principle, madness, obsession and lunacy. Among her attributes are the key (mystery, enigma, a task to be performed, and the means to do it), the lash, the dagger, the torch. The crossroads includes the union of opposites, the mother as both object and epicentre of all union. They are sacred to triform Hecate; in the underworld, dogs were sacrificed to her and the bodies of hanged men were dumped (box 10, folder 7). All these associations appear in the poem. The owl's predatory strike, her 'choice', corresponds to the boy's eating of the pomegranate. The feeling he has of being threatened frightens the speaker. What he discovers is the principle of devouring, the hunger that must be recurrently satisfied, which is visible in the owl, her mouth ready. The description that follows affirms that reality in life's great stomach.

> And all mouths everywhere so
> in their need, turning on each furious
> other. Flux of forms
> in a great stomach: living meat torn off,
> enduring in one mess of terror
> every pang it sent through every thing
> it ever, in shudders of pleasure, tore. (114)

The idea is expressed again in the allegorical Aztec-like 'Sacrifice' when the woman victim speaks, exulting in the violent action when love seizes her heart. She, too, loses her mind as she descends into this abyss of pain and recovery. 'Love dying down, as love ascends.' The predatory bird is transformed into an 'angel' whose 'great flushed pinions' are the result of the bloody encounter. In Kinsella's mind such transmutation permeates and helps to unify 'From the Land of the Dead'.

The various meanings of the land of the dead are absorbed. Within waste and ash where death holds sway may be found particles in the process of change. These encounters with the unknowable, the threatening, as well as with the infinite and complex congruencies of matter, are experiences private to the poet. Although it seems that the emphasis is on the boy and the old woman, the real concern is with the self, with the process of growth and the way we learn. The poems that bring the two figures together create a radical contrast. What he buys from her in the pomegranate is knowledge of life and death and her capacity to absorb experience. Paradoxically, in her proximity to darkness and death, in her imminent decline he finds life. Through his nauseating contact with her drying mud he finds her heart beating in his mouth. She is the pungent source of knowledge.

Kinsella thought hard about the ways in which ordinary incidents and people may be given mythological and psychic resonances. In the list that he gave at McGill University he mentioned the breaking open of the egg, Persephone's time in Hades, and the archetypal night sea crossing. In his notes he focuses in greater detail. He makes the point that the image of the egg equals both the mind and the imagination. It refers to imaginative gestation and the subconscious realm of the egg, which is the alchemical container, the vessel of transmutation, the land of the dead, under Hecate and the rejuvenating receptacle of souls. The cavern is 'in the hen' and also 'in the egg'; it is associated with 'the centre and with the cave of the heart, which is the centre of being/the egg of the world.

Although these are notes taken before they are processed by the imagination, they indicate how Kinsella's associative intelligence works, gathering clusters of associations about an individual image. The image of the egg connects with all the references to hollow receptacles – mind, heart, imagination, womb, cavern, cave. The idea of process includes its synonyms – fertilization, rejuvenation, the coming to life, recovery, return – so that the collection itself, its egg of being, becomes alive with potential, with transfers of meaning from one poem to another through a number of recurrent images.

When he makes notes on the archetypal night sea crossing, there is a similar listing of meanings; it is, he says, a symbol of immanence, sin, occultation and expiation. Typically, a sea monster in the West swallows a hero. The animal goes, with him inside, to the East. The essential features of the myth are devouring, confinement, feeling entangled and threatened, enchantment. Kinsella remarks on the process as an introduction to death, as an initiation, a symbolic journey that starts in the darkness of the profane world (the unconscious, the mother) and gropes towards the light. The archetype is the journey to the Centre or the holy land or the way out of the maze. The hero escapes not by becoming immortal but by becoming fascinated by the mystery; death is also hell, the unconscious and the awareness of all latent potentialities of being that are needed to reach the heights of Paradise. Restless heroes are always travellers. Intellectual search is a journey. So are dreams. But *the true journey*, he says emphatically, is neither acquiescence nor escape but *evolution*. Dreams are as real as experience in the everyday world. When the dream world erupts, Kinsella does not try to suppress it.

He relates entanglement to the fear of being devoured by the mother, disguised as witch (wolf, ogre, dragon) who swallows children. It has both psychic and cosmic significance. The psychic includes the unconscious, the repressed, the forgotten, the past; the cosmic includes the collective dream that separates one cycle of life from another and encompasses the mass of nerve ends out of which rise, here and there, vegetable or animal forms or whole beings enmeshed in a cage. The snake, the serpent of night, refers to primordial, pre-conscious instincts. He connects the primordial seed with the serpent's egg and speaks of the second birth – the first as egg = zero, the second as hatching or the first heartbeat of the embryo; the O is unseeded, the 1 is seeded.

On the following page he is still exploring in compressed fashion the implications of the numerological progression. On the count of one – the ego punkt – separates from mother and that involves awareness, form-ation of ideas, polarity (that is, masculine and feminine); pure abstract spirit, science (three-dimensional thinking). Masculine is uneven (all human males have uneven number of chromosomes – and nearly all biological species). Each previous thing remains inside the subsequent: zero – feminine = mother; one is male and female in the beginning; phallus, uneven and evil (eve), snake, both *latent*. One – snake, masculine and feminine; two – feminine, feminine snake inside; three – masculine, uneven, with feminine and masculine inside; four – feminine, including male which includes feminine which includes dual. It is a process of differentiation – the image, irradiated with increasing light, sharpening and clarifying its contours. Four is the state of physic totality: corporeity, a form adequate to physical creation, is added to three, the serpent of eternity, uroboros, which eats its own tail; turns feminine but includes male. Kinsella saw 'From the Land of the Dead' as the beginning of a series that would start on the count of zero and end on the count of Quincunx. The numerological plan seemed natural. Individual life begins as one person, joins with another, becoming two, and then producing a third. It also had reverberations with the symbolism of numbers in Irish tradition, of five, seven, nine or twelve, in which five is dominant (box 10, folder 18).[4]

Kinsella regarded himself as an intuitive who wants to see inherent potentialities. That sense of potentialities is a strong imaginative force throughout 'From the Land of the Dead' and accompanying poems in *New Poems*. The 'wavery albumen bodies' in the embryonic abyss is the first confirmation that new life, fresh symbiotic relationships may be created. In 'Invocation', the sexual encounter with the Persephone figure embodies the living particles with the living blossom of a creative appetite:

> living particles –
> cells: eyes: tongues – drifting out
> in a cloud toward either bank, to meet
> the living blossoms clustering down in answer
> to the current
> – cells of ruby blood, jewels
> to kiss and melt; crystal eyes
> to fasten against, fluttering; pink tongues
> to cling lingering among – [5]

'Hen Woman' orchestrates a set of items all of which fuse in the imagination of the observer. In 'Good Night' there is a drawing together of forces in the room, the sounds of the house 'all flowing into one another' and being absorbed by the alert, intoxicated observer. The room becomes a womb, the rock transformed and resembling Fintan's cave in a neighbouring poem. It is a moment of vision.

> If you look closely
> you can see the tender undermost muscle
> forming out of the rock
> the veins continuing inward
> just visible under the skin
> and (faintly lit from within)
> clusters of soft arms gathering down
> tiny open eyes, fingertips,
> pursed mouths from the gloom,
> minute drifting corruscations of hair,
> glistening little gnat-crescents of light! [6]

These too become part of the self – 'and feed us and feed in us/and coil and uncoil in our substance'. The Darwinian perception in 'St Paul's Rocks: 16 February 1832' has a corresponding significance. A cluster of rocks emerges briefly from the mists, 'white and glittering'. Even in that inhospitable, barren place, life takes hold.

> Colonies of birds eat the abundant fish;
> moths feed on the feathers; lice and beetles
> live in the dung; countless spiders
> prey on these scavengers; in the crevices
> a race of crabs lives on the eggs and young.

The verbs are insistent – 'eat', 'feed', 'live', 'prey', 'lives'. The scene is rendered in convincing detail. The lesson is read.

> In squalor and killing and parasitic things
> life takes its first hold.
> Later the noble accident: the seed,
> dropped in some exhausted excrement,
> or bobbing like a matted skull into an inlet. (127)

In a similar mode 'Crab Orchard Sanctuary: Late October' reads the signs of the season's ending: vacated bodies drift on the driveway, 'a myriad/leather seed-cases lie in wait'. 'They will swarm again ... and wither away again'. The cycles of life and death go on. There is a 'process' as the fox confirms in 'The Route of *The Táin*': 'Flux brought to fullness; saturated;/the clouding over; dissatisfaction' followed by the emergence of 'meaning'.

'Worker in Mirror, at his Bench' has a different approach. In a self-deprecatory mood, Kinsella reflects on what he does and on how he is seen by others. The ways in which things coalesce in the natural world resembles how material forms within the artist. A poem is assembled, the poet fits pieces together; he tinkers with material, penetrating its substance, eliciting its significance. It has no practical application, he is simply trying to understand something; the process is 'tedious', 'elaborate', 'wasteful'; the 'passion is in the putting together'.

> Take for example this work in hand.
> Out of its waste matter
> it should emerge solid and light.
> One idea, grown with the thing itself,
> should drive it searching inward
> with a sort of life, due to the mirror effect.
> Often, the more I simplify
> the more a few simplicities
> go burrowing in their own depths
> until the guardian structure is aroused. (124)

While he mimics the 'Understanding smiles' of others, this is how the creative process works for him; and he is content, however conscious of the achievement of others. 'Yes, I suppose I am appalled/at the massiveness of others' work.'

> I tinker with the things that dominate me
> as they describe their random persistent coherences.
> Clean surfaces shift and glitter among themselves. (124)

Notes

1   Kinsella's contribution to the panel discussion was published in Joseph Ronsley (ed.), *Myth and Reality in Irish Literature* (Waterloo, Ontario: Wilfrid Laurier University Press, 1977), pp.1–16. In preparation, Kinsella had made extensive notes on Carl Jung's theories and read in particular Jolande Jacobi's *The Psychology of C.G. Jung* (London: Routledge & Kegan Paul, 1942), but the discussion, as I recall, was diffuse.

2   (Box 10, folder 12); see Jacobi, *The Psychology of C.G. Jung*, p.43.

3   *Lebor Gábala Érenn: The Book of the Taking of Ireland (Book of Invasions)* 5 vols. ed. and trans. Stewart Macalister (Dublin: Irish Texts Society, 1938–1956).

4   See Alwyn and Brinley Rees, 'Numbers', *Celtic Heritage. Ancient Tradition in Ireland and Wales* (London and New York: Thames & Hudson, 1973).

5   'Invocation' in *Notes from the Land of the Dead* (Dublin: Cuala Press, 1972), p.13. The text is not included in *Collected Poems* (2001).

6   'Good Night', in *Collected Poems 1956–1994* (Oxford and New York: Oxford University Press, 1996), p.110. The text is not included in *Collected Poems* (2001).

Part II
STYLE AND SUBSTANCE

Butcher's Dozen, 1972
A Selected Life, 1972
Vertical Man, 1973
New Poems, 1973
The Good Fight, 1973
One, 1974
A Technical Supplement, 1976
The Messenger, 1978
Song of the Night and Other Poems, 1978
Songs of the Psyche, 1985
Her Vertical Smile, 1985
Out of Ireland, 1987

INTRODUCTION

Between the years 1972 and 1987 Thomas Kinsella wrote some of his greatest work and experienced a major setback to his career. During the period he wrote two elegies for Seán Ó Riada, the incomparable *Her Vertical Smile*, and published his translations from Irish, which will be considered in Part III. The setback came from the realization that the numerological system, which had originated in *Notes from the Land of the Dead* (1972) and is the determining force in *One*, *A Technical Supplement* and *Song of the Night and Other Poems*, had become too restrictive. Even though they did not fit into the system, events such as the assassination of John F. Kennedy, the premature death of Seán Ó Riada and the death of his own father could not be excluded.

The two Ó Riada elegies, *A Selected Life* and *Vertical Man*, not only express the poet's feelings of loss and grief at the death of a friend and fellow-artist but consider the role of the artist, the ongoing struggle of writing, and the nature of success. These become the identifying and unifying concerns of the period. In *Vertical Man*, through his vision of the metaphorical beam of light, Kinsella's understanding of the numerological system is glowingly expressed. That the poem also considers the sense of struggle and failure involved in the artist's life is a natural consequence. The question of what the artist may achieve is raised to metaphysical and philosophical heights in *Her Vertical Smile* in which Gustav Mahler's character and accomplishments are celebrated and measured against Kinsella's own idea of what may be achieved. The elegy on the death of his father, *The Messenger*, resumes this philosophical assessment by considering what a man may accomplish and what ideals may motivate him. Death itself is the basic context at the heart of which lie the questions of individual decision and character.

The Good Fight considers the topics in its contrasting characterizations of John F. Kennedy and Lee Harvey Oswald, the one charismatic and confident, articulating an optimistic vision for the people, the other outcast and solitary, brooding upon his sense of inadequacy and uselessness. Plato's ideas about leadership and personal balance are offset by the post-Jungian awareness of the dark forces that operate within the psyche. The manner in which a final position evolves out of the interplay of different voices is characteristic of Kinsella's method at this stage. The later work, *Out of Ireland*, with its multiple perspectives and final view of the artist, is an extended and more complex treatment. In his *De Divisione Naturae* (On the Division of Nature), possibly the greatest theologico-philosophical achievement from Augustine to Thomas Aquinas, John Scotus Eriugena's claim that all men return to God is powerfully imagined, but Kinsella puts his faith in the quotidian pairing of love and art. The plain language employed to describe Seán Ó Riada's dance of life is more attractive than the overblown language employed to express Eriugena's uncompromising morality. The moral force of Ó Riada connects him with the god Mercury, whom Kinsella describes as 'impish, teasing, diabolical... hoodwinking, droll, inexhaustibly inventive... Ambivalent, malicious. But also with highest spiritual qualities... Mercury is the serpent that fertilizes, kills, and devours itself, completing a circle, and brings itself to birth again!' (box 17, folder 13). Not all these terms are directly applicable to Ó Riada but some appear in later portrayals of the composer.

New Poems is in effect a manifesto of the major change in Kinsella's development. But the Ó Riada elegies, written in contrasting tones, one austere and formal, the other more openly expressive, have a new style, more literal and more understated, and need to be considered separately. They register the forces of creativity and destruction as a dialectic of opposites.

Some of the poems in *From the Land of the Dead* had a loose shape. As Kinsella remarked, 'they swim about with no apparent control'; but in *One*, poems 'can organize their own behaviour'.[1] The elegies are in fact examples of technical mastery. Kinsella uses external detail in a metaphorical manner, with the result that an image that might seem to be incidental is in fact an integral part of the imaginal design. The third elegy, *The Messenger*, is of particular interest for its dramatic interplay of scenes and for what it says about the poet's moral values.

Two collections, *One* and *A Technical Supplement*, advance the numerological system. In *One* the male element appears throughout and the idea of source takes the poet back to the *Book of Invasions* and to the principle of man's propensity for onward movement. In a new world, prehistoric people, behind them the force of history within the male creative drive, settle in, work the land, and discover a saturated source from which new life comes. The system carries forward in *A Technical Supplement*, which enacts the division of one into two, and that was as far as it went. At one level the collection is an allegory about poetic procedures and responses. Sometimes the lessons are hard, as is shown in the systematic description of slaughter in the abattoir or of one lizard swallowing another, live. The introductory portrait of William Skullbullet warns of artistic struggle; its injunction, 'let us see how the whole thing/works', prefaces the scrutiny that follows. The penetrative drive of the intelligence is expressed through the metaphor of surgical investigation. Out of fierce engagement understanding may come. Inert matter may respond. The metaphor is seen in the working of the land by early inhabitants in 'The Oldest Place' and in the bursting of new life from the carpenter's block in 'His Father's Hands'.

Poems in *Song of the Night and Other Poems* celebrate the correspondences between man and the natural world and do so on the basis of noting and absorbing the particularities of external settings, such as a family camping beside the ocean in Carraroe, County Galway. In 'Tao and Unfitness at Inistiogue on the River Nore', the poet perceives the visible world in a kind of Taoist contemplation. The 'Carraroe' section of 'Song of the Night' also follows a strategy of exact observation and precise description. Its dynamic bringing to life of inanimate and insensate material resembles the net of correspondences sought by French Symbolist poets. In addition, the poem connects scenes of unearthly manifestations with the powerful feelings evoked by the music of Gustav Mahler. The composer's exclamatory style helps to release a correspondingly powerful poetic response to nature's dramatic tableau of beauty and poignancy. The hurtling violence at its climax is not only a reminder of a counter force but of the fruitful presence of opposites, something unavailable in the pent-up fury of the opening 'Philadelphia' section.

While grounding poems in the actual, Kinsella also gives them a sense of the mythical. At times he transmutes the ordinary into the extra-ordinary. Obscure intimations of psychic experience recall his previous psychological explorations that are specifically evoked in the inward-turning *Songs of the Psyche*. He returns once again to the land of childhood but the perspective has altered. Now in middle age he still searches for wisdom and understanding, but the search is fraught with the realization that the numerological system has failed. The beam of light is associated with theories of psychoanalysts which have turned out to be inadequate. By making that realization part of the sequence, Kinsella dramatizes himself once again as one who suffers. Just how traumatic is the experience is made clear in the savage humour of 'Self-Release'. In keeping with the honesty and clarity of these revelations, the portrayal of family life in *St Catherine's Clock* is unflattering. Banal domestic details are refracted through the stylized historical world of Malton prints as Kinsella identifies where he comes from and limns its social contexts. As always in poems of this period the individual is defined in specific circumstances.

The unifying themes include not only the comprehensive and particular considerations of heritage through the translations and through the historical and autobiographical poems but questions about the role of the artist and what he may achieve. Those questions are present in the

Ó Riada elegies, part of *The Messenger*, and integral to the social, political
and historical contexts that frame all these poems; they are orchestrated
in *Her Vertical Smile*, where evil is present in the large-scale destruction
of modern warfare. Great artists incorporate as much as they can of the
human story, its glorious moments, its artistic triumphs, its absurd
enthusiasms, its doomed adventures. Mahler, for Kinsella, is the model
artist. Even if he cannot bring himself to endorse unreservedly, the
composer's artistic vision, he is investigative, persistent, ready to take
risks, capacious and concentrated in rendering his artistic vision.
Ultimately, as the poem says, things come from nothing and go back into
nothingness. The readiness is all. So too is the ability to encompass
experience, to absorb and counter evil within the creative energy of the
work of art. The task for Kinsella is to render and match the depth,
splendour and complexity of Mahler's music in the language of the poem
from the evocation of the grieving Earth Mother's song to the
contrapuntal orchestration of the Eighth Symphony. The theme of artistic
endeavour, associated with Ó Riada and Kinsella in the room in Baggot
Street, forms a natural part of the poem. Just as Mahler's music alternates
between energy and desolation, the poem enacts a metaphor of promise
and disappointment. It unites the collapse of the old Austrian Empire
with the death of the composer and raises the questions of the possibility
of an ordered world and whether or not it had a Divine Creator. The
poet's identification with Mahler, so single-minded and so driven, is
central, as is his lament for the slaughter of war and his response to the
mingling of hope and disappointment, the gap between what he, the
artist, initially envisions and what he finally accomplishes. The melancholy is fed by the collapse of Kinsella's system and by the conviction that
the curse of destruction comes from within. He questions the confidence
of artists and psychoanalysts: 'Who are we to look for/harmony and
fulfillment?' (box 18, folder 6). The mockery in the poem's 'Coda'
qualifies the commemoration of achievement, while not dismissing it. In
their clownish fall the conductor's trousers replace the sartorial elegance
of Mahler and his wife. Kinsella modifies the mystical vision expressed in
the ascent of Faust and in Michelangelos's picture of Creation. Mahler's
transcendent music dissolves grief and death. Kinsella's poem evens the
score through ironic counterpoint. In his notes the poet ridicules Mahler's
excess.

Notes

1   Daniel O'Hara, 'An Interview with Thomas Kinsella', *Contemporary Poetry: A
     Journal of Criticism* 4 (1981), p.17.

4

THE ENTIRE FABRIC

From the beginning Thomas Kinsella has situated poems in particular places and over the years the sense of bonding between poet and place has deepened. The earlier lyrics set in Basin Lane, Baggot Street, King John's Castle – the poems 'Lead', 'A Country Walk', 'Downstream', 'Phoenix Park', 'Nightwalker', and many others – have created a sense of location in his work that is as tangible as the use of place in the work of James Joyce or Austin Clarke. In return visits, particularly in poems since 'From the Land of the Dead', the confined Basin Lane region of his childhood has gained in significance, although other settings, such as Percy Place, Philadelphia, Carraroe, Coolea, Co. Cork, and Vienna have also become significant. In these poems of place, as in almost all his poetry, the use of particulars is primary. Whether he is recording impressions of personal places or imagining artistic, particularly musical, achievement in Coolea or Austria, the basic ingredient is the skill with which specifics are made part of the rhythm and texture of the work. From lyric notation to comprehensive sequence, from literal investigation of the immediate to metaphysical questioning, his achievement is grounded on detail.

The manner in which places have been treated has varied. 'King John's Castle' (*Another September*) interprets the castle's force objectively. Although more personal, 'A Country Walk' (*Downstream*) also views the surroundings from a distance. In later poems, dramatizing the self within specific places, often the distance between self and surroundings is diminished, but at times, as in the description of the Tighe house in 'Tao and Unfitness at Inistioge on the River Nore' (*Song of the Night and Other Poems*) or of his father's career in *The Messenger*, he writes objectively. Even though 'Nightwalker' reduces that gap, using external images to reflect internal states, the style maintains a distance between the reflecting consciousness and the world about him.

With the first lines in *New Poems*, which includes nearly all the poems in *Notes from the Land of the Dead* and a few others, that space has almost been erased. The nightmarish, allegorical falling out of consciousness into the depths is rendered in what he sees, registering his profound sense of loss; particulars function as metaphors. Some lines have a compact force in their dynamic, fragmented style in which truncated clauses, empty spaces, and a striking literalism contribute to the nightmarish drama.

> So sunless.
> That sour coolness...So far from the world and earth...
> No bliss, no pain; dullness after pain.
> A cistern-hiss...A thick tunnel stench
> rose to meet me. Frightful. Dark nutrient waves.
> And I knew no more. (96)

In 'Hen Woman', 'Ancestor', 'Tear', 'The High Road' and 'A Hand of Solo', Kinsella fuses myth and actuality. While he gives material a context in reality through the use of concrete images, sometimes listed abruptly, he incorporates both the myth of Persephone and narratives of prehistoric peoples who seek an earthly paradise but find 'a new beginning' in a process mimicked in the rhythm and the litany of negatives.

> A new beginning. An entire new world
> floating on the ocean like a cloud,
> distilled from sunlight and the crests of foam.
>   ....
> Paradise. No serpents. No noxious beasts.
> No lions. No toads. No injurious rats
> or dragons or scorpions. Only the she-wolf.
>
> Perpetual twilight. A last outpost in the gloom.
> A land of the dead. Sometimes
> an otherworldly music sounded on the wind. (111–12)

Kinsella's work now renders the trivial and ordinary but gives them a sense of otherness. Dense details about specific, ancestral women in *New Poems* accumulate toward mythic association. They are recognizable members of his family in the much-revisited confined space, but, as in 'A Hand of Solo', the scene melts at the edges.

> Uncle Matty slithered the cards together
> and knocked them. Their edges melted. Soft gold.
>
> Angus picked up a bright penny and put it
> in my hand: satiny, dream-new disk of light...
>
> 'Go on out in the shop and get yourself something.'
> 'Now Angus...'
>   'Now, now, Jack. He's my luck.'
> 'Tell your grandmother we're waiting for her.' (100–101)

Playing cards turn to gold, the penny becomes dream-new, the child is a bringer of luck as he goes to meet the hag-like elder whom he must encounter, time after time, if he is to be renewed. Mysterious female figures are a source of repugnance and insight; the meeting of youth and age is richly laden. The details of place, room, shop and people are explicit, but the game of cards opens towards wonder and insight. A child's kiss for his grandmother is more than it seems. So established are Kinsella's skills in transmuting the ordinary that it is easy to overlook how language itself, however plain and naturalistic, accommodates a variety of different, even ambiguous meanings: the fall into the abyss through the grill or shore seems destructive but is also positive; the zero state is the egg of being; Fintan, survivor of the flood, lives on in his cave, another place of origin. The land of the dead is also the land of the living. The paradigm of fall and renewal, of encounter, setback and recovery, is played out over and over in successive situations, in a variety of styles. Whereas earlier poems express the sense of threat and destruction, the awareness of erosion affecting all things and all relationships, in later poems that expression is balanced against the facts of creativity and often conveyed in an idiom that is dynamically both positive and negative. In 'The Oldest Place' (*One*) the barren land becomes fertile; the material itself glows in response, adapts in its mass.

> And there was something in the way the land behaved:
> passive, but responding. It grew under our hands.
> We worked it like a dough to our requirements
> yet it surprised us more than once
> with a firm life of its own, as if it
> used us. (166)

The inert becomes alive, the solid fills with life. The standing stone is 'packed more/with dark radiance'. The carpenter's bench gives birth to 'squirming' little nails. The buried Mister Cummins is saved from the dead. Things flicker, hiss, wriggle, squirm, beat, creep, coil and uncoil, shut and open, shine, glitter, glow, and are infused with meaning and promise.

In 'Minstrel' (*One*) the details of a personal place establish a melancholy setting: 'A mist of tears lay still upon the land.' Even the banal items in a poem replete with ordinary, domestic details – 'down', 'bare', 'dry', 'stained' – give a context for the intense, predatory-positive activity of the narrator 'bent like a feeding thing/over my own source'. Out of childhood's insignificant pocket comes the hint of the unusual: the white ash falls, a shadow or chill of night advances, the 'I' figure becomes alert, is drawn into a cosmic connection. Such intimations of universal order have been present in 'Baggot Street Deserta', in 'Downstream', in *Vertical Man*; here they are affirmed in a comprehensive context and delicately expressed as a gradually unfolding awareness until the entire universe is poised in an act of union and communion.

> Outside, the heavens listened,
> a starless diaphragm
> stopped miles overhead
> to hear the remotest whisper
> of returning matter, missing
> an enormous black beat.
>
> The earth stretched out in answer.
> Little directionless instincts
> uncoiled from the wet mud-cracks,
> crept in wisps of purpose, and vanished
> leaving momentary traces
> of claw marks, breasts,
> ribs, feathery prints,
> eyes shutting and opening
> all over the surface.
> A distant point of light
> winked at the edge of nothing. (170)

This kind of perception, already affirmed in 'Baggot Street Deserta', is dramatized profoundly in *Her Vertical Smile* where its detail is mediated through the music of Gustav Mahler, who sought to compose works that reflected the entire world, including cosmic experience.

From the beginning, mortality has been part of the 'evil' that Kinsella perceives. Much of the material in 'Cover Her Face' (*Downstream*), for example, is deeply painful; the poem makes us see the actuality of death. 'Office for the Dead' (*Nightwalker*) gathers images for a similar occasion – 'grief-chewers enter', 'a silver pot tosses in its chains', voices 'grind across the body'. The poem's music is a harsh accompaniment to the service. But memories of the dead woman survive, momentarily offsetting the disharmony, before the poem turns again in a balancing conclusion to the 'throb of chain', the 'gasp of smoke', the thurible like 'An animal, dragging itself and breathing'. The satirical *Butcher's Dozen* mounts an angry and contemptuous response to Lord Widgery's whitewashing report about the shooting dead of thirteen Civil Rights marchers by British paratroopers in 1972. 'Death Bed' (*New Poems*) faces the inscrutability of death. An old man dies, the sons try to 'weave' his death into their lives. They watch in vain for a sign that might issue from his mouth, but are left with the blankness of death. The numbed state of the poet/mourner in 'Cover Her Face' is comparable to theirs, as is his inability to find answers or any comfort in the church service. 'Office for the Dead' was equally bereft of religious solace.

Kinsella is the central figure in *A Selected Life*, the first of two elegies about Seán Ó Riada. His is the observing, reflecting consciousness whose purpose is to describe and absorb the significance of the experience. The first section, '1 Galloping Green: May 1962', begins with a vibrant portrait of Ó Riada the musician – alert, intent and purposeful. The language is compact and forceful, the slant rhymes carefully worked, every word chosen for a precise function.

> He clutched the shallow drum
> and crouched forward, thin
> as a beast of prey. The shirt
> stretched at his waist. He stared
> to one side, toward the others,
> and struck the skin cruelly
> with his nails. Sharp
> as the answering arid bark
> his head quivered, counting. (139)

A hard staccato command of notes arrests the attention – 'clutched', 'crouched', 'stared', 'struck'. All the tightly packed, forceful images attest to raw, animal intensity.

In the second section, '2 Coolea: 6 October 1971', the poet turns to the miserable weather and sodden landscape that serve as metaphors for his feelings and set the elegiac mood. This section is in two parts. In the first the 'fine drizzle', the 'tattered valley', and the 'mourning suit' are introductory motifs, their functional significance becoming clearer in the following lines where 'A crow scuffled in the hedge/and floated out with a dark groan/into full view'. The imaginative context, almost entirely monosyllabic words – 'drizzle', 'field', 'crow', 'rock', 'scraped', 'beak', 'croaked', 'a voice out of the rock/carrying across the slope' – mimic the speaker's numbed emotional state. In a technique akin to the way a piece of music develops, the line of implication grows in a gradually increasing clarification that ends in the voice from the rock saying, 'Foretell'. The consciousness registers but is not released from the misery it describes, and from what the crow forecasts in the ongoing musical progression – river, field, house, parked cars, bare yard, family and friends gathering, a shelf with concertinas in the dust, 'the pipes folded on their bag'. These melancholy particulars lead to 'The hole waiting in the next valley./That'. The stark image and the stark thought it conveys are as much as the speaker can achieve. The single word 'That' is like a struck musical note.

'Down in the village the funeral bell began to beat.' Hearing it, we realize how soundless this part of the poem has been, except for the dissonant 'dark groan' of the crow. The dead rat gives evidence of the crow's literal and metaphorical function. The destructive appetite the bird embodies is more clearly exposed as the poem advances. Through a bareness of means, an avoidance of rhyme, a colourless tone, a detached persona, the consciousness registers what it sees. The observer moves his gaze from place to place, from detail to detail, the participial verbal forms, present and past, slide through the setting. Interruptions to this pattern – the description of the dead rat, the description of the drizzle's sudden thickening, the use of full stops – have a dramatic effect.

A rat's torn body and a flesh-picking crow are harsh indicators of the day's significance. Kinsella works through such literal, unflinching details to focus on the miserable event. Coming after the sight of the rat's torn body, 'flesh-picked' by the crow, the direct address to Ó Riada: 'And you. Waiting in the dark chapel./Packed and ready' adds an intimate, realistic note. The conjunction of the 'you' referring to the crow and this 'you' underlines the predatory nature of life, including artistic life.

In the next part of section 2, the musical analogy is heard in the address – 'And you. Waiting in the dark chapel'. The dead composer is now brought forward, his 'few essentials' summarized: 'a standard array of dependent beings', 'sundry musical effects', 'a lurid cabinet', and 'a workroom, askew'. The emotional diminishment is starkly evident in the description of the Ó Riada family: 'a standard array of dependent beings,/small, smaller, pale, paler, in black'. Such depersonalized language reduces them and identifies in them humanity's vulnerability. Shrunk to pallid black shapes, the pulse, colour and variety of a family have been obliterated.

If the opening lines of the poem captured Ó Riada's vitality, these identify instruments whose potential he had revived: tin whistles, uillean pipes, melodeon, bodhrán, harpsichord.

> – sundry musical effects: a piercing
> sweet consort of whistles crying,
> goosenecked wail and yelp of pipes,
> melodeons snoring in sadness,
> drum bark, the stricken
> harpsichord's soft crash... (140)

The listing also records what Ó Riada has left behind – family, musical effects, his capacity to make the nation his audience, his workroom. The animated listing recalls his vitality and bears witness to loss. Even when the poem evokes distinction, beauty and musical power, the language is restrained as in the description of the sounds of the instruments. After these mimetic summaries, the poem salutes Ó Riada's music, including the score for *Mise Éire*, which reflected aspects of Irish history and spoke to a whole people. 'Men's guts ignite and whiten in satisfaction.' Ó Riada, Kinsella implies, was a national figure. His death is a national loss.

In the final essential, the workroom, he is the artist 'fumbling' at his table, pools of ideas forming. We hear the sounds of the instruments, are given a mocking account of European music, Ó Riada's early love, and in the concluding phrase – 'Let us draw a veil.' – we move to section 3 which returns to the bare language of the first half of the poem.

Section 3, 'St. Gobnait's Graveyard, Ballyvourney: that evening', is a farewell movement in seven stanzas: the theme is the return to normalcy, a process shown in grass 'disentangling', crows 'dissolving', their appetite 'Fed', and includes the buried man. In direct appeal for the first time, the voice enjoins us to 'Shudder for him', then offers a glimpse of the young Ó Riada, the promising musician-friend as Pierrot, and follows that with a harsh summary of a man's life; Pierrot, the promise, this, the conclusion:

> swallowed back: animus
> brewed in clay, uttered
> in brief meat and brains, flattened
> back under our flowers...(141)

'swallowed', 'brewed', 'uttered', 'flattened', the Earth's appetite is the negative side of the predatory, creative force shown in the opening portrait. The lines highlight human fragility and the brevity of existence.

Ó Riada himself, once vibrant and creative, is silenced, family reduced, instruments put away, achievements left behind, aspirations but a memory. Creativity and destruction co-exist: the positive is vibrantly struck in the opening portrait of Ó Riada and evoked in memories of his achievements, but these are countered by the metaphorical detail of drabness, wet weather, silent instruments, colourless family. The two are deeply realized. Kinsella moves from the particulars of the event to its universal application, defining a tableau of what reality is, life and death both present. That is the poem's philosophical basis. While he salutes Ó Riada's attractive humanity and artistic achievement, he does not offer transcendent consolations. Bluntly stated, there is life and there is death, inseparably linked.

The final two stanzas recall Ó Riada on his death bed, 'Gold and still', his wry humour, and end in a series of toasts, and the kind of robust curses good friends exchange.

> *Salut.*
> Slán.
> *Yob tvoyu mat'.*
> Master, your health. (142)

In these concluding lines, showing his pain, Kinsella utters words of affection and concern in a fragmented, undeveloped, allusive, modernist manner.

The poem moves adroitly between personal and impersonal pronouns from the 'he' in section 1, referring to the dead composer in the vigour of youth, to 'my glasses' and 'my mourning suit' in section 2 that place the poet as the focussing observer, to 'It flapped', 'scraped' its beak and 'croaked' which contain the developing theme to the identification of

> I have interrupted
> some thing... You! Croaking
> on your wet stone. Flesh picker. (140)

The lines – 'And you. Waiting in the dark chapel./Packed and ready. Upon your hour.' – give an equivalent value to the new second person pronoun, not diminished by colloquial usage or literary allusion.

When the poet in section 3 moves to the burial of his friend, the direct injunction to an implied you/reader, 'Shudder for him', sounds a note of horror at what has happened. The poem completes its deployment of pronouns with a specific memory of Ó Riada as Pierrot before returning to Kinsella's memory of the man on his deathbed, to gruff humour, and the affectionate insults that in their explicitness express the fullness of loss.

In *Vertical Man*, '4 Philadelphia: 3 October 1972', the two friends meet again on the anniversary of Ó Riada's death. The contexts are ritualistic and sacramental as Kinsella arranges an altar made up of Ó Riada's death mask, the sleeve of his recording of 'Vertical Man' with its portrait of the composer, and drinks a toast to the 'master'. He senses Ó Riada's ghostly presence, recalls youthful feelings when he plays Gustav Mahler's *Das Lied von der Erde*, wryly notes the romantic nature of Hans Betge's song *Der Abschied* ('The Farewell'), and replaces that with his own vision, borrowed from Betge's 'Song of Sorrow', of an ape-shaped figure howling over Ó Riada's grave. As part of this propitiation and in the contexts of sentences from Plato's *The Laws*, Kinsella offers Ó Riada his understanding of the artist's struggle to create, how 'tasks arise, dominate our energies/are mastered with difficulty and some pleasure,/and are obsolete'. Each fresh composition is a new beginning, 'as lonely, as random, as gauche and unready,/as presumptuous as the first' (144).

In that spirit Kinsella recalls the sequence he had been working on that morning which eventually became the collection *One*, and describes his vision of its 'plot'. It is a numinous moment.

> At the dark zenith a pulse beat,
> a sperm of light separated
> and snaked in a slow beam down
> the curve of the sky, through faint
> structures and hierarchies
> of elements and things and beasts. It fell,
> a packed star, dividing
> and redividing until it was
> a multiple gold tear. It dropped
> toward the horizon, entered
> bright Quincunx newly risen,
> beat with a blinding flame and dis-
> appeared.
>   I stared, duly blinded.
> An image burned on the brain
> – a woman-animal: scaled,
> pierced in paws and heart,
> ecstatically calm. It faded
> to a far-off desolate call,
>   a child's.
>
> If the eye could follow that, accustomed to
> that dark.
>   But that is your domain. (144–5)

The vision is animated by the idea of potential as the sperm of light separates, snakes and penetrates the subconscious through archetypal images that are distinct and evocative. It outlines the numerological system upon which the poet's work has been and is being grounded, the separation from the mother, the division into two, then three, then four, culminating in five.

Kinsella's notes identify the moment as taking place on the count of snake, the snake being phallic and a symbol of self-fecundation when the ouroboric serpent of eternity bites its own tail. The axle of light, he explains, preceding good and evil, represents pure force, energy and passion. It goes from the dome of heaven through the core of space, which has seven enfolding layers or spheres into the Pythagorean hole (or circle). The snake represents primordial, pre-conscious instincts. The egg separates from the dark mother and becomes aware; the sperm is masculine and feminine, both latent. It goes through pain, ambivalence and ecstasy, from mind to tears, from lead to gold. The sphinx-woman symbolizes the pain involved in creativity, as in the separation, but also the calm that may ensue. The child has this in the future. The Great Goddess brings new birth through pain, as the image, a combination of snake, fish and sphinx, rises to consciousness, is irradiated with increasing light, sharpens and clarifies its contours until it is visible in every detail of the archetype as a potential 'axial system' that pre-exists and is immanent in the psyche (box 10, folder 16). It is not engendered at the moment it rises, but is already there in the darkness. As it rises to consciousness it is irradiated in the manner Kinsella describes.[1] In a coming to consciousness by differentiating, the male element, the father principle, frees itself from the dark unconscious by moving from dark to dawn. In the process it passes through 'Structures and hierarchies/of elements and things and beasts', which embrace not only the signs of the zodiac but also Jung's diagrams of the psyche and all the images that may rise. The term 'things' carries the implication of material from below and beyond the rational. The moment in which the Quincunx rises corresponds to all those moments of beginning in Kinsella's work, such as the snake wriggling in *One*, the maggot ascending to Amergin's brain in 'Finistère', the nails being born from the carpenter's bench, one and phallic, in 'His Father's Hands' (*One*).

In uniting with the newly risen Quincunx, the sperm finds its mark, at the cosmic centre of the X, which represents four points with the fifth at the centre, that is the Quincunx itself, the division of Ireland into five provinces, the five wounds of Christ, and church architectural designs. The reference to the letter Chi (X), the Greek form of the name of Christ (*XPI*), recalls the Chi–Rho page of the *Book of Kells*, which is full of images of people and animals and spirals, beautifully refined, as they flow across the vellum in dazzling colours. In practice, Kinsella never reached numeral three. The plan remained incomplete. Four would be a totality, an achieved stability, a total career. He would have understood the outside world. The Quincunx would represent the penetration of that, into the centre, to find the ultimate basis. 'It is the circle and the zero, and everything else.'[2]

The vision yields to the impulse to detain Ó Riada's ghost so that they can relive their youthful enjoyment of Mahler's *Das Lied von der Erde*. It is a chilling moment. 'The room filled with a great sigh' as the poet lowers the needle onto the record-player, to recall the beginnings of their long friendship with an eerie realization of the ghost's presence – 'a contraction of the flesh'. In a glowing re-enactment he plays Mahler's great work.

> I arrested the needle. The room filled
> with a great sigh.
> 　　　　　　In terror and memory
> I lowered the tiny point toward our youth
> – into those bright cascades!
> 　　　　　　　　　Radiant outcry –
> trumpets and drenching strings – exultant tenor –
> *Schadenfreude*! The waste! (145)

This, too, is a vision, a crossing the line between here and the other world, followed by dejection. 'Abject. Irrecoverable.' The past cannot be brought back. Hans Betge's song says that life is a black business, but there are compensations – the blue sky, the good earth, spring. Kinsella undercuts that optimism with his vision of the grotesque figure.

> 　　　　　　　　　　...– ape-shaped! –
> demented, howling out
> silent foulness, accursed silent screams
> into the fragrant Night...(146)

These contrasting images and reflections mingle powerfully, qualifying each other to the point at which Kinsella sums up: 'A black bloody business,/the whole thing'.[3]

The three concluding vignettes introduce a lighter, positive note: the first of Ó Riada's making a gesture,

> He stepped forward, through the cigarette smoke.
> to his place at the piano
> – all irritation – and tore off
> his long fingernails to play.

The second is of Jerry Flaherty's singing, whose style Kinsella has imitated in these elegies in which his grieving voice rises from darkness and is recurrently checked.

> From palatal darkness a voice
> rose flickering, and checked
> in glottal silence. The song
> articulated and pierced.

The third vignette is of Ó Riada and Kinsella as young men fishing for shrimp.

> We leaned over the shallows from the boat slip
> and netted the little grey shrimp-ghosts
> snapping, and dropped them
> in the crawling biscuit-tin. (146)

That last image is alive with potential. In Kinsella's personal idiom words like 'crawling', 'wriggling' and 'flickering' indicate creativity, so that this portrait of the two young men not only brings Ó Riada into vivid existence but attests to their common bond as artists. The first person pronoun is the linking point, beginning with time and place – 'I was pouring' – then sensing the ghost – 'it is hard to keep/a vertical man down' – followed by the toast. The line of development is pliant and tensile, with the observing 'I' as the conductor for the thread of feeling running through the valley of grief. The first person is used again in 'I arrested', 'I lowered', and the poignant pouring out of those 'bright cascades!' Kinsella's account of his visions requires the conviction of the personal voice. The poem is a convincing portrait of the self that suffers and the self that sees.

Vertical Man has a static intensity. Elements exist in tension: the images of death and burial are laid beside the images of expectancy and success; the present elegiac occasion is contrasted with past moments of promise; the idea of artistic potential and achievement is conjoined with the idea of artistic struggle and uncertainty. The glories of musical harmonies, of earth's goodness, of springtime renewal are offset by the horror-image of the ape-like creature howling in the cemetery. Lines are characterized by a series of delicate adjustments in tone and rhythm and by taut injunctions directed as much to the self as to the reader. In a variety of tones – cold description, intimate mockery, warm recall – it creates a balance between what death takes and life leaves and transmutes grief into an affirmation of carefully measured, realistic endurance.

The poem is a deeply moving, personal and carefully worked meditation on what the artist may achieve within the beauty and brevity of life and in the face of the abyss of death. Confronted by the hazard of each new beginning, he is buoyed at times by the satisfaction of getting work done, responsive to natural beauty, responsive also to the cares of existence – 'the misery of this world'. That perception is set against primordial suffering, including death: the ape howling, yelling and shattering the sweet fragrance of life. Kinsella's work has many occasions where he draws attention to the pain of existence, the strain of keeping his composure, his awareness of death; but this image of the ape, this forked animal letting loose the anguish, raises it to a level reminiscent of the archetypal images of Job on the rubbish heap and Lear on the heath.

To measure the scope and variety of the work, its ideological constructs, its faith in the imagination, its trust in love, its balance of good and evil, creation and destruction is to begin to appreciate Kinsella's achievement. His poetry alternates between reined-in rhythms, disjointed phrases that halt and impede emotional release – he is reluctant to exult, to release – to moments in which the feeling runs freely and sequences flow. There are passages of great emotional range and power, but there are also poems where the consciousness is fractured, the mind under stress, where mental instability is dominant, where the shocked sensibility recoils from what it encounters.

The Messenger is a tribute to a different kind of man, the poet's father, a political activist, a socialist, an independent individual who worked in Guinness's brewery. The book's cover imitates the cover of the well-known Catholic magazine, the *Irish Messenger of the Sacred Heart*, but instead of its symbols of papal keys, Church insignia and figure of Jesus Christ, it has images that represent John Kinsella's professional and political allegiances: the harp of the Guinness firm, the plough and the stars of Irish socialism, and the figure of the messenger god Mercury. The poem begins by evoking the poet's unease, half-sickness and chill expectation, which are occasioned by the father's death. 'It is more than mere Loss.' It goes deeper in sombre, funerary images to the very source of life:

> (your tomb-image
> drips and blackens, my leaden root
> curled on your lap)...(209)

Mortality strikes to the bone. Something that eats so deeply discourages the natural urge towards goodness which is rendered in images of moist movement, a worm winding, an egg gleaming, 'a pearl in muck/glimpsed only as the muck settles'. This is a pearl of great price – the force and actuality of goodness, associated with the father and with beginnings.

The immediate memory is of the father in old age, 'unmanned', given to anecdotes about his time in Guinness's. The tone is a mixture of admiration for the father's capacity to fight the employer, pity for the insignificant issue in the quarrel, and admiration tinged with irony in the account of him leading 'fellow pensioners' against the far-off boardroom door. At the funeral, someone from the firm commiserated with the poet, adverting to the family's long connection with Guinness's and issuing words of conventional comfort – 'He will be well remembered.../He lived in his two sons.' – a comfort vehemently rejected.

> – In his own half fierce force he lived!
> And stuck the first brand shakily
> under that good family firm...(210)

The poem lifts then to scenes that memorialize the dead father – his formation of the first trade union in Guinness's, his successful fight against the power of the Masons and the Knights of Columbanus, his formation of a pensioners' union that secured small benefits for the workers. It is for those he was 'well remembered'. He was then 'in full vigour, his fiftieth year'. But the triumph was hollow and temporary. 'There is an urge, and it is valuable,/but it is of no avail.' (211)

In another example Kinsella recalls a feat of courage when, with a shout of laughter, in view of the other workers, his father walked across a steel beam high up in the Racking Shed, daring whatever might happen. What befell, in the poem's rhythm between promise and failure, was illness, his life's journey interrupted. Nothing can prevail against the inevitable decline. It is the poem's insistent message. The lines at this point, dividing left and right and forming an appropriate heart-shape on the page, salute courage and vitality, but juxtapose them with the 'full stop' that followed, 'a slammed door' on 'bright prospects'. The heart-ache lies in the positioning between salute and sadness.

In response to the disappointment seen in his father's life, it is characteristic of Kinsella that he should turn inward, withdrawing from objective narration to subjective reflection in which he absorbs the disappointment. 'The Self is islanded in fog', but despite being 'meagre and plagued with wants', it is secure. It has a mechanism for coping with events, both good and bad. What it refuses is absorbed into the psyche. When it awakens, it is a guardian monster with conflicting emotional claims: 'appalling, appealing; exacting sympathy/even as it threatens'. These contradictory demands are inherent and manageable. The dragonfly metaphor with halved head, bellowing with 'incompleteness', summarizes the idea.

The 'beast' comes between father and son, present in enigmatic, riddling questions about knowledge, secrecy, lethargy, anger, duplicity. Or the beast might ask, ambiguously, 'Guess who'd love to gobble *you* up!' The questions both deflect and attract. The final one – 'Who'd like to see what *I* have?' – elicits a definite '*I* would'; and the son follows the father, now in the image of Mercury, 'into the fog, the wings down at heel'.

But that positive adventure ends in collapse, the poem goes back to its beginning, and the father, in a series of images that recall the grave-yard monument, becomes immobile and incommunicable. The harshness of the final line – 'surrendering his tissues and traps' – disguises the son's pain and deflects sympathy. In a further distancing, he watches his own hand as it reaches for the goodness of the father.

> The eggseed Goodness
> that is also called
> Decency. (214)

Section 2 illustrates the 'pearl' of goodness in two examples. What we see first is the father as a young man opposing the Blueshirts, a fascist organization. He is pointing upwards, symbolically. Remembering, the poet fixes the moment in the 1930s.

> I am there. A dark little
> blackvelvet-eyed jew-child
> with leaflets. (214)

He is helping. The face of the Labour leader James Larkin is leaning down.

The second incident takes place in a church when his father, taking his son by the hand, leaves in protest at a priest's interference in politics, 'a black mouth shouting/Godless Russia after us'. (215) These are testaments to his father's goodness, his advocacy for the rights of workers, his resistance to ecclesiastical power at a time when the Labour movement was reluctant to take on the Catholic Church in Ireland. Written '*In memory of John Paul Kinsella* (died May 1976)', the poem pays tribute to the father for specific qualities, even as it laments their ultimate failure. The feeling of futility is countered by the two incidents at the end. The graveyard had its blackened monument; the poem commemorates a decent man who will be remembered now through his son's elegy.

Essentially, two styles predominate in Kinsella's work, the literal and the allegorical. The exact use of significant detail is seen in the description of the dead rat in *Vertical Man* and throughout *A Selected Life*. Everywhere in Kinsella's work between 1972 and 1987 are examples of the plain factual style. Such poems move dynamically through successive passages of unadorned language and by means of the disciplined handling of small units of line and word, the controlling presence of sensibility and tone, the use of space. The literal style often carries an allegorical level of meaning. Kinsella's poems of this period invariably have that allegorical dimension no matter how bound they may seem to be by the nuts and bolts of the ordinary. The more explicit allegorical style may have an old-fashioned, seemingly awkward, quality. References to ghosts and dreams, to vapours, cauldrons, nightmare, phantasms of one kind or another belong, one feels, to another age or to outmoded conventions of the Romantic and the Gothic. Nevertheless their place in Kinsella's poetry is deliberate and organic.

The allegorical style is sometimes found in the form of a prologue, and/or an epilogue. At the beginning of *The Good Fight* the overall theme is announced in the first stanza, which was not included in the Carcanet edition of *Collected Poems*.

> Once upon a time a certain phantom
> took to certain-red-smelling corridors
> in sore need. It met, with a flush of pleasure,
> the smell of seed and swallowed
> life and doom in the same animal action.[4]

The enactment of a fundamental appetite by a storybook phantom introduces what the rest of the poem elaborates. The seed of life and death corresponds to the contrasting figures of John F. Kennedy and Lee Harvey Oswald, whose positive and negative aspects are both presented as an instinctive hunger. The transitional stanza in parenthesis that follows underlines the meaning of the first: man is by nature ready to absorb the seed, the 'Mere substance'.[5]

The allegorical style is present at greater length in the 'Prologue' to *One*, in which the pattern of hunger, digestion, absorption and renewed hunger is outlined in a sequence of deepening dream. The self as dreamer accompanies the self as interpreter, a device by which the self here and in other poems is dramatically captured and understood. The 'Prologue' initially mimes the hungering instinct in the image of a bird arising 'out of this black lair' and fulfilling its hunger in ecstatic, buoyant activity, feeding on 'little hearts beating in their/furryfeathery bundles, transfixed.' When that hunger has been appeased, the action is stilled. Then comes the dreaming in which the self is 'sprawled out/winding across the heavens'. This shift in language and perspective from reality to fantasy represents one of the demands of this poetry, as it adjusts from the literal to the fantastic.

The allegorical mode enables Kinsella to illustrate the procedures he wishes to investigate in the poems that follow: the diagram is charted within the dream sequence as exposition. The language of the sequence is active, varying in rhythm from the swift movements of the initial metaphor of ecstatic feeding to the quietness of satiety, from the horror vision of the 'natural threat out of the void' to the interpretation. The second stage of the dream also unites the fantasy of the 'cosmic grip' with the process of physical decay and again gives the interpretation. The third stage is the division of the self, the separation into 'two discs of light', and this also is followed by interpretation. The third stage concludes with the struggle towards rejuvenation and with a return to the joyous hunger of the opening lines. The final injunction – 'Sleep on these things' – is directed to the self and to the reader, as much as to say: reflect on this allegory, therein lies meaning.

At times the serious, even portentous, manner becomes noticeable: the impulse is to instruct the reader or to emphasize a particular reading. At the same time Kinsella can be self-mocking, as in 'The Entire Fabric' (*One*), in which the 'confident quackery' and the theatricality of the scene, with its magician, painted woman and smoking cauldron, poke fun at similar occasions in the poetry, where the same components are presented seriously. The scene is drawn from the Hall of Knights in Goethe's *Faust*. There Faust returns to the upper world with his prize, the key, and summons up Paris and Helen, archetypal lovers who fuse the erotic and the redemptive. In this case, coming right after the 'Prologue', the poem serves as transition and introduction to those that follow. That 'the entire fabric sang softly' is exactly what Kinsella wants to happen and that intention is not lessened by being presented here in a light-hearted manner. The total infusion of poetic life into a poem or a sequence of poems is the kind of linguistic achievement that his best poems attain. When matter or substance in a Kinsella poem takes on a life of its own, alters, glows, stirs – the images vary – the mystery at the heart of things happens; the creative imagination fuses life into inert matter.

The informing design of his poetry at this period is based on a numerological system extending from zero to five, the Quincunx. It begins in 'From the Land of the Dead' where the egg of being, the O, was manifested and where the poems explored the first stirrings of life, embryonic forms, small movements and indications of potential. *One* continues the plot by concentrating on the unitary, the male element. Its exploration of the poet's familial and racial past focuses on his father and grandfather in particular and ultimately on the first peoples to arrive in Ireland. The book begins with the affirmation of man's adventurous spirit in 'Finistère', a womb journey through the salt chaos of the ocean to the moment of arrival in Ireland. Amergin has come from the regions of death and sets his right foot on Irish soil (box 14, folder 13). The rhythms often embody the movement of the travellers, whose instinctive response to a force they do not understand but strongly feel is imaged in drawings on megalithic monuments – 'river ripple earth ramp/suncircle moonloop'. The poem concludes with Amergin's majestic hymn to creation.

> Who
>   is a breath
> that makes the wind
> that makes the wave
> that makes this voice?
>
> Who
>   is the bull with seven scars
> the hawk on the cliff
> the salmon sunk in his pool
> the pool sunk in her soil
> the animal's fury...(164)

The poem's last line gives the open-ended answer: '(I went forward, reaching out)'.

'The Oldest Place' continues the account of prehistoric peoples settling in, suffering privation, persisting, undergoing the fundamental process of search, absorption, suffering, death and renewal which the 'Prologue' had outlined. Even in this primitive engagement that miracle of response within the material occurs.

> And there was something in the way the land behaved:
> passive, but responding. It grew under our hands.
> We worked it like a dough to our requirements
> yet it surprised us more than once
> with a firm life of its own, as if it
> used us. (166)

The details are drawn from the *Book of Invasions*, so that the literal and the mythological coalesce. The image of the standing stone surviving in the barren plain is emblematic of its indestructible life force, round which matter gathers, decays and renews itself. It is one of several phallic images in the book. Whereas in 'From the Land of the Dead' such renewals took place in underground pits or caves, womb-like receptacles, in this book the source is the pillar-stone, block, phallus, the one. The dream sequence at the end of 'The Oldest Place' affirms the mystery of life in death; the gifts deposited on the pillar are recognitions of its rejuvenating power; it becomes 'packed ... with dark radiance'.

> And I dreamed
> that my ghost moved toward it, hand on heart,
> the other hand advanced.

> And its glare
> gathered like a pulse, and struck
> on the withered plain of my own brain. (167)

There are intimations of renewals in the concluding lines in the references to 'restless metal', 'abnormal stirrings', 'complex emptiness shimmered', and the female presence in 'shawl'. 'His Father's Hands' completes the sequence with its Jungian sense of the weight of history behind the individual. Kinsella's historical sense is of a living, ongoing force affecting successive generations, modified from time to time but connected. The process concludes here with the emergence of life from the block of wood, which has been worked on by three generations. In a female context, saturated with potential, it yields its extraordinary birth.

Extraordinary... The big block – I found it
years afterward in a corner of the yard
in sunlight after rain
and stood it up, wet and black:
it turned under my hands, an axis
of light flashing down its length,
and the wood's soft flesh broke open,
countless little nails
squirming and dropping out of it. (173)

A Technical Supplement, a sequence of twenty-four poems, moves towards the division of the unitary into two. The metaphor of the blade or knife, as an instrument of investigation and division, recurs. The material examined is of many kinds, some pleasant, some objectionable, both positive and negative. The factor of dynamic response is crucial. Kinsella is open and flexible, confident in his own technical ability. At the basis of his approach is the idea that one understands experience best by taking it exactly on its own terms. The poems function accordingly.

Following an introductory 'Prologue', the opening prayer addressed to 'Blessed William Skullbullet', the cartographer Sir William Petty, is an exaggerated appeal in which the language calls attention not to benevolence but to mad and furious activity. The image of the cartographer as fisherman wrestling with his catch emphasizes stress and strain.

Blessed William Skullbullet
glaring from the furnace of your hair
thou whose definitions – whose insane nets –
plunge and convulse to hold thy furious catch
let our gaze blaze, we pray,
let us see how the whole thing
works (177)

The implication is that this will require considerable effort. The material under scrutiny has a 'furious' life of its own; it is difficult to manage; out of the interaction between the burning intensity of the fisherman and the contortions and reactions of the 'catch', insight may come. The images within the poems of pain, incisions, penetrations and cutting, the dismemberment of animals, the swallowing of one creature by another all relate to these introductory images of violent engagement. Kinsella chooses cool appraisal, a distancing from the uncontrollable involvement imaged in the portrait of Skullbullet, whose name suggests rigidity and hardness, an inability to be supple and pliable. The title of the collection points towards rationality.

Petty also used the body as a metaphor for society, as does Kinsella in the opening poems of the collection. The parallel between anatomical dismemberment and critical analysis is clear. The human body and the work of the poet need to be seen as a whole, not in isolated parts. It is a point of view to which Kinsella returns over and over within his own poetry and in comments on it.

Poetry as intense confrontation of material is most readily seen in the poems about the operation of the knife. The vividness and accuracy of the description compel the reader to witness the activity in all its gory and shocking detail. Each stage of the process in the slaughterhouse has the verifiable accuracy of a scientific record; this is indeed how this particular activity works.

> The next opened it downward to the throat,
> embraced the mass of entrails, lifted them out
> and dropped them in a chute. And so to one
> who excavated the skull through flaps of the face,
> hooked it onto the carcass and pushed all forward
> toward a frame of blue flames, the singeing machine. (181)

Similar too is the unblinking account of one lizard being swallowed by another. The nature of this hunger is akin to other examples of dynamic energy in this book and elsewhere – the shark in the aquarium, Oswald in his room, the artist at his bench. Fierce concentrated energy consumes matter, the substance from which energy comes; eyes blazing, light beaming, mouths eating are all metaphors for the same capacity. But *A Technical Supplement* also incorporates waste, and concludes that everything is grist to the imaginative mill; all energy has a function. The energy is the essential element.

Poem 10 reflects on the domestic scene as a kind of parable on refuse, showing what has to be done, how waste must be dealt with, how the garden must be prepared for cultivation – 'sieve, scour and roughen; make it all fertile and vigorous'. No. 11 considers how the poet must act. Here the various forms of outward-directed action are turned inwards, towards division. The process is the same. The transformation of the inner substance in poem 16 makes a new beginning possible; the stages correspond to those described previously in the third dream of the 'Prologue' or in the narrative of the effigy in poem 3 or in the block that gives birth.

> A few times in a lifetime, with luck
> the actual *substance* alters; fills with
> expectation, beats with a molten glow
> as change occurs; grows cool; resumes. (187)

The artist, as poem 19 makes clear, is attempting to arrest something from flux, from 'the streaming away of lifeblood, time-blood'. The dynamic encounter with experience of whatever kind in its total absorption and the possibility of its being recycled results in the creative process. The final three poems point towards the separation; the dividing blade is now within, an integral, painless part of the self, the 'split id', the 'knifed nous'. The pattern of the redemptive fall continues. 'The divider waits, shaped/razor sharp to my dream print.'

> Turning slowly and more slowly
> we drifted to rest in a warmth of flesh,
> twinned, glaring and growing. (193)

In prefacing *A Technical Supplement* with Denis Diderot's letter to Voltaire in which he admits to weariness with his work on the *Encyclopédie* and to a recurrent yearning to 'live in obscurity and die in peace', Kinsella voices his own negative feelings at this time about the uselessness of what he does, when all men end up as ashes. 'That there is more spleen than good sense in all this, I admit – and back to the *Encyclopaedia* I go.'

There are resemblances between Diderot's comprehensive attempt to bring together in one work all the knowledge of the time and Kinsella's attempt to encompass so much of human experience and to see in this collection 'how the whole thing/works'. Kinsella respects those who undertake comprehensive examinations. Diderot in the eighteenth century wanted to bring together all forms of knowledge, to show its underlying system and to indicate how it might be passed on into the future. Sir William Petty wanted to make a map of Ireland; he saw the land as fixed and unchanging, but for the poet the land is lived upon and in flux. Just as Diderot turned away from weariness, Kinsella turned away from his negative response to his own undertaking. For him the driving forces of persistence, endurance and momentary insight are fundamental. The anatomical metaphor found in this collection, some of which is highlighted in the accompanying plates from Diderot's *Encyclopédie* – some illustrations of surgical procedures – is an analogy for the analysis of the nature of understanding and the ways in which poetry works. The Peppercanister collections are intended to embody a construct of significant elements.

Sometimes, Kinsella adopts the metaphor of falling, of allowing his mind to drift, in order to indicate that his poetry, at that point, is dealing with dream material or with material from the unconscious. The work then gives the impression of following some psychic course that is not only inherently puzzling but by its very nature random or even chaotic. In fact Kinsella usually alerts the reader to understand his poetic procedures, to concentrate on his uses of language, to note how the overall structure works. In the Peppercanister collections the technique is one of recurrent refocusing in which situations, incidents, characters and ideas are seen with different degrees of clarity and force. The repetitions are repetitions in which the same subject is made part of the life of the poetic sequence; it functions within a particular context and at the same time, because it occurs elsewhere, it has significance beyond its immediate contexts; its force is both particular and more general. Elsewhere it may appear in more expanded or more contracted form, or may be realized in a different style, seen within a different imaginative perspective. And this condition of singularity and complexity, of oneness and multiplicity, of isolation and participation attends each one of the poetic sequences that is part of the ongoing poetic sequences in the Peppercanister collections.

The Good Fight uses the assassination of John F. Kennedy to consider philosophical, moral, psychological and artistic questions. Plato's *The Republic* and, to a lesser extent, the *Laws* serve as a foil for these considerations. His discussion of the moral and political question of what is justice both illuminates the assassination and at the same time fails to explain why it happens, as though the great rational dialogue proceeded without considering all the pertinent factors, a view of *The Republic* in keeping with recent commentary.

It is the interaction of its main figures, John F. Kennedy, Lee Harvey Oswald and Robert Frost, their individual wills and values, and their interpretations of human psychology that gives the poem its particular force. By his vigour and idealism, his ability to imbue a people with a vision of what is possible, John F. Kennedy evokes the promise of New Frontier politics. In its positive rhythms and choice of words, his voice embodies the forward-looking drive of the political leader: 'we will march along', 'bend their wills together', 'admit no limit'. The call is to urgent 'adventuring', 'aspiring to the sublime', 'to greatness'. 'Let us make ourselves vessels of decision.' 'The old order changes!' These passages pulse with the dynamism of Kennedy's language and are interspersed with Kinsella's voice as he reflects on this language and the limits within which Kennedy framed his appeal. Side by side with the heightened, motivational political rhetoric is the calm analysis of the poet, who measures Kennedy's final speech and its definitions of national and human possibilities, positive and optimistic, based on the idea that 'All reasonable things are possible', against Plato's observations on the dangers and pitfalls of leadership. The Greek philosopher's comments on imperfect societies and his criticism of democracy in the famous similes of the ship's captain and the large and powerful beast qualify the Kennedy image, and ominously confirm what happens to Kennedy.

References to great crime, evil, Reason and the Spirit subject to Greed place Oswald's deed in the context of the evil to which men and societies are prone, but at the same time project it as a crime of a different origin, one not accounted for in Plato's rational scheme. In addition, Kinsella subjects Kennedy's inflexible ideals to sardonic dismissal.

The contrast between Kennedy and Oswald is dramatic. The portrait of Lee Harvey Oswald begins with objective third person narration as Kinsella describes him settling into the room from which he will shoot at the President but this point of view changes to the first person voice of the alienated being. It is a moving threnody for how it feels to be a nobody and how that feeling motivates him to do something to counter the negative state.

> I have seen very few
> cut so dull and driven a figure,
> masked in scorn or abrupt
> impulse, knowing content
> nowhere. (153)

Oswald is broodingly self-aware and at the centre of his own drama of changing response. His baffled loneliness is as imaginatively realized as is Kennedy's confident enthusiasm. He is the victim of an obscure force – 'there is something he must do'; the tasks are 'assigned' to him; he works his way into them, prepares his state of mind. The portrait dramatizes Oswald in an objective manner, then moves to a subjective view. His diary shifts the focus inward. The 'I' figure is both narrator and protagonist, able to separate himself from the objective mode in order to understand himself better. Whereas Kennedy lives his life and finds fulfilment in terms of public performance and acceptance, Oswald sees and understands himself as a lonely outcast, a lost person, victim of his own energy. His self-analysis is perceptive, a painfully revealing self-portrait balanced against Kennedy's limiting inability to move except within the theatre of public acclaim. Oswald comes to suspect that being enclosed in silence, as he is, is not normal; therefore he entertains the idea of ending his plight by suicide or by reaching out to make dramatic contact with another.

In complex ways the poem creates a dramatic and subtle contrast between the two men. It also raises, outside of Plato's range of reference, the question of decision. Who determines human action? What makes Kennedy behave as he does? What causes Oswald to act? Why did this event happen? Robert Frost at the end of the poem calls both men 'vessels of decision', implying outside causes. The unwillingness to define human action in exclusive rationalistic terms is post-Freudian.

Plato could rely on reason; Jung knew there were other forces to be considered when trying to understand human nature. Jung himself raised similar questions about his traumatic childhood experiences: 'Who spoke to me then? Who talked of problems far beyond my knowledge? Who brought the Above and Below together...?'[6] Oswald's own explanation, however valid psychologically, does not confront such fundamental issues. Nor does Plato's analysis get to the root of them; his ideals of the right balance between reason, physical desire, and ambition are mocked by the disjointed, exclamatory style.

> (His 'philosophic nature'
> – balance, you will remember;
> apportionment, as between Mind and Body!
> Harmony, and proper pitch!
> The Dance!) (157)

Only in the poem's concluding section, after it has registered the devastating effects of the assassination on the public, does Kinsella put forward a personal view through the persona of Robert Frost, who has been stunned by the calamity of the assassination. The twentieth-century, post-Jungian intellectual knows what man is capable of, the evil that men do. The best one can hope for is to understand, and that understanding must be based on seeing what Kennedy and Plato omitted.

> That all *un*reasonable things
> are possible. *Everything*
> that can happen will happen. (157)

The impulse to understand is important but so is the capacity to take experience exactly on its own terms. Frost's words identify Kinsella's artistic faith:

> it is we, letting things *be*,
> who might come at understanding.
> That is the source of our patience.
> Reliable first in the direction
> and finally in the particulars of our response,
> fumbling from doubt to doubt,
> one day we might knock
> our papers together, and elevate them
> (with a certain self-abasement)
> – their gleaming razors
> mirroring a primary world

> where power also is a source of patience
> for a while before the just flesh
> falls back in black dissolution in its box. (158)

The important point for Kinsella is the extraction of order from actuality. Kennedy, whom one might have expected to be the creative figure, lacks the right attitude: he imposes a design, plays the game of appropriate response, fails to relate to reality on its own terms, and therefore does not understand it. Nor does Plato's speculative mode encompass an accurate perception of reality. Oswald, in his patient adjustment to the task assigned, in his slow and careful preparation for what he has to do, is close to the artist. Both are fulfilled in particular responses to which each is committed, like the shark for which movement is life and inaction death. The poem is not only about political, philosophical and psychological interpretations of human behaviour but about creativity. It defines Kennedy's limitations, portrays Oswald in a manner that indicates the radical isolation of the modern artist, and in Robert Frost shows the possibilities of creative endeavour. With patience, intelligence and luck the artist may 'knock' his papers together in the kind of organic relationship of particulars that we find in Kinsella's work. The Joycean, sacramental associations of the razors, elevation and mirroring affirm his respect for that writer's acceptance of the actualities of life, 'the primary world', as the ingredients of art and his sense of the disciplines required. As Kinsella said in an interview with John Haffenden in *Viewpoints* (1981), the direct dealing with matter requires great sophistication and equipment. The organs of perception and understanding, as well as the technical skills, must function effectively. There is a note of humility in the lines quoted above, the recognition that failure is always possible and death is inevitable. The artist creates amid the streaming away of lifeblood, time blood; he gathers from the continuity of human experience, creates his metaphoric vision and declines into final darkness, bequeathing, like Gustav Mahler, his particular song of the night.

Notes

1   Jacobi, *The Psychology of C.G. Jung*, p.43.
2   Badin, *Thomas Kinsella*, p.196.
3   *Collected Poems* (1996), p.151. The lines are not included in *Collected Poems* (2001).
4   Ibid., p.153.
5   Ibid.
6   C.G. Jung, *Memories, Dreams, Reflections*, trans. Richard and Clara Winston, ed. Aniela Jaffé (London: Collins, 1963), p.30.

SONG OF THE NIGHT

The sea, which has a strong presence in Kinsella's work from 'Ballydavid Pier' (*Nightwalker and Other Poems*) and 'The Shoals Returning' ('Wormwood') to 'At the Ocean's Edge' (*Personal Places*) and 'High Tide: Amagansett' (*Godhead*), is the decisive force in 'Carraroe' (*Song of the Night and Other Poems*). This fully achieved poem is alive with descriptive detail and mimetic rhythms expressing movement and release, the force of water and light, the strong oceanic power working at the shore. The scene is described in terms of myriad movement, of wave and light, of the humans, the lamp, the light, the voices of the children, the cleansing of the utensils, the seething flight of the sand eels. Based on a description of a family scene beside the western ocean at Carraroe in County Galway, the title poem illuminates the correspondences within man and nature and concludes with an eerie sense of the power within nature. The poet/observer views the landscape, feels, sees and responds to its components, including the actual force within the movements of water and cloud.

> ...At night-time,

> in the wind, at that place,
> the water-wash lapped at itself under the rocks
> and withdrew rustling down the invisible grains.
> The ocean worked in dark masses in the bay
> and applied long leverage at the shore. (206)

With a similar intensity of perception, the poet notes the activities of his children:

> ...Splashes and clear voices echoed
> as the spoons and knives were dug down
> and enamel plates scooped under water
> into the sand, and scraped and rinsed. (207)

The myriad flickerings of sand eels, the excited responses of the children, the blaze of the lamp are part of a sequence of similar images. Through a fine net of correspondences the poem pulsates with an animated, mirroring effect. The dynamic intensity of its descriptive accuracy discloses the multiple energies of a setting in which ocean, sky and people are brought into creative communion. The spectacular ending – in which exclamation, wonder, the sense of tears at the heart of things are openly manifested – conveys a climax of feelings that rises naturally from the setting. The hurtling violence that tears through the scene is a poignant reminder of darkness, of forces beyond our control that make our deepest experiences of beauty and of artistic achievement both joyous and sad. This recognition of positive and negative force is made possible in this setting. Denied in the pent-up pressure of the city in the 'Philadelphia' section, it is made manifest in 'Carraroe' through the dramatic interaction of its natural elements.

> The bay – every inlet – lifted
> and glittered toward us in articulated light.
> The land, a pitch-black stage
> of boulder shapes and scalps of heaped weed,
> inhaled.
>
> A part of the mass
> grated and tore, cranking harshly,
> and detached and struggled upward
> and beat past us along the rocks,
> bat-black, heron-slow. (208)

Against this emphatic physical reality comes the arresting moment of 'A new music', with Gustav Mahler's Seventh Symphony, known as 'Song of the Night', providing a parallel imaginative treatment. The tone lifts to wondrous exclamation – music, bird, people, setting – in an act of contemplation and comprehension. Kinsella's handling of the material, an interweaving of themes, analogies and commentary, resembles Mahler's arrangement of Hans Bethge's '*Der Abschied des Freundes*'. His language is aimed not so much at pictorial description as at the expression of powerful feeling. He inflates and intensifies the force of the lines, alternating between the music itself and the lines of critical appraisal, repeating Mahler's ejaculatory style of musical rhetoric in the language of the poem. There is a specific echo of his 'Song of the Night', whose third movement is called *Schattenhaft* ['like a shadow']. The common ground is the pressure of motion – in the ocean and in the behaviour of children and adults; rhapsody rises to fervent emotional heights.

> A new music came on the wind: string sounds hissing
> mixed with a soft inner-ear roar
> blown off the ocean; a persistent
> tympanum double-beat ('... darkly expressive,
> coming from innermost depths...') That old
> body music. *Schattenhaft*. SONG OF THE NIGHT.
> A long horn call, 'a single note
> that lingers, changing colour as it fades...'
>
> Overhead a curlew responded.
> 'poignant...' Yes.
> 'hauntingly beautiful...' Yes! (208)

That ending contrasts with the passage in *Vertical Man* that results in the 'Radiant outcry' of Mahler's *Das Lied von der Erde*.

The Taoist concept of nature might serve as an allegory for Thomas Kinsella's idea of a poem, for while it would be far-fetched to discuss 'Tao and Unfitness: At Inistiogue on the River Nore' as an expression of the ideal poetic response, the Taoist perception of nature and Kinsella's understanding of how a poem works are analogous. For the Taoists, the universe is a living organism, its woods and rivers infused with a mysterious spirit, its rocks and mountains endowed with a life force. They feel a stillness at the heart of nature and apprehend mysterious correspondences within it. To perceive the stillness, they say, one must cultivate stillness. Kinsella's poem is a parable of such perception, underlined by a sequence of quiet directives, such as 'Move, if you move, like water.' The subject is delicate, the means recalcitrant.

One constant is the distinction made between ordinary observation and intuitive communion. The attractive casualness of the former, a relaxed noting of place and people, is subtly offset by the gentle quietism of the latter. More directly, within the same pattern, the disruptions of history yield to intelligent inaction. Within each section of the poem the two kinds of response contribute with growing certitude to the profounder nature of the second until there is a fusion of sensibility with the natural phenomena. The final image of the man in the boat completes the vision of oneness with nature.

> The flat cot's long body slid past effortless
> as a fish, sinewing from side to side,
> as he passed us and vanished. (205)

Kinsella's sensibility not only responds with sensual immediacy to forces within the universe, it also registers psychic experience with equal fascination and precision. Kinsella's explorations of the dark waters have persisted. The interconnecting imagery of his work is closely linked with his openness to these half-understood but meaningful experiences. References to shadows, darkness, hidden rooms, pits, recesses indicate the unconscious within which frightening and potentially significant experience may be encountered. 'C.G. Jung's "First Years"', also in *Song of the Night*, acknowledges the obscure, powerful intimations of primordial experience. It begins ominously – 'Dark waters churn amongst us/and whiten against troublesome obstacles' – pointing in deceptively simple terms towards the unconscious. The details of the poem – the nurse, the Jesuit, the enthroned phallus – are taken from the first chapter of Jung's autobiographical *Memoirs, Dreams, Reflections*, to which Kinsella adds his own similar memory. The mysterious nature of such childhood experience is recognized, in agreement with Jung's conclusion: 'it was an initiation into the realm of darkness'. (30)

Published in conjunction with *Her Vertical Smile* in the pairing pattern that is now Kinsella's preferred method of publication, *Songs of the Psyche* begins in a realistic manner. After a gap of seven years during which he worked on his translations for *An Duanaire* (1981) and prepared *The New Oxford Book of Irish Verse* (1986), Kinsella re-enters the world of psychological exploration. The book is in three parts: 'Settings', three poems which focus on what Jung calls the land of childhood; 'Songs of the Psyche', an 'Invocation' and thirteen sections that pursue an 'inward' journey; and 'Notes', eight poems of definition and summary.

Through the identifications of childhood experience in 'Settings', Kinsella moves towards the exploration of the psyche. The child is seen in the context of school with its associations of learning, history, ideas and expectation. Then he comes into contact with the adult world of books, work and death, in a combination of promise, fear and partial understanding. In 'Model School, Inchicore', the ordinary is freighted with potential: the plasticine rolls into the shape of a 'snake', the chalk makes 'a white dot' on the blackboard, the boy feels he is going to know 'everything'. It is a dynamic shorthand that describes the boy's lessons: the snake of wisdom, the macrocosm in the microcosm, the centre that contains everything. In the background, are deliberate echoes of Joyce's *A Portrait of the Artist as a Young Man*, the expanding consciousness, the brooding sensibility there and here, boys enthralled in the illusions of childhood, in excited contemplation of possibility, in delighted play. These associations lead on to the reflective self, thinking in an autumnal setting about existence, about judgment or accountability. The poem concludes with references to the nib of the pen that will record, penetrate and even kill, and to the ink that shrinks things to an exact, unromantic shape.

The primary effect is of an inquiring, eager-minded child. Scenes in 'Model School, Inchicore' evoke this state.

> In the second school we had Mr. Browne.
> He had white teeth in his brown man's face.
>
> He stood in front of the black board
> and chalked a white dot.
>
> 'We are going to start
> decimals.'
>
> I am going to know
> everything.
>
> *
>
> One day he said:
> 'Out into the sun!'
> We settled his chair under a tree
> and sat ourselves down delighted
> in two rows in the greeny gold shade.
>
> A fat bee floated around
> shining amongst us
> and the flickering sun
> warmed our folded coats
> and he said: 'History...!' (221–2)

The imagery of sun, tree, 'greeny gold shade', 'flickering sun' contributes to the sense of excited possibility, with the ironic qualification of the excessively nationalistic nature of Irish education at the time. We are back to the beginning, before the encounter with the old women, as far back in an adjoining poem as the possible moment of conception. These poems about the child's first inklings of the possibilities of gaining knowledge, including 'forbidden knowledge', are part of the pattern of mankind's lust for fresh discovery that characterizes other poems, such as 'Finistère'. But the paradigm keeps appearing. There are the sunlit possibilities of his first school and his attraction to knowledge: the inquisitive boy 'stuck' in the back room, frightened by darkness and noise like a bat fluttering, is in search of knowledge. In 'Bow Lane' the roller-blind in the uncle's wardrobe rustled like a bat; in 'Phoenix Street' the father's 'dark nest/stirred with promises'. The compressed allusions stir with Jungian parallels.

> And I have opened the black-stained
> double doors of the triangular
> press up in the corner,
> and his dark nest
> stirred with promises...(223)

Kinsella recounts the bewilderment of childhood, the uncertainties, the guilt, the exaggerated feelings, the nightmare, the sense of recurrence. His sensibility is coloured by apprehension of the harsher side of experience, including destruction, erosion and death; one of the defining strengths of his poetry is that he does not shrink from describing that bleaker reality. A significant strand in his development has been the increasingly comprehensive manner in which he has written of opposing forces, the positive and the negative. As Jung maintained, the world exists only because opposing forces are held in equilibrium. The initial search for order has been deepened and extended. Universal patterns declared in 'Baggot Street Deserta' or 'Downstream' have become part of the imaginative life of later collections, such as *Her Vertical Smile*, *Out of Ireland* or *The Pen Shop*.

Songs of the Psyche portrays the self as graceless in middle age, but determined to explore the psyche in a close and conscious parallel with 'From the Land of the Dead'. Its search for wisdom evokes the ritualistic method of the Old Irish poet in his similar pursuit: '(Chew nine times/on the chosen meat/and set it down/outside her door.').[1]

This section of the book is a dramatic narrative, a night journey towards the dawn of discovery. He is only 'half safe' and needs to achieve wholeness by turning inwards. In the course of the narrative Kinsella accepts that he cannot continue with the numerological system that has underpinned his work for over a decade. His notes speak of the collapse of the plan. Many years later he described the system as numerological, emblematical, historical and philosophical, 'extremely satisfying' but 'totally useless'. At the time he had high hopes for it. 'It was a plan for a career.' It had given depth and resonance to the poetic sequences *Notes from the Land of the Dead*, *One* and *A Technical Supplement*. It was, as he said, useful for enlarging his state of mind, but it was not effective for individual poems.[2]

Now, in *Songs of the Psyche*, he re-imagines the plot envisioned in *Vertical Man*, where it 'snaked in a slow beam' down the sky, figuring a compact Jungian message – 'structures and hierarchies/of elements and things and beasts' – undergoing division and redivision in its descent into the newly risen Quincunx which Kinsella associates with the 'woman-animal', the muse and earth goddess. Now he recreates the 'plot', packs the moment with previous affirmations – the pillar on the plain, the block of wood, the Cross. The 'beam of light' once again snakes across 'in multi-meanings' and disappears. It is followed by mythical figures and creatures: Prometheus stealer of fire, Heracles, who slew a dragon, and 'helpful animals'.

> Then stealers of fire;
>   dragon-slayers; helpful animals;
> and ultimately the Cross.
>
> Unless the thing were to be based
>   on sexuality
> or power. (232)

The allusions come directly from Jacobi's *The Psychology of C.G. Jung*, where he summarizes archetypes of the collective unconscious. There is, he writes, a dominant archetype underlying the doctrine of various psychologists: Freud concentrates on sexuality, Adler on the striving for power, Jung on 'tetrasomy', that is, on 'four-bodiedness' seen, for example, in the Cross. For Jung, four is the archetypal expression of the highest significance for the psyche. With this fourth term, he says, 'pure spirit' takes on 'corporeity' and a form adequate to physical creation.[3] But, as Kinsella now decides, none of these archetypes is totally sufficient. It is a significant moment in his development and one of considerable strain since he not only realizes that the numerological system has to be abandoned but makes that discovery part of the poem, projecting himself as a man stuck in a system that has failed.

'Songs of the Psyche' is introduced by 'Invocation', a prayer to Psyche for non-moralizing judgement: 'Sweet mother, sweet muscle,/predatrix, ...rarely seen/yet persistent,'. The 'subsequent' does bustle 'in the previous'. Intimations of what lies ahead are sensed in childhood, as these Jungian contemplations suggest. The poem becomes a descent into the dark, nutrient waters of the unconscious. In a 'reverie' of submission, invoking the number nine as a guarantee of safety and return, Kinsella begins his Dantesque journey to Middle Earth, to his encounter with the grin of the goddess.

> I have kissed the inner earth
> and the grin of stone upon stone
> and it was time again
>
> to surrender
> to your
> beaten smile ... (228)

He must find her 'again' as he did in 'From the Land of the Dead'. Now he returns with a clearer sense of how the creative process works: 'a matter of negative release'. The allusive, allegorical method unfolds a familiar philosophical concept of the interlocking forces of the creative and the destructive; the metaphorical figures are joined once again in a mutually wounding relationship, both 'tender' and 'brutal', consumed in the flame imagery of 'Phoenix Park' and of Eriugena. They have a compulsive need to absorb: 'they have eaten/and must eat'. Similarly, in the re-use of the metaphor of the intertwined trees, Kinsella restates his philosophy of the centrality of love and persistence. The flower colours – gold, red, dark blue, jet black and pale for 'unfinished children' – represent emotional and artistic growth, changes of mood as caused by life's experiences. The Persephone-like figure in the following poem is an image of promise and truth – she is the other half he needs, the 'monster' he must discover in his unconscious – but the romantic contexts are qualified by the reference to the leeches. Poem 13 returns to the imagined self, recreated from 'stupid youth', to a renewed sense of possibilities.

> *I came to myself*
> *in the middle of a dark wood,*
> *electric with hope.* (232)

He restates his understanding of a process of fall and recovery, of 'storm' leading to 'peace' or to 'sleep/or a dream,/or a system of dreams'. The poem ends on images of coming into being, of embryonic stirrings, of light, of 'multi-meanings', evoking then more heroic metaphors of achievements, all leading to the Cross. Beginnings and possibilities are affirmed, then qualified by the thought that 'the thing' may be based not on the light of the creative imagination but on 'sexuality/or power'.

The eight poems in 'Notes' are tense clarifications, as though the poet is taking stock of where he stands after the strain of the descent into the unconscious. It is a new beginning. The process of descent into the mother liquid is recurrent. Even God, as 'A New Beginning' declares, had to lean 'over the mothering pit', to engage with the physical. In 'Opposites' love produces 'refreshment/in the recognition of pattern'; it is open to experience unlike 'Grudging memory', which is locked in on itself. 'The Little Children' uses the metaphor of allowing a child to 'topple forward', in play and fright. This is a miniature account of the encounter 'in laughter and panic/into darkness and fire'. The artist is similarly engaged

> in a series of beginnings
> with feathery touches and brutal fumblings,
> in stupefying waste, brooding and light. (234)

'Brotherhood' records and accepts discord; it is 'no time for kindness' when the poet weighs up the reason for the division between the two brothers: 'your behaviour and your work/are incomprehensible to me'. 'Talent and Friendship' argues that neither talent nor friendship is simple; both are affected by change, either may fail. In a reference to both, Kinsella concludes 'There is no mantle/and it does not descend.'

The last three poems – 'Self-Scrutiny', 'Self-Release' and Self-Renewal' – are more expansive in style, less compressed in structure. The mood is sombre as the 'threadbare body' gathers about itself and becomes conscious of its composite parts – in the reality of death which is conveyed in the finality of eyes now 'wet with delicacy' that will inevitably close 'under unopenable marble'; the closure, the end of feeling, and finality are brilliantly imagined. All the 'parts' have similar messages: the ear brings 'the snarl of mutabilitie' straight to the brain; the tongue brings 'understanding' of the way things are the more it experiences its apparent existential freedom; thumbs and fingers applied to the temples press home the degree of limitation that attends human indecision.

That sense of pressure and inner strain is taken up in 'Self-Release', in which the poet is on the verge of a mental breakdown. It is a powerful portrayal of inner agony and frustration, a satirical modest proposal for surgical self-laceration. If he applies such fierce treatment, then he will be 'charming', a 'startlement to all,/internationally and beyond'. The sarcasm reinforces the desperation.

> Possibly you would rather I stopped
> – uttering guttural Christ curses
> and destroying my nails down the wall
> or dashing myself to pieces once and for all
> in a fury beside your head?
>
> I will ease it somehow.
> I could pull down a clean knife-shaft
> two-handed into the brain and worry it
> minutely about until there is
> glaze and numbness in 'that' area. (236)

In 'Self Renewal' he swings open the two-sided mirror, 'Reverently'. He recognizes – 'the pale secrets of all/the lonely'. It is a moment of intense clarity, as the self and the *anima* come face to face in a perception of division, firmness and hurt. But it is also a moment of renewal as they 'recover themselves a little'. As a result of the clear-eyed inspection, 'they felt more able/to slip off about their business'. The particular business that Kinsella moves to is to see how the artist engages with politics and history. In Jung's opinion the archetypes should save the individual from his isolation. In 'Self-Scrutiny' this is not the case. The system has failed. The individual slips off about his business without the support of the Jungian system. Kinsella has been aware for some time of the constrictions of writing to a system. Now in language that indicates the strain, he says that the system itself is as exploratory as the poetry he is trying to fit to it. In addition, ordinary experience has started to take over and he has begun to write poetry of 'detail and immediate beauty' (box 62, folder 1). Much of the poetry of *Songs of the Psyche*, in particular the recollection of boyhood experience, may be said to be poetry of detail, although that is hardly new. As for poetry about immediate beauty, there is little of that. The work is more concerned with moral reappraisal and has greater intellectual weight.

When the later autobiographical poems deal with historical material, as they do in *St Catherine's Clock*, the exact details are noted rather than interpreted. In the case of family portraits we are given unflattering images. There is hurt and conflict between the aunts and a mixture of pretension and pride.

> Sometimes some of the aunts
> wouldn't talk for weeks,
> in a bad temper after passing remarks.
>
> They chewed their lips
> and passed each other by
> with stiff faces.
>
> But some of them would keep
> muttering together in the middle room.
> And one of them would suddenly
>
> laugh up out of her throat,
> and all the put-on pain and the high snout
> would go out of their stares. (265)

A distinctive social world emerges in small instances of human behaviour, in exact realities.

St Catherine's Clock resumes that investigation of home but from a longer perspective. The image of the pointed instrument – pen, syringe, clock-hand, pike, fishing-hook, imagination – reoccurs in its five poems, as does the image of the prowler or nightwalker. The collection returns to the world of family and depends not on the contrapuntal relationship

of image and idea, but on the unifying force of a single historical direction and of a preoccupation with the bloodline. The glistening point, of
the pen or of the syringe, is both positive and negative. The blood is that
of the drug addict, of Lord Kilwarden and his nephew, of Robert
Emmet, of the family line.

On the way to his boyhood home Kinsella sees, remembers, recreates
scenes from the area. The stylized Malton print, smoothing over colonial
violence, is also of the area of St Catherine's Church in Thomas Street,
where Kilwarden was killed, where Emmet was hanged, where the
population dipped their handkerchiefs in his blood, and introduces the
casual historical scene: horsemen, children or dwarfs, dogs, a redcoat, the
cailleach (or hag) crossing the street. Through the use of literal detail and
a broken structure, a redefinition of the historical and personal past, it
is in effect insisting on the violence. Ahead lies familiar territory: Bow
Lane and Basin Lane, aunts, uncles, cousins, 1938. The family is
rendered in tenacious, realistic detail, with an objective, ironical, amused
tone. Kinsella does not stylize them or romanticize them in the manner
of a historical print. They are explicitly ordinary, not drawn into a
diagram of youth and age, not subsumed into Celtic or classical mythology, but brought into life by a selection of unflattering detail – an aunt
with 'a slow bum', aunts who quarrel and sulk, boys who take part 'in a
savage dance' and experience the familiar pain of adolescence. The
context makes a confused, poignant portrait of shared boyhood.

Returning to the world that shaped him, Kinsella gives it a new
dimension of feeling, sometimes in exact and revealing Dublinese. He
points to what was there: 'I always remembered/who and what I am.'
And there is more to know: the poem obliquely hints at mysteries, at
deficiencies in feeling, at uncertainties of identity. It moves then from
these intimations back to Emmet, back to Thomas Street, back to the
blood of the martyr and the dipped handkerchiefs, back to the beginning
in 'Baggot Street Deserta', back to *Her Vertical Smile*, to that period in
his early manhood when the poet studied and worked to prepare himself,
before love entered his life with the arrival of Eleanor. The imagery of
the river carrying the soul towards some haven, some magnificence, some
discovery brings the sequence to an end. In this surge of promise the
language rises above the imagery of back lane, belching aunts, schoolboy
awkwardness and confusion, the riddle of identity and purpose. The
tooth on the measuring-wheel of St Catherine's clock adjusts the focus,
and the image of Swift in the final poem – another prowler and, like the
poet, another link with the region – also indicates the ingredient of
satirical, creative imagination in concentrated focus on Irish life.

The method of varied dramatization found in *Songs of the Psyche*
corresponds to the compositional techniques both of *The Good Fight* and

Out of Ireland, a poem in five parts with an 'Entrance' and 'Exit', which resemble those in *The Good Fight*. In that poem Kinsella deploys ideas through particular figures – Plato, John F. Kennedy, Lee Harvey Oswald, Jung, Robert Frost – in a drama of ideological responses to a few central issues, such as government, morality, choice and fate. In *Out of Ireland* various voices – of the crow, the Black Robber, the Sheila-na-Gig, the grave, Eriugena, the early Kinsella, Ó Riada, the Catholic Church, superstition, the musician, the dance – provide a set of challenging ideas, none fully answering the problems of existence or the question of an adequate, artistic response. Kinsella's borrowing from his own work, from 'Phoenix Park' and from *Vertical Man* through images, setting, style and philosophy, becomes part of the dramatic development of the poem.

The movement is backwards in time through a carefully planned sequence of poems, including 'Entrance' and 'Exit'. The former introduces a familiar Kinsellan world; it reasserts his faith in writing, in love, in clear-eyed inspection, in the two cultures. Like chords in a musical composition, the lines echo what has gone before; the spare style avoids fluencies and colorations of language, but every image is precisely functional. Partly concealed rhymes, assonance and alliteration unobtrusively modulate the sound and the sense. The second poem, 'Native Wisdom', sets together a number of seemingly dissonant images: the dark crow of death, the Black Robber, the Sheila-na-Gig, and images of opening – of the vagina, of the grave – and all of them with the same invitation: 'Come and buy.' This repeats the invitation of Irish scholars on the Continent during the Carolingian revival and their claim to knowledge based on experience and on the identification with place. The poem is grounded on a spare style, within which it presents these vibrant, contradictory, tempting claims which form contrasting pieces of wisdom, of mortality, of good and evil, of sexuality, of salvation.

In 'Harmonies' and 'The Furnace', Kinsella transfers Eriugena's Neoplatonic speculation, which was intellectual, allegorical and at times mystical, into a different kind of language. Through images of union, sweet breathing, ascent, departure and gathering, 'silent in a choir of understanding', he adapts some of Eriugena's discussion of the 'Return'. Eriugena's philosophy of the return of all mankind to God subsumes the various entreaties of the preceding poem in a harmonious resolution of dissonance, contradiction, and ambivalence. 'The Furnace' celebrates the idea of the return in images of intensity, flowing fire, the searching for a Shape, and foresees his own eventual melting 'to ineffable zero'. It adopts and provisionally accepts Eriugena's mystical account of man's final union with God as an analogy for the poet's own faith, articulated in the 'Wormwood' sequence, in 'Phoenix Park', in 'Nightwalker' and elsewhere: his trust in love, persistence and the understanding of what may be gained. Kinsella's account of Eriugena's 'harmonious certainty', a philosophy of ascent and return, eloquently expounds a transcendent experience in which Earth's pains are overcome and all Mankind is joined 'in a choir of understanding'. 'The Furnace' becomes a hymn of praise to the imagination's combustible power. Descending from its paean to acknowledge the presence of sin in Eriugena's thinking, the visionary style yields to normalcy; the 'dry kiss' on the beloved's 'rain-wet hair' is an acceptance of reality.

In a language of musical lament for 'a forgotten young hero', 'The Dance' returns to Ó Riada. The notes of fading and loss are momentarily countered by a revivifying passage of dance in which the young man is a Pierrot figure, dancing, 'beckoning with a comic thumb' as he leaves. The entire passage of lively recreation concludes with grieving solemnity. Ó Riada says '*Come and buy/ my terrible new capabilities*', but slithering away he escapes questioning, his music bright and teasing with its 'shifts and rhythms', establishing its distinct sounds on the traditional instruments. While different from the polyphony of Eriugena's linguistic music or the wilful assertions of the other figures, the characterizing of Ó Riada is attractive; he is entertaining, vulnerable, humane and redemptive, the style plain and simple by contrast with the overblown language used to represent Eriugena's vision.

Eriugena had his Old Testament morality. Where Ó Riada dances, Eriugena places 'impediments' on mankind for 'failure/to walk in the Divine Law'. There is no dance of life:

> and it grows dark and we stumble
> in gathering ignorance
> in a land of loss
> and unfulfillable desire. (259)

Bound by an Old Testament view and punished for failure, 'we' exist in a land of the dead. Ó Riada's sprightly comedy is more attractive; the images of 'the goats'/dainty, unbothered feet' and others along the way to 'the stony places,' provide a defining, evaluating context. 'The Land of Loss' returns to Eriugena, to his writings, his rejection of the Church, his death at the hands of students. The bleak outline of the life and the work serves as a philosophical basis, but a minimal basis, on which one might rely.

We may wait in the 'Exit' for the Final Day in 'suspended under-standing'. In a modest conclusion, Kinsella invites us, through the words of a song made after disagreement has been overcome, to join him in the dance, to close the gate on the land of loss. The gesture of closure is repeated in *The Pen Shop* where death is also given a farewell kiss. A follower more of Ó Riada than of Eriugena, Kinsella will use his 'weapon/in the goat-grey light', will use his pen to ward off false prophets, to describe strictly in Ó Riada idiom the complexity and beauty of existence. The figures in 'Native Wisdom' were open; now 'we' are open.

> Lidless, lipless, opensocketed
> and dumb with suspended understanding,
> waiting for the Day ... (260)

That 'Day' reminds us of the child pondering at the end of the Model School poem on God's judgment and on human responsibility. As Kinsella exits from this sequence, he takes up his pen. The image of the pen, the nib, of writing, of inspection, of thinking has been recurrent and will permeate *The Pen Shop*.

Negotiating between successive voices, revealing what they have to say and their attitudes through explicit statement and metaphor, *Out of Ireland* moves from 'half-certainties', including the incompleteness of the 'Phoenix Park' assertion of faith in love and the romanticized view of the artist, to the decisiveness of 'reach me my weapon', through the declensions of the claimants, the breath-taking magniloquence of Eriugena, the exuberance of Ó Riada's dance and his down-to-earth knowledge, although the certainty he claims is also beyond proof. What gives *Out of Ireland* its power is the exactness of its language, its dramatic contrasts of tones and rhythms, the ease and precision with which it engages our attention and moves us through a variety of nicely judged perceptions to the chaste diction of the final stanzas. Like instruments in an orchestra or characters on stage, these conflicting appeals, sequential and contrapuntal, sound their voices with accumulating force. It is attractive also because in addition to these aesthetic values it has a satisfying and stimulating intellectual diversity, subtly presented. Made to discriminate between the voices and to recognize what Kinsella finally offers, our understanding and his are 'suspended'; there is no ultimate, satisfying certainty, but there is a way for the artist to live and that way is defined in persuasively modest terms.

The undefined 'us' in this poem connects with Kinsella's habit in several poems of moving from the 'I' persona to the general 'we'. It is particularly effective in the collection *One*. In 'Finistère', for example, he celebrates the voyage of people from continental Europe to Ireland. The 'I' speaker is both Amergin, the male principle, and the undivided one. It is he who responds creatively to the idea of voyaging into the Atlantic, he who observes a 'point of light'. The poem moves with rhythmic intensity, changing at once from 'I' to 'we', as the people set out. As they step ashore the speaker/narrator recites Amergin's 'Hymn to Creation', an affirmation of beginnings. The fluid interaction of 'I' and 'we' is perfectly adapted to the pervasive thrust of these poems, their explorations of heritage in the immediate past and in distant sources. At the heart of this backward turning is the concept of process, the ways in which things develop, a country's past, language and culture, the creative process itself. The collective voice is that of humanity, all people, at all times, mankind making its way forward from pre-history to the uncertain conclusion at some time in the future. The idea receives a more understated treatment in *Marginal Economy* (2006) where a primitive people, stripped of religious and philosophical supports, modestly eke out a living and do not expect much. Their voices are muted, aware of the dangers of optimism and under no illusion as to the arrival of the Word.

Perhaps no single sequence so powerfully and so fluently reflects Kinsella's sense of the presence of evil as *Her Vertical Smile*, a poem with an Overture, two movements divided by an Intermezzo, and a Coda. Set in Vienna at the time of the collapse of the Austrian Empire, the beautifully poignant 'Overture' responds to the Earth Mother's song in Mahler's *Das Lied von der Erde*. The opening four stanzas interpret the song, ascribe tonal and emotional qualities to it, creating a portrait of a grieving woman, burdened by sorrow, looking inward and withdrawing into the 'heavens' whence she came. The poem delicately evokes the plaintive conclusion of *'Der Abschied'* where the voice of the sorrowing woman, slowly repeating the single word *'ewig'* ('eternal') nine times, becomes so inaudible that it seems, like one of Samuel Beckett's disembodied voices, gradually to come from beyond life. She sings for her son (both Mahler and Ó Riada), but her lament is also an elegy for the end of the world, 'that last lovely heartbeat', the transition from the particular to the universal effected with ease in the fluid rhythm of the run-on lines. Kinsella wonders if God will sit there on the Last Day 'listening to the last echo fade', unmoved, detached, and recalls the young Kinsella and Ó Riada in drab surroundings excited by the same song and filled with desire to emulate such heights of feeling, such an absolute testing of their talent. The poem combines rhapsody and parody in its portrayal of the young men's excited response to the music of old Vienna at the turn of the century, to music that expressed the idealism of the First World War. It is at once poignantly beautiful in its lyric, rhythmic mimicry of the music and in its nostalgic, ironic deflation of youth's enthusiasms and hopes, a telling contrast between the magnificence of the score and the response – 'If only we could wring our talent out/wring it and wring it dry like that' – to the seedy setting: 'A butt flung into a dirty grate.' Mention of God prepares for the poem's later questioning of the purpose of life, just as the picture of Kinsella and Ó

Riada, who will create 'out of nothing', prepares for the poem's later reflection on the role of the artist. Mahler also wrote from nothingness into nothing. In his music, splendour and exceptional energy oppose the desolation of Li-Tai-Po's poem in Bethge's translation.[4] In changing rhythms, abrupt transitions, alternating tones and connecting imagery, *Her Vertical Smile* plays out incidents, metaphors and occasions of hope and promise against those of disappointment and destruction.

The portrait of Mahler the conductor, surrounded by intense, young admirers, is brilliantly focused, vividly emblematic of the man's essential appeal: the readiness to embrace risk, the concentration, art as an investigative force, undeflected, absorbent, recreative. The description of the dance that follows moves quickly into parody: the glamour of war and the music of war are recreated realistically but with mock-heroic effect – 'it's off to the mutton–chop slaughter'. The collapse of the Austrian Empire and Mahler's death are brought together, raising questions of order and purpose, the destructive failure of death, the possibility of a shaped, purposeful world, beginning with the creation of man. Ultimately the beginning is less important than what man does with life. The section ends by bleakly questioning the purpose of war and is followed by one of Thomas Mann's ennobling letters. Aroused by the unexpected violence of Allied propaganda against Germany, Mann abandoned fiction and wrote in Germany's defence. His letter, a brief reminder of former values, expresses Mann's belief in the redemptive renewal of war. It was written in December 1914.

The poem returns then to Mahler on the podium, 'The Elect', concentrating on his masterly execution to show the artist engaged, sensing what lies within the psyche – 'fishchill/a remote stink'. The rest of the poem acknowledges the powerful presence of these instincts that consume the self and pulsate through the body. The moment is metaphysically significant. For Kinsella, acknowledging 'foul feeders on carrion/circling our farthest reach/with a refusing snarl', this is another reality, matching the energy of old Vienna, to which he dedicates himself. It is composed of 'an outer carrion/bone-walking in a dream bedlam', from which he may yet make 'a gavotte' to feed the 'everlasting Ear'. The image of putrid matter from which life may be created is replaced by a pictorial scene of a man and a woman, elegantly dressed, walking beside the sea. The poem ends by welcoming the Fall, expressing the readiness to sing. The Song is directed outward and inward. The 'Coda', invoking the magic number nine, ends the poem in a combination of the serious and the burlesque. *Her Vertical Smile* is a disguised elegy, in which loss and death, the destruction of an empire, the death of an artist friend, the purpose of power, sexuality and life are all brought into focus.

The grieving tone permeates the first movement. Kinsella broods on
history, on mankind's capacity for creation and destruction. No longer the
excited youth – his is the generation that witnessed atomic destruction –
he writes a philosophical poem, moving between commentary and evaluation, which engages profoundly with reality and sees in Mahler's
counterpoint of creation and destruction a true reflection of the nature of
life, but modifies the composer's transcendent solution with his own
restrained treatment and balanced conclusion. Through successive evaluations and imaginative leaps, the poem examines the central and unifying
issues of adult measuring of evidence, together with an appropriate
artistic answer to the conflicting signs of human behaviour.

In a change to a sturdier rhythm with interrupted, sometimes staccato,
lines, Kinsella begins the first movement with a portrait of Mahler con-
ducting the first performance of his Eighth Symphony. He is a model
artist – committed to his work, theatrical, strong-willed. In fact he never
ceased to search for new ways in which to express his complex vision,
his 'strange work', as Kinsella writes, characterized by 'a readiness to
embrace risk':

> tedium, the ignoble,
>   to try anything ten times
> if so the excessive matter can be settled. (240)

Although the excessive matter cannot be finally settled, not even in
ten symphonies, the last incomplete, Mahler explores deeply into the
Muse-Mother in the familiar Kinsellan concept of

> every rhythm drained
>
> into nothing, the nothingness
>   adjusting toward
> a new readiness. (241)

The excited young respond – Kinsella to Ó Riada, the audience to Mahler
– their naive enthusiasm 'there at the heart of old Vienna', expressing the
optimism of the time. Kinsella's notes convey the exuberance he
associates with Mahler.

> ... aetat funfzig: all youth and maturity gathered in risk, willing
> and able to risk anything, any silly melodiousness, over-power-
> ing and tinkly; all future years poised on them also...
> Millions poised whirling in the air above him: cascading notes,
> interdrenching down, out, pouring in toxic elation, outrageous,
> all Europe in total revolving fanfare, melodious howlings...
> (box 21, folder 4)

The poem repeatedly bears witness to the power of music over an audience and the ability of the true artist, poet or composer, to engage fully and responsibly with the potential for profound understanding inherent in the making of a work of art. That the premiere took place in Munich, not Vienna, hardly matters. For the poem's imaginative purposes Vienna, at the heart of the Austrian Empire, where Mahler was conductor of the Vienna Philharmonic Orchestra for ten years and where his musical genius both sustained and transformed the ways in which music was composed, is central and has extensive historical and cultural implications. At 50 years of age Kinsella identifies with the driven temperament of the composer, also aged 50 in 1910, who experienced the spiritual anguish of the twentieth-century artist deprived of a supportive system of belief. In his notes Kinsella asks himself, 'Why am I the one? How come I am so driven? Single-minded, single-bodied. Out of where? Into where? That *this* direction was chosen, into close pursuit of which it appears I am fated, and born' (box 20, folder 12).

The association with Richard Strauss's *Der Rosenkavalier* is apt. No other opera captures so perfectly the mood of Europe on the verge of the First Great War, the gaiety and splendour, the sense of time running out, the young in one another's arms, those vile bodies. The lines beginning the second part of the first movement recreate the mindless antics of privileged Viennese, the mechanical harmony of marching men, the bannerets with their racing pulses, heads filled with notions of 'glory'. The jaunty rhythm, deflating as it records, gives way to the journalistic flatness describing rivers as natural boundaries, marking a place of disaster. In a detached musing Kinsella grants that we 'might search for harmony there' among 'the tangled woebegone', but it would be in vain. Aware of the emergence of destructive machines, the threat of war, and the litter of metaphorical pigs to which the Empire is about to give birth, we might listen to 'the logic of majesty' that makes music out of war: 'drum-roll', slow march. In a natural transition to the last years of the Austrian Empire recreated in a combination of glorious surroundings and buffoonery, Kinsella uses exact detail to create yet another social setting. The tone is one of lament for the almost farcical nature of man's trust in, and attraction to, militaristic glory – the splendour of dress, the yearning for fame in battle – and the inevitable conclusion 'when the awful day is over'. There is no mistaking Kinsella's deep sense of lament at such recurrent instances of vainglory and loss.

Giving imaginative life to this 'curse', Mahler's vision of a happy outcome creates in his listeners 'the pulse of order' but that solution, expressed through a rapturous matriarchal litany in the symphony's jubilant, accelerating ascent as Faust is raised to an affirmative, mystical vision of '*Das Unbeschreibliche*' ['the indescribable'], is startlingly juxtaposed in the poem with Michelangelo's patriarchal depiction of the Creation (God's finger also present in the symphony's hymn *Veni, Creator Spiritus*) where, in Kinsella's view, the figures are a little ridiculous. Neither of these perceptions, as far as he is concerned, is fully satisfactory. The curse, he maintains, as he had in early intimations of figures from Hieronymus Bosch let loose upon the world in modern warfare, comes from within.

Considering these matters – Mahler's and Michelangelo's depictions, old Vienna destroyed, the collapse of the Austrian Empire, the pigs of war let loose – Kinsella asks the rhetorical question: what shall it profit an elder that civilization will be destroyed? The question extends over eight mocking, descriptive stanzas with brilliant detail and hypnotic rhythm. What is the value when we ourselves will turn it into mud and gore, when the 'bannerets' become bodies dangling on the barbed wire of trench warfare, when the rivers of blood are 'of our own making'. This vision of destructive, animalistic behaviour counterpoints the brilliant, social activities of old Vienna and is effective because quietly made in contrast with the heightened rhetoric used for social and militaristic achievement. At the height of his powers Kinsella reiterates the vision of evil he had defined in more restricted fashion in 'Downstream', 'Old Harry', and other early poems.

These meditations are briefly interrupted by the contrasting portrait of an artist who supported war. Thomas Mann's letter, for all its personal warmth, goodwill and enthusiastic support of the German army, expresses another optimism destined to disappointment, its idea of the outcome profoundly ironical. Returning in the second movement to Mahler and the Eighth Symphony, the poem celebrates the maker and the music. Mahler's 'double beat' moves between creation and destruction, bringing new life out of nothingness. The poem, too, reiterates the idea of an art that draws upon the dark underside of existence. The next six stanzas describe its birth: the 'teeming' self, the reality of 'aches and needs', the voracious appetite, absorbing, advancing 'in unsureness or error'. In admonitory mode Kinsella creates his image of ugliness, waste and death from which 'we might yet make a gavotte!' The portrait of Gustav and Alma Mahler walking on the strand depicts a closeness between the sexes and a trustworthy natural world, but the tone is slightly mocking, the scene too good to be complete, not a temptress in sight, the 'Fall' about to begin. Failure, as the Coda reminds us, is always possible. Mahler dissolves grief and death in transcendent music. Kinsella relies on the defusing corrective of ironic counterpoint.

Notes

1   See Derval Tubridy, *Thomas Kinsella: The Peppercanister Poems* (Dublin: University College Dublin Press, 2001), pp.125–7.
2   Badin, *Thomas Kinsella*, p.196.
3   Jacobi, *The Psychology of C.G. Jung*, pp.47–8.
4   Hans Bethge's *Das Trinklied vom Jammer der Erde* translates the Chinese poem.

Part III
TRANSLATIONS: FROM PAGANISM TO CHRISTIANITY

The Táin (Táin Bó Cuailnge), 1969
The New Oxford Book of Irish Verse, 1986
An Duanaire. 1600–1900: Poems of the Dispossessed, 1981

INTRODUCTION

Thomas Kinsella began his translations from Irish literature with three works: *Longes Mac Unsnig: Being the Exile and Death of the Sons of Usnech* (1954); *Thirty-three Triads, Translated from the XII Century Irish* (1955); and *The Breastplate of St Patrick* (1954), revised as *Faeth Fiadha: The Breastplate of St Patrick* (1957). Initially published separately by the fledgling Dolmen Press in limited editions, all three appeared in *Poems & Translations* (1961), which began with 'Death of a Queen', a poem about Deirdre, and concluded with the account of her suicide in *Longes Mac Unsnig*.

The Breastplate of St Patrick, a powerful incantation against those who would harm the saint and his clerics, gave Kinsella a feeling for the character of Old Irish literature; but it was *The Sons of Usnech*, an eighth-century prose narrative interspersed with passages of poetry, that gave him a sense of the impressive achievements of early Irish literature. Economical in language and tight in structure, it is a direct, passionate narrative about the beautiful Deirdre, the jealousy of Conchobor mac Nessa, King of Ulster, who had reared her for himself, and her elopement with Noísiu and his two brothers. Guaranteed a safe return from Scotland, they were betrayed by Conchobor, despite the pledge of safety given by Fergus, former king of Ulster. As an introductory tale for *The Táin* (*Táin Bó Cuailnge*), it explains why Fergus has left Ulster and fights for Medb of Connacht, but in its own right is a tragic tale of love and loss, told with great sophistication. It showed Kinsella that the version in Old Irish was much different from the romanticized treatment by Lady Gregory, W.B. Yeats, J.M. Synge and others. It also directed him to the realities of a pagan, heroic, aristocratic society and led him to translate the *Táin Bó Cuailnge*, its single epic, and thereafter to a sustained programme of translation from literature in Irish. The question is: why did he become so engaged?

His lecture to the Modern Language Association (MLA) in December 1966, printed in *Éire-Ireland*[1] and much reprinted, explains it as an attempt to define his literary identity. He establishes three points of reference: his contemporaries, tradition in Irish, and tradition generally. By 1966 the renewals associated with Dolmen Press had not resulted in a community of literary lives. *The Dolmen Miscellany of Irish Writing* (1962), representing the new writers and edited by Kinsella and John

Montague, was careful to assert that they did not form a movement. The result is that Kinsella feels a sense of isolation in his own time. When he examines Irish tradition, his second point of reference, and looks for the past in his own experience, the results are similar. Whereas the contemporary English poet may find his forbears in the long tradition of English poetry, the Irish poet finds only one major poet, W.B. Yeats, and behind him the virtual silence of the nineteenth century, where there are only a few indispensable poems and nothing that adds up to the conventional literary achievement of a period. But when he tries to identify himself by looking back further, he discovers a poetry that is 'suddenly full of life':

> ...in the service of real feeling – hatred for the foreign landowner; fantasies and longings rising from the loss of an Irish civilization (the poets putting their trust in the Stuarts or the Spanish or even the Pope of Rome); satires, love songs, lamentations; outcries of religious fervour or repentance. (9)

The poets may, as he says, represent the tragic end of Gaelic literature, but they are at home in the language and among them is Aogán Ó Rathaille, 'a major poet'. Further back there are riches and variety in abundance in a tradition that had survived for over a thousand years.

> Poetry as mystery and magic, in the earliest fragments and interpolated in the early sagas; poetry as instant crystalline response to the world, in a unique body of nature lyrics; poetry as a useful profession, the repository of historical information and topography and custom; love poems and devotional poems of dignity and high technique; conventional bardic poetry heavy with tradition and craft. (9)

Early and medieval literature in Irish had what was missing from his time – continuity, a shared literature and a shared history. He recognizes 'a great inheritance and a great loss'. The tradition is broken; he can reach it only across the silence of a century and across the divide between one language and another. Because he writes in English, he is separated from Irish tradition and feels the discontinuity. To make living contact with that inheritance he would have to write in Irish. His translations are, therefore, attempts to reach across to the past, to retrieve and absorb what has been lost, and to make it available to others. When he tries to explain why he is so deeply involved with the laborious work of translation, he can only say that it is an impulse 'to make an offering to the past'. That is why he made those initial translations from early Irish, despite being linguistically ill equipped to do so, and that is why he had worked on the *Táin Bó Cuailnge*, off and on, for fifteen years. It is a process of self-search and, he confesses, 'a labour of some kind of love'. (10)

Kinsella's passionate brooding, felt in the force of words like 'broken', 'mutilation' and 'isolation', is also shown in his enthusiasm for poetry in the Irish language. As successive acts of definition, the translations together with his sustained examination of the past in his own poetry give his work a unique character. In his two lists, one for Irish poetry in the seventeenth and eighteenth centuries and one for the earlier periods, he identifies the material that forms the contents of his two anthologies, *An Duanaire. 1600–1900: Poems of the Dispossessed* and *The New Oxford Book of Irish Verse*. In the two chapters that follow their contents are discussed chronologically, beginning with the pagan world of the *Táin*[2] and the pre-Christian poetry of the *New Oxford* before progressing through the entire history of poetry in the Irish language in *An Duanaire*.

Notes

1 'The Irish Writer', *Éire-Ireland* 2, 2 (Summer 1967); rpt. from W.B. Yeats and by Thomas Kinsella, *Davis, Mangan Ferguson? Tradition and the Irish Writer* (Dublin: Dolmen Press, 1970). Followed by a lecture on 'Irish Poetry in the Nineteenth Century' given at the Merriman Festival, September 1968; and in an expanded form as 'The Divided Mind', *Irish Poets in English. The Thomas Davis Lectures on Anglo-Irish Poetry*, ed. Seán Lucy (Dublin and Cork: Mercier Press, 1972). Subsequent references are given in the text.

2 Kinsella's translation of the *Táin* was beautifully illustrated by Louis le Brocquy.

6

TRANSLATIONS:
THE TÁIN and *THE NEW OXFORD BOOK OF IRISH VERSE*

The *Táin Bó Cuailnge* tells of an incursion made by Medb, warrior Queen of Connacht, goddess of sovereignty and war, into Ulster to capture the Brown Bull of Cúailnge. She is a decisive woman, but Cú Chulainn, a young Ulster warrior, who is not hampered by the debilitating sickness that afflicts the other Ulstermen, holds up her journey to the north. He kills hundreds of her soldiers and further delays the advance by engaging her champions in a series of man-to-man combats, emerging triumphant each time. In a substantial flashback, the narrative also tells of his boyhood deeds. After a great battle the Ulstermen finally emerge from their sickness and defeat the forces of Connacht. The two bulls fight. The Brown Bull of Ulster kills the white bull of Connacht, the White-Horned, and in what has been interpreted as a Celtic reflex of an Indo-European myth of cosmic creation, scatters fragments of its body throughout Ireland, but then dies from the exertions.

The *Táin* is found in a number of manuscript sources. In the twelfth-century *Book of Leinster*, which is the one most frequently translated, the story is complete but the style overblown. The earlier form, which Kinsella chooses, is in the *Yellow Book of Lecan*, where the story is unfinished but the style simpler. Inconsistencies, repetitions and some extraneous matter mar the text, but he gets rid of the inconsistencies and repetitions as far as possible and clears up the obscurities with the help of other sources, usually the *Book of Leinster*. His purpose in translating this prose epic is to provide a readable text, a living version of the story which does not deviate significantly at any point from the original. When translating verse passages, Kinsella takes greater freedom, although the sense and structural effects are adhered to; but when he deals with *rosc* or *retoiric* [obscure passages], he relies consistently on a 'stepped' [indented] form. His aim is to produce passages that are roughly the same length as the originals and that match them in ambiguity and obscurity, thereby reflecting the main components of *rosc*.

He also translates a number of tales that serve as introductions to the *Táin*. These include an account of how Conchobor mac Nessa, King of Ulster, was begotten and how he took the kingship; the account of the debility suffered by the Ulstermen, as a result of which they were unable to oppose Queen Medb's invading army; the story of the exile of the Sons of Uisliu which explains why some of the Ulster chieftains are with the Connacht forces; and the account of Cú Chulainn's training in arms with the Scottish warrior-queen Scáthach.

For the modern reader it is a strange world – a pagan aristocratic society of kings, queens, warriors, lavish ornaments, great possessions and epic contests. Conchobor, who lives in a well-stocked and resplendent palace, is greatly respected and protected; he is the rightful king, a brave fighter, who gives wise judgements, and under him the kingdom flourishes. He is held in such high esteem that 'every man in Ulster that took a girl in marriage let her sleep the first night with Conchobor, so as to have him first in the family'. Queen Medb of Connacht is also a powerful ruler who leads the armies of the four provinces of Ireland against Ulster. She is commanding, haughty and sexually attractive – her husband, Ailill, and King Fergus sleep with her and she holds out the promise of sexual union with heroes who will fight Cú Chulainn for her. In her drive to possess the fabulous Brown Bull of Cooley she is prepared to sacrifice hundreds of soldiers and a succession of heroes.

It is a world of omens and prophecies, mysterious beings, strange beliefs and dramatic conflict. When Deirdriu is born, there are dire warnings. A tragic figure fated to cause trouble, 'the loveliest woman in all Ireland', she is proud and stubborn, capable of independent choice and fierce fidelity. Raised secretly by Conchobor, who wants her for himself, she announces that the man she wants must have three colours: hair like the raven, cheeks like blood, body like snow. Noísiu, introduced in a brilliantly condensed passage and emphatic style, is the man.

> This man Noísiu was chanting by himself one time near Emain, on the rampart of the stronghold. The chanting of the sons of Uisliu was very sweet. Every cow or beast that heard it gave two thirds more milk. Any person hearing it was filled with peace and music. Their deeds in war were great also...[1]

Deirdriu compels Noísiu to take her. When he is murdered by Fergus's son Eogan, she is forced to live a year with Conchobor, who then gives her to Eogan, whereupon she kills herself. She is one of a number of strongly defined women figures with diverse personalities.

When love occurs it is expressed in arresting language as when Deirdriu sees Noísiu or when Cú Chulainn goes to court Emer. They speak together 'in riddles'.

Cúchulainn caught sight of the girl's breasts over the
top of her dress.

'I see a sweet country,' he said. 'I could rest my weapon there.'

Emer answered him by saying:

'No man will travel this country until he has killed a hundred men
at every ford from Scenmenn ford on the river Ailbine, to Banchuing
– the 'Woman Yoke' that can hold a hundred – where the frothy Brea
makes Fedelm leap.'

'In that sweet country I'll rest my weapon,' Cúchulainn said.

'No man will travel this country,' she said, 'until he has done
the feat of the salmon-leap carrying twice his weight in gold, and
struck down three groups of nine men with a single stroke, leaving the
middle man of each nine unharmed.'

'In that sweet country I'll rest my weapon,' Cúchulainn said.

'No man will travel this country,' she said, 'who hasn't gone
sleepless from Samain, when the summer goes on its rest, until Imbolc,
when the ewes are milked at spring's beginning; from Imbolc to
Beltaine at the summer's beginning and from Beltaine to Brón
Trogain, earth's sorrowing autumn.'

'It is said and done,' Cúchulainn said. (27)

When Cú Chulainn goes to the warrior-queen Scáthach to be trained,
she prophesies what is to come. The language is resonant with the
imagery of events from the *Táin*. She chants to him through the *imbas
forosnaí*, a form of divination that makes what she says all the more
convincing and chilling, pointing ahead to images, deeds and places that
will recur in the main narrative.

> with your red stabbing spiked spear
>   grief and sorrow where you roam
> murderous on Murtheimne Plain
>   playing at the stabbing game... (35)

Cú Chulainn's fight with his son Connla, whom he does not recognize,
is the basis of W.B. Yeats's play *On Baile's Strand*. Significantly, in a
foreshadowing of a major contest in the *Táin*, when they try to drown
each other in the sea, Cú Chulainn saves himself from death by using
the *gae bolga*, a javelin cast that Scáthach had taught to no one but him.
'He sent it speeding over the water at him and brought his bowels down
around his feet'. (44)

Fifty pages of the text are devoted to these preliminary tales. The
other 200 take up the story of the *Táin*, which begins with the humorous,
well-judged 'Pillow Talk' in which Medb, Queen of Connacht, and her

husband, Ailill, compare their possessions in a lengthy, impressive and colourful inventory. When it is finally discovered that Ailill has a bull for which she has no equal, the initial motivation for the epic is established. She sends for the Brown Bull of Cooley, near Dundalk. The owner is willing to give it until he hears one of her henchmen remark that if he didn't they would take it by force. That gets his back up and her messengers are sent home empty-handed. But Medb will not take no for an answer and gathers her great army. Already there are omens. Fedelm, the poet of Connacht, whose eyes have triple irises, foresees the destruction of Medb's army. 'I see it crimson. I see it red,' (61) but Medb does not believe her.

When Cú Chulainn impedes her army's advance, Fergus warns them. Cú Chulainn may be only a boy but he is formidable: 'no point more sharp, more swift, more slashing; no raven more flesh-ravenous, no hand more deft...You will find no one there to measure against him...'. (75–6) At this point the story relates his boyhood deeds. As everywhere in the epic, the deeds have an awesome quality. This return to the past prepares for his later exploits: if he could be so unusually capable as a boy, even as a child, he could exert prodigious skills as a young man. The episodes from the past are like folk tales in which the hero's legendary deeds accumulate into a compelling portrait. When Conchobor's boy warriors try to resist him, he easily overcomes them. 'They flung three times fifty javelins at him, and he stopped them all on his shield of sticks. Then they drove all their hurling-balls at him, and he stopped every ball on his breast. They threw their hurling sticks at him...'. It is then that his 'warp-spasm', described by Fergus in impressively concrete terms, came upon him:

> ...it seemed each hair was hammered into his head, so sharply they shot upright. You would swear a fire-speck tipped each hair. He squeezed one eye narrower than the eye of a needle; he opened the other wider than the mouth of a goblet. He bared his jaws to the ear; he peeled back his lips to the eye-teeth till his gullet showed. The hero-halo rose up from the crown of his head. (77)

Then he attacked the boys.

Kinsella achieves a crisp narrative momentum, mingling description with dialogue and a swift sequence of scenes, stories within stories, including the reality of battle and one-to-one combat with wounding, beheading and the taking of trophies. The imagery is grounded in reality, concrete, specific, however transformative the narrative becomes at times. There is no shirking of coarse elements – bodily functions, the butchery and brutality of conflict. The element of *dindshenchus* (the lore of place) is central to the *Táin*. The advance of Medb's forces is connected all along the way with specific locations. Much of the narrative is a verification of place-names, confirming deeds done in particular places, or providing names of men killed in places named after them thereafter so that the reality of past events and people is affirmed. The poem creates the impression of a historical and topographical reality even though, as scholars generally agree, the characters and events are purely imaginary. At the same time the epic is of historic importance because it contains genuine traditional material and gives a picture of early Irish life and civilization that resembles in many ways the account of those of Gauls and Britons before the Roman invasion of their territories.

The use of omen and prophecy is recurrent. The druid Cathbad foretells Deirdriu's appearance before she is born; Scáthach prophesies Cú Chulainn's future; Fedelm foresees the destruction of the *Táin*; the Morrígan, crow of death, speaks in a *rosc* to the Brown Bull in the language of bloodshed and violence.

> 'affliction and outcry
> and war everlasting
> raging over Cuailnge
> death of sons
> death of kinsmen
> death   death!' (98)

There are magical incidents: the flight of nine scores of birds with a silver chain between each couple, two birds of prey who suddenly take human shape as two pig-keepers, the Morrígan's transmogrification from mysterious young women to eel to she-wolf to hornless red deer to squint-eyed old woman milking a cow with three teats.

Despite the explicit realism of the style, the storyteller declares an impossible number killed by Cú Chulainn, as in the case of those destroyed by the River Cronn. These extraordinary events add to the heroic status of the narrative and the heroic status of the warriors. There are constant triumphs and defeats. Cú Chulainn is larger than life, an invincible fighter, skilled in the arts of war, roaming the countryside ahead of Medb's invading army, picking off the enemy. No wonder Fergus warns his son not to go out against him.

> 'Mighty son,
> don't venture out
> it is only asking
> to have your head

> knocked from your neck
> > by the boy with no beard
> who comes from the heights
> > howls on the plain
> summons up rivers
> > shakes the woods
> wrenches into shapes
> > mighty acts
> men in great numbers
> > drowned in the waters
> Ailill hurt
> > and Medb mocked
> faces cast down
> > in the bristling battle.' (109)

The text becomes a kaleidoscope, an ever-changing panorama through which the compelling figure of the epic hero drives with 'ferocity and grimness, force, fury and violence' (117), who chants over the slain. His feats of arms are magnificent:

> – the apple-feat, the feats of the sword-edge and the sloped shield; the feats of the javelin and rope; the body-feat, the feat of Cat and the heroic salmon-leap; the pole-throw and the leap over a poisoned stroke; the noble chariot-fighter's crouch; the *gae bolga*; the spurt of speed; the feat of the chariot-wheel and the feat of the shield-rim; the breath-feat; the snapping mouth and the hero's scream; the stroke of precision and the stunning-shot; stepping on a lance in flight, and straightening erect on its point; and the trussing of a warrior. (128)

There is unstinting admiration for Cú Chulainn's prowess as a fighter, as though the epic were primarily a vehicle through which to show such feats.

In view of his display of killing-power, the four provinces ranged against him need a champion of comparable skill and power to fight him in single combat. Finnabair, the seductive daughter of Medb, is always offered as a prize and successively various champions go out to fight and are killed. Sometimes Medb offers her own 'friendly thighs' as an inducement. Cú Chulainn's father comes from the Otherworld to relieve him so that his wounds can be healed. After three days of rest and healing he emerges refreshed, ready for further engagements. In a palpable heightening of language, the narrative takes hold, advancing inevitably towards the fight between Cú Chulainn and Ferdia. There is the colourful and detailed description of the charioteer Laeg as he dons his war-harness, followed by a description of Cú Chulainn – his warlike battle-harness, his heroic deep battle-belt, his silk-smooth apron, his dark apron, his warlike weapons, his crested battle-helmet, his concealing cloak. His first warp-spasm transforms him into

> ...a monstrous thing, hideous and shapeless, unheard of. His shanks and his joints, every knuckle and angle and organ from head to foot, shook like a tree in the flood or a reed in the stream. His body made a furious twist inside his skin, so that his feet and shins and knees switched to the rear and his heels and calves switched to the front. The balled sinews of his calves switched to the front of his shins, each big knot the size of a warrior's bunched fist. On his head the temple-sinews stretched to the nape of his neck, each mighty, immense, measureless knob as big as the head of a month-old child. His face and features became a red bowl: he sucked one eye so deep into his head that a wild crane couldn't probe it onto his cheek out of the depths of his skull; the other eye fell out along his cheek. His mouth weirdly distorted: his cheek peeled back from his jaws until the gullet appeared, his lungs and liver flapped in his mouth and throat, his lower jaw struck the upper a lion-killing blow, and fiery flakes large as a ram's fleece reached his mouth from his throat. His heart boomed loud in his breast like the baying of a watch-dog at its feed or the sound of a lion among bears. Malignant mists and spurts of fire – the torches of the Badb – flickered red in the vaporous clouds that rose boiling above his head, so fierce was his fury. The hair of his head twisted like the tangle of a red thornbush stuck in a gap;...The hero-halo rose out of his brow, long and broad as a warrior's whetstone, long as a snout, and he went mad rattling his shields, urging on his charioteer and harassing the hosts. Then, tall and thick, steady and strong, high as the mast of a noble ship, rose up from the dead centre of his skull a straight spout of black blood darkly and magically smoking like the smoke from a royal hostel when a king is coming to be cared for at the close of a winter day. (150, 153)

There is a magnificent description of his attack, followed by an incantatory enumeration of the nobles and chiefs he has killed in his first full battle with the provinces of Ireland. Cú Chulainn comes through unharmed. Afterwards he is described in his normal state – a beautiful 17-year-old boy with 'three distinct heads of hair – brown at the base, blood-red in the middle, and a crown of golden yellow.' (156) The tone is one of wonder at the mythic splendour of this young man.

The narrative so far has been like the expository part of a play in which the champion and the predicament are set out so that when he comes on stage we are ready for him, able to understand and appreciate the kind of person he is. So when Cú Chulainn's friend Ferdia rises to the challenge and faces Cú Chulainn, we are fully aware of the nature of this duel. He is a worthy opponent, since he, too, has been trained by Scáthach. They chant challenges in a ritual of defiance and confidence building in a language of violent assertion. Cú Chulainn implores Ferdia not to fight him: they are old comrades; they used to fight side by side, but Ferdia will not be deflected. It is a mighty contest, lasting three days. Each day they choose weapons – darts, heavy spears, swords – and fight fiercely. Each night, with a courtesy that heightens the personal tragedy, they embrace and their horses are put in the one paddock. They exchange healing herbs and foods so that it may not be said that either had an advantage over the other. With the spears they pierce holes in each other. Cú Chulainn is not invincible, but eventually he sees a change in Ferdia and regrets he has come to fight him for the prize of a fickle woman. Ferdia sees he will be killed. Cú Chulainn regrets this. They fight with swords; there is much 'hacking and hewing and striking and destroying, and cutting bits and pieces the size of baby's [*sic*] heads from each other's shoulders and backs and flanks'. That night they do not embrace. They are 'two wasted men'. (192)

The next day Ferdia puts on his battle-harness, carefully described; each performs a 'thousand thrilling, multiple and miraculous feats...'. (194) They fight in the ford where, as both know, Cú Chulainn can use the *gae bolga*. The story has moved to its intensifying climax. It celebrates the two great warriors in a crescendo of praise – the two first and foremost warriors, two blazing torches, two lavish gift-scatterers, two keys to Ireland's valour. It is an intense conflict brilliantly described, gripping in its clarity and precision of detail. The narrative is a bravura piece, using language to great effect, simile, exaggeration, emphatic building.

Ferdia does well. Cú Chulainn enters into his warp-spasm. They fight at close quarters, head to head, toe to toe, shields and weapons split apart; so closely do they fight that they drive the river back on each side, so closely that the horses of Ireland break loose in panic. When Ferdia is likely to kill Cú Chulainn, the epic hero calls for the *gae bolga*. When he casts it from the fork of his foot, it penetrates Ferdia's body despite his sturdy apron and 'went coursing through the highways and byways of his body so that every joint filled with barbs'. (196–7)

Overcome with grief rather than triumph, Cú Chulainn mourns Ferdia and the false promises that lured Ferdia to fight him, eulogizes 'his beauty and bravery', their days together. After this climax the story returns to particular incidents and becomes loosely structured again. The Ulster army arrives in impressively described companies. The opposing armies face each other. The suspense and excitement grow. The Morrígan speaks 'in the half light between the two camps':

> 'Ravens gnawing
>   men's necks
> blood spurting
>   in the fierce fray
> hacked flesh
>   battle madness...' (238)

Ailill chants the list of nobles who will fight – all who have survived the slaughter by Cú Chulainn. Conchobor names the chieftains he wants in his army. The Ulstermen are composed of many companies, each described, as are their leaders, in an epic catalogue. The story becomes an extensive panorama. While the ending is disappointing, given the intensity and elevated language of the climax, in effect its failure to round out the narrative at an appropriate level throws what has gone before into greater relief. The story has been a vehicle for the portrayal of the epic hero who is a law unto himself and who behaves like a champion in the knowledge that his skills and exploits guarantee his fame.

The New Oxford Book of Irish Verse

When Christianity came to Ireland in the fifth century the merger of Latin culture and Gaelic civilization resulted in a period of learning and artistic achievement through the next two centuries. As Thomas Kinsella points out in *The Dual Tradition* (1995), Christian and non-Christian elements worked together to produce a literature in the Irish language which was made up of devotional and occasional poetry from the Christian background and a collection of non-Christian oral literature.

One of the earliest Christian poems is '*A Poem in Praise of Colum Cille*' (No. 4), which has elements of the bardic panegyric. It celebrates a man of God whose virtues are clear and who has been welcomed into Heaven 'where the wise do not die'. His attributes are presented in homely metaphor – 'He was a roof to the naked,/a tit to the poor.' The serious tone allows for no disagreement.

> He has died, our lawful leader,
> he is gone, our witness to the Word:
>   the wise one who took away our terrors,
> the strict one who taught us truth in words,
>   the teacher who could chant for us
> the tribes of the whole world.
>   We are a harp without a peg,
> a church without an abbot.[2]

The mode is incantatory: 'He was learned and clean-lived./He was loving;...He was eager. He was noble...He was gentle'. If we hear in these rhythmic outpourings an anticipation of Eibhlín Dhubh Ní Chonaill's 'Lament for Art Ó Laoghaire' in the eighteenth century, this may suggest the continuity of an oral tradition in which the expression of grief included a recreation of the dead person's life and personality.

The anonymous verses, '*The Boyhood of Christ*' (No. 6), from the seventh century and '*Saint Patrick's Breastplate*' (No. 7), from the eighth, have also survived. '*The Boyhood of Christ*' is childlike in its account of the Christ child shaping birds from clay and then causing them to fly by clapping his palms. The poem about St Patrick is made up of a series of parallel statements. It is an act of comprehensive armouring of the self with religious and natural forces. It summons 'these powers' against all forms of temptation – 'every implacable power/that attacks my body and soul' – and has a persuasive simplicity and fervour.

> Christ beside me,
>   Christ before me,
>   Christ behind me,
>
> Christ within me,
>   Christ beneath me,
>   Christ above me,
>
> Christ on my right hand,
>   Christ on my left,
>
> Christ where I lie,
>   Christ where I sit,
>   Christ where I rise... (13–14)

In the religious poetry the poet is sometimes a hermit. In '*An Ivied Tree-Top*' (No. 15), he celebrates the security and beauty of his home, his cell in Tuaim Inbir. The selection of monastic poems (Nos. 18–25) contains many of the identifying qualities of poetry of the period in which religious feeling and the response to the natural world, seen as an aspect of God's creation, are intertwined. Poems in praise of nature become poems in praise of the Christian God. In No. 18, the poet expresses satisfaction and delight in his monastic cell, his isolation in his place of repentance and self-denial, where his upright conscience has no fear of Heaven. He has mortified the flesh, subdued desire, denied the world, so can devote himself to God with 'earnest devout confession'. Itemizing his habits of abstinence – dry bread to eat, fresh water to drink – he is content, confident of where he stands in relation to God.

> A salt and meagre diet
> with mind bent on a book;
> no disputation, visitation;
> conscience serene and calm.

'How wonderful it would be', he says, if Christ were to visit him:

> my Maker and my King,
> my spirit turned toward Him
> and the Kingdom where he dwells. (29)

As they worked at their illuminated manuscripts, scribes sometimes wrote short poems on the margin and these glosses give insight both to the mind of the monk and the perception of the relationship between him and the natural world. The four '*Glosses*' in Kinsella's anthology are examples of this type of poem, unique to Ireland, which are notable for vividness of imagery, sharp observation of detail, sensuous enjoyment of the visual world and a spirit of natural divinity that informs them. Their simplicity of utterance gives them an enduring freshness.

> How lovely it is today!
> The sunlight breaks and flickers
> on the margin of my book.

Or

> The little bird
> let out a whistle
> from his beak tip
>   bright yellow.
> He sends the note
> across Loch Laíg
> – a blackbird, a branch
>   a mass of yellow. (30)

The characteristics of Old Irish poetry – brief images without elaborate description – are illustrated in several poems. The anonymous nature poem *'Toward Winter'* (No. 14), contains clearly defined images of the countryside – animals, birds, stormy conditions – 'The night is cold on the Great Bog./The storm is lashing–no small matter'. The 'we' of the poem are 'battered', 'swallowed' like twigs, suffer 'Want and Winter'.

In No. 20, the well-known *'Pangur Bán'*, a witty, human portrayal of a monk and his cat, as fresh and pleasing today as it was 1,200 years ago, compares the activities of the former in his pursuit of knowledge with the activity of the latter in his quest for mice.

> He directs his pure bright eye
> along the wall surrounding us.
>   I direct my clear eye,
>   weak though it is, at hard knowledge. (31)

'The Hermit Marbhán' (No. 24) is characterized by spontaneity and freshness of expression. The poem is in the form of a dialogue between King Guaire, King of Connacht, and his half-brother Marbhán, whose rhapsodic depiction of life as a hermit makes up most of the poem. In fact, the King speaks only the framing first and last stanzas; the former by asking Marbhán why he sleeps in the fir-grove, which allows the monk to elaborate upon his reasons for doing so, and the latter a confession by the King that he would give up his kingdom to be with his half-brother in the life he has so convincingly described. The poem's enumeration of the attractions of the hermit life subsumes many of the metaphors, motifs and affirmations of similar but usually shorter poems on the same theme:

> they come, the white ones,
> gulls and herons,
>   till the harbour echoes
> and (no sad music)
> the brown hen fowl
>   in the russet heather. (35)

In effect, the hermit lives in an earthly paradise with an abundance of natural provision, the colours of nature, the music of birds, the voices of the wind, and in peace. The paean concludes, fittingly in accordance with the philosophical outlook that infuses all these poems.

> I thank the Prince
> Who grants all good
>   to me in my hut. (36)

The absence of conflict, the sense of serenity, the certainty of closeness to God and his creation give the psychological portrayal an idealizing quality. There is neither uncertainty nor feeling of absence from family or friends. The conventions of the poetry exclude such considerations. The natural world is sharply etched and the better appreciated because the poet/monk is alone with his thoughts. Since he devotes his life to God and God has created the world, there is a congenial fusion of the physical and the spiritual; the phenomenal realm is a confirmation of God's presence.

A conscious simplicity of expression is found in much of this poetry and while the imagistic depiction of the natural world, rather than sustained description, is also evident, the poet expresses his own emotional response to nature's prodigality. It is subjective, emotionally charged. The process of idealization of the hermetical retreat from society, quite natural to the hermit, also includes other figures, such as Suibne Geilt, who has been driven into the wilderness by personal misfortune.

The ninth-century '*The Hag of Béara*' (No. 16) imagines one of the most celebrated figures in early Irish literature. Often seen as a goddess of sovereignty, in the earlier versions she is a woman who has retired from the world and lives a life of penance. Her lament is an eloquent portrayal of a complex emotional state. As in the case of the poet/monk who feels at one with his natural surroundings, she identifies with the ebb tide. The sea will experience the tide's return, but her decline will not be reversed. She once enjoyed the company of kings, now she is alone. Now she is resigned to God's will and to death. Now her arms are thin, once they clasped 'the bodies of mighty kings'. Interweaving the sacred and the profane, the verses alternate between images of plenty and images of want, memories of love and thoughts of loss, ebbing and flowing in accordance with the movements of her mind. Throughout, the language is spare.

> Winter begins to waken
> the sea's great roaring wave
> and I cannot look forward now
> to company high or low. (25)

Part of the attraction of the poem, in addition to its personal voice, is the restraint with which she elaborates her plight, returning successively to metaphors of activity and inactivity until in the wave imagery of the concluding stanzas she pours out her sense of deprivation and loss. Bleak recognition expands from the reflection on her own situation to a general consideration of the human lot.

> Everything is wretched
> and the wretchedest thing is Man.
> He sees the flood-tide ebb
> but his ebb without an end.
>
> Happy the isle in the ocean wide
> where the flood follows the ebb.
> As for me, after my ebb
> I can look forward to nothing.
>
> There is scarcely a single house
> I still can recognize.
> What once was full in flood
> has ebbed to the full at last. (27)

The excerpt, from the *Prologue* to *The Calendar of Oengus* (No. 25), also from the ninth century, creates a sustained contrast between the destruction of earthly mansions and the indestructibility of God's structures. Tara is perished, Armagh remains; King Loegaire has fallen, his fame quenched, Patrick's name 'is spreading still'. Written in the tenth century, '*Manchán's Prayer*' (No. 44) is on the other hand a fervent prayer to God by someone who lives in conscious, appreciative harmony with his natural surroundings. The poet expresses a lyrical and contemplative response to the life of solitude, which is enriched by the variety of creatures that also live in the wild wood. He prays for 'a hidden hut' and the 'sensible disciples' he will gather:

> a lovely church, with linen,
> a home for Heaven's King,
> with bright lamps shining down
> on the clean bright scriptures...(53)

The poems from the twelfth century attributed to Colum Cille (Nos. 54–58) have the same combination of precise images from the natural world as are found in early poems. In No. 54, a poem of exile, the poet remembers the delights of Irish places, the sounds of birds, the sight of stags and the 'fields of Ireland I have loved'. It begins:

> O Son of God, it would be sweet,
>   a lovely journey,
> to cross the wave, the fount in flood,
>   and visit Ireland... (64)

No. 55, 'Mary mild, good maiden', a prayer to Mary, is a hymn of praise. No. 56 laments the lost homeland in a tone of unmistakable grief.

> I stare back across the sea
> at the plain of plentiful oaks,
> my clear grey eye in tears
> seeing Ireland fall behind me. (68)

It is the exact listing of images and their clear delineation that makes the poem so persuasive. They have a declarative power: 'If I owned all of Alba...I would rather my chosen place...The reasons I love Doire...I could find...I am sad...I swear...I care not...I am Irish...We are parting in misery...I stare back.' These statements accumulate in steady affirmation of how he feels so that the persona is sharply defined in the psychology of loss and longing.

Two characteristics may be observed about this religious poetry. The first is the mind-set that remained in place for hundreds of years, defining the poet and his outlook in a consistent world-view that interonnected personal life, nature and God in a mutually supportive system. The second is the psychology involved in the self-awareness of the poet, the understanding of relationship, the perception of his own system of self-discipline and its effects and purposes within a guiding ascetic ideal.

In the contexts of so much undivided loyalty to asceticism and belief, the ninth-century *'Liadan and Cuirithir'* (No. 40) is outstanding for its portrayal of the conflict between desire and spirituality. Líadan had agreed to marry Cuirithir, but became a nun instead. Then he became a monk. After a while when she visited him in his cell, he had to sail away to avoid her. She stays there until she dies. The poem is her lament for what happened, a story of love, denial and human frailty. Part of the poem's attraction is the brevity and starkness of the narrative.

> It is miserable
> what I have done.
> I have tortured the thing I loved. (46)

It was, she says, foolish to deny Cuirithir out of fear of God. Her account is the more powerful because understated, its brief lines taut with condensed pain.

> A little while
> I was with Cuirithir.
> He thought well of my company. (47)

In No. 42, 'I am ashamed of my thoughts', the anonymous poet writing in the tenth century fears that his uncontrollable thoughts will endanger his salvation 'on Doom's endless day'. The main body of the poem is a series of images to express the wayward courses of his thoughts:

> Though you try to restrain them
>   or fetter their feet
> they're too fickle and thoughtless
>   to try to stand still. (50)

But the poem ends with an appeal to Christ to restrain them and bring the monk close to Heaven.

An even more insightful portrait of mental conflict is found in No. 43, also from the tenth century, which is a troubled consideration of the unavoidable 'horror' of death: 'Alone up here on the mountain'. It begins with a plea for protection to the 'Sun-King', but goes on to admit philosophically in stanza after stanza that there is no defence against death.

> There is no safe place on earth
> when a mortal man is doomed.
> And who has ever heard
> of a path where the saved will die? (51)

A man's fate is in the hands of the Lord. No one can shorten a person's life, except with His permission.

What is interesting here is the psychological complexity, the awareness and the imagination's consideration of the issue of death's certainty. The tone is measured and calm, the speaker secure in God's protection, while at the same time regarding death as the ultimate horror. He can consider the ways in which death may strike, realize that there is no defence against it, but hold firm to the knowledge that every imagined fatal incident can succeed only when God decides. As in the reflections of the Hag of Béara, the speaker is dramatically positioned between two forces; it is there that the poem finds imaginative space in which to illuminate the tension between 'dread' and confidence.

It is only when we come to the twelfth-century poem about Suibne Geilt, the wild man in the woods, the feathered outcast, that the voice attends to feelings of alienation and suffering. The combination of place and feeling is part of the imaginative force of '*A Selection of Verses attributed to Suibne Geilt*' (No. 60), in which the state of exile is rendered through the imagery of harsh weather and exposure. The feeling of being alone with nature is deeply rendered, but the humanity of one driven from society, alienated from the church and bereft of wife is equally powerful.

When the poet wants to illustrate personal alienation he does so in terms of disjunction from that closeness to nature which was part of the religious and nature poetry. Whereas in other poems, such as Colum Cille's poems of exile, place gives security of identity, in Suibne Geilt's situation, forced from home and kingdom, place is part of the nightmare of insecurity and wandering.

> I have lost my sense and my wits.
> I shift restless everywhere
> from Line Plain over Lí Plain
> and from Lí Plain over wild Liffe. (72)

The poem veers from expressions of fear and distancing to expressions of preference for the sounds and movements of creatures 'racing the red stag over the moors'. His chosen place is Glen Bolcáin. There he is nourished.

> Its pure green water is good
> and good its rough clean wind.
> Its cress is good, the green cress,
> and its tall brooklime is better! (73)

Elsewhere the sense of communion with the natural world is absent. Nature is not a manifestation of God's creation; it is a place of disharmony and uncertainty. He *now* flees to escape the animals.

The medieval period brought a reform of the monasteries and the Norman invasion with the result that the native cultural and social order was affected by continental influences. The native monasteries gave way to continental foundations and a new grouping of learned families came into existence which initiated a strict metrical code and a standard literary language that was followed by all learned poets from the early thirteenth century to the middle of the seventeenth. Praise poetry returned, but at the same time there was a considerable amount of less conservative work, such as love poetry, which was affected by the conventions of *amour courtois*. As in the past, poets depended on the continuation of a society in which patronage was available, but in the seventeenth century the native order began to weaken in the face of Tudor and Elizabethan aggression, and aristocratic poetry came to an end.

Kinsella's selections from the professional bardic poets include four from Muiredeach Albanach Ó Dálaigh, who lived in the early thirteenth century and who belonged to a great poetic family. Amongst his surviving poems are an address to the Virgin Mary and a lament for his wife. The poem to the Virgin Mary, 'Mighty Mary, hear me', written in the style of *amour courtois*, is unusually personal in its descriptive details as the poet adapts the conventions of the praise poem to a religious subject. The result is somewhat inappropriate in its personalization of the Mother of God as though she and Christ Himself were figures in an Irish royal house.

> Pure, wholesome, yellow hair,
>   a vine of curls about your head;
> round, thin-fingered, pure palm,
>   O firm, slim, well-shaped foot. (90)

His lament for his wife on the other hand – 'Last night my soul departed' – has force and conviction. It breaks through the formulaic restrictions that hamper much bardic poetry. A note of genuine feeling emerges; the language is simple and unadorned, the metaphors homely.

> I am, but I do not live,
>   since my round hazel-nut has fallen.
> Since my dear love has left me
>   the dark world is empty and bare. (96)

It says something about the conventions of the time that his poem to his knife, full of praise imagery, seems almost equally appreciative: 'Her point keen and slender,/dainty and sleek her flank.' (97)

In the late sixteenth and early seventeenth centuries, poets began to respond to the disruptive presence of the Tudors. Laoiseach Mac An Bháird did so through the metaphor of a sheltering tree that has been removed – 'a blast has wrecked its root'. Eochaidh Ó Heoghusa, poet of the Maguires of Fermanagh, records the final phase of the unsuccessful struggle for survival of the Gaelic aristocracy and in No. 110, '*A Change in Style*', deals sourly with the fall in poetic standards. Before the collapse of the old order he worked hard – 'every poem composed in the past,/it almost broke my heart'. Now he will relinquish standards and write to please the popular ear.

> I've deserted the stricter ranks
>   of a discipline sharp and clear
> for an average soft sort of work
>   that earns me better attention. (158)

Fear Flatha Ó Gnímh's '*After the Flight of the Earls*' (No. 112) refers to the time of land confiscation and plantation. The poem catalogues evidence of change – the heroes gone to Spain, no regard for festivals, the youth destroyed, the chieftains ousted.

> The race of Murchadh and Ó Mordha,
>   warriors brave in battle,
> scarce one of that noble seed
>   holds a sod of his native land. (163)

In '*The Passing of the Poets*' (No. 113), he laments the disappearance of poetic composition. It would, he says, have been better to turn to a different trade – training horses, steering a ship, roping a plough to a bullock.

> The honour of verse is faded
> and esteem for its guardians gone.
> The schools of the land of Ireland
> would do better to dig in the dirt. (165)

His contemporary Mathghamhain Ó Hifearnáin has a similar story. He cannot sell his work. Nobody wants it. The generous patrons are gone. He is ignored 'by Gael and stranger'.

> I ask, who will buy a poem?
> It holds right thoughts of scholars.
> Who needs it? Will anyone take it?
> A fine poem to make him immortal. (167)

These momentous events become the subject matter of poetry in the sixteenth and seventeenth centuries, at which point the poetry in *The New Oxford Book of Irish Verse* begins to overlap with poems published in *An Duanaire*.

Notes

1   *The Táin, Táin Bó Cuailnge* (Dublin: Dolmen Press, 1969, 1985; London and New York: Oxford University Press, 1970), p.12. Subsequent references are given in the text.

2   *The New Oxford Book of Irish Verse* (Oxford: Oxford University Press, 1986), p.4. Subsequent references are given in the text.

7

AN DUANAIRE. 1600–1900:
POEMS OF THE DISPOSSESSED

An Duanaire. 1600–1900: Poems of the Dispossessed, an anthology of one hundred poems with the Irish on one page and Kinsella's translations on the facing page, seeks to demonstrate the nature and quality of the Irish poetic tradition from the defeat of the Irish forces at Kinsale in 1601 to the continuing presence of an Irish literary tradition in the Irish language at the end of the nineteenth century. That defeat signalled the collapse of the old aristocratic Irish order in which the poet had a rightful place. The completion of the Tudor conquest and the Ulster plantation led to the replacement of Irish chieftains, the patrons of the poets, by English and Scottish settlers. The confiscation of land led to the spread of English as the language of the country.

The Flight of the Earls in 1607 was regarded at the time as a catastrophe and was widely lamented. The traditional bardic order was on the point of extinction, the Irish patrons disappeared; the poets were exposed to a hostile Protestant government. The driving of leaders into exile and the collapse of the bardic schools hastened a process initiated by a renaissance which led to the liberation of the Irish poetic canon and a notable diversification in poetic activity, although the theme of cultural loss and alienation persists in the poetry for 200 years. At the same time, with the disappearance of native nobility and the weakening grip of the learned families on the canon, there gradually developed new classes of poets who replaced bardic rigidity with different types of metre and genres, in particular the accentual forms that now became prominent. In an English-dominated Ireland the contrast for the poets lay between imperilled Irish culture and boorishness, between revered tradition and ignorance. The poets put the contrast in the starkest terms. They resented the new owners of the land, the Protestant upstarts.

The theme of the steady decline of Irish language and culture and with it the dispossession of the poets recurs in the poetry throughout the seventeenth and eighteenth centuries whose events are mirrored in the poetry – the Cromwellian wars, the War of the Two Kings and the formation of the Protestant Ascendancy. By the end of the eighteenth century a new generation of poets emerged which included Eibhlín Dhubh Ní Chonaill and Brian Merriman, who composed outside of the written tradition and whose work was transmitted primarily in the oral tradition.

During the seventeenth and eighteenth centuries as the political situation fluctuated in England, Irish aspirations rose and fell. There was the apparently unquenchable hope of the arrival of a saviour from the outside, a Redeemer's Son, a Stuart Pretender, help from Catholic Spain or Rome itself. That vision of political redemption and as a consequence the restoration of the poet to his rightful place as it had been before 1600 reached its full development in the eighteenth century, but becomes in the long run an outworn myth and a poetic cliché. Its conventions of a weeping country personified as a beautiful woman ravished by a foreign boor and the figure of a dejected poet could express personal distress. Conventions can be superficial in the hands of some poets, while deeply personal and expressive in the hands of others. We read the poetry of the period not primarily for its political or historical realities, although they are clearly present, but for its literary qualities.

The new poetry in the seventeenth century was composed in an accentual form that was often ornate and highly wrought and therefore difficult to translate. Since Kinsella believed that translations in rhyme bear little relation to the original, his translations arc unrhymed, but do 'indicate the major basic rhythms of the originals' (xxxix) and seek 'a high standard of fidelity' to their 'actual contents' (xxxvii). The idea for the anthology originated with T.K. Whitaker, the selections were made by Seán Ó Tuama, the translations by Kinsella in consultation with him. Its purpose is to persuade readers who once had knowledge of the Irish language to return to the originals, to meet again poems they had studied in school and to experience them once more. Selective, therefore, rather than comprehensive, it throws light back upon the Irish poems, rather than upon the English translations. It is an attempt to reach across the linguistic and cultural divide, to retrieve what is in danger of being lost and to make it part of modern Irish consciousness. The anthology is divided into three sections: I, 'Transitional Poetry', Nos. 1–21; II, the largest section, 'The New Poets', Nos. 22–68; and III, 'Folk Poetry', Nos. 69–100. It extends Kinsella's translations from the seventeenth century in *The New Oxford Book of Irish Verse*.

Part I deals primarily with anonymous poetry written in the first half of the seventeenth century. There are three different kinds of poem – those in the *amour courtois*, the courtly love tradition, those in a religious mode, and those that illustrate the Fenian tradition. Much of this material is in the courtly love manner, in which by convention the speaker loves a woman who is married to someone else. It is a poetry that requires an exquisite dialectic in the expression of an emotional poise between erotic attraction and moral restraint. In poem No. 2, '*Meabhraigh mo laoidh chumainn-se*, Take my song of love to heart',

Kinsella retains the linguistic simplicity of the original and some of its alliterative pattern and verbal play:

> *Meabhraigh mo laoidh chumainn-se*
> *a bhean an chumainn bhréige*:

> Take my song of love to heart,
> lady of the lying love...[1]

The negative injunctions – not to talk, look or tell – disguise the gentle concern: she is to pretend on the outside but love, as he does, on the inside. To keep their secret they must enter into a compact to hide their love. Paradoxically, the poem declares love by seeming to deny its reality; it is in the denial that we detect love's presence.

The courtly love conventions are particularly evident in No. 4, '*Ní bhfuighe mise bás duit*, I will not die for you', in which the poet-lover, addressing the woman, declares indifference to her beauty. Others – weaker men – may have died for her, he will not. The delight in the poem lies in his itemizing of her beautiful features – lips, teeth, hand, breast and so on – in an apparent mode of rejection. He may declare 'I will not die for you', but the evidence, provided by him, counters this. His real state reveals itself in the fourth stanza in which he continues to describe her attractive features to which he will not yield, unless, of course, God wills it.

> Your rounded breasts, O skin refined,
> your flushed cheeks, your waving hair.
> – certainly I will not die
> on their account, unless God will.

But, if God should will it, he will die for her. With refined irony, his address, revealing how closely he has observed and relished, while avowing immunity, is, paradoxically, enormously flattering. The voice is personal, creating in its insistent and recurrent allusions an undeniable portrait of her attractions and his acute appreciation of them, even as he pretends to deny their power. He gives himself up to the play, to the religion of love, but the love-sickness he seeks to escape has him in its power, or so he pretends. They may be anonymous but these poems are sophisticated creations, delighting in their subtle casuistry.

The issue of jealousy is present in a number of these poems, Nos. 5–7. In a succession of fearful mini-parables, '*Rainn Fhir an Éada*, Song of the Jealous Man' (No. 5) illustrates the state of the jealous man. A sequence of plain statements about five wild creatures alludes to uneasy watchfulness. The word 'sleep' is repeated as an end-rhyme in each stanza, as are the words '*ní chodlann*' (will not sleep) in each stanza in the Irish. Inevitably, the bonding alliterative music is repeated in stanza four.

> *Ní chodlann an míol maighe*
> *biorach buadhach barrbhuidhe,*
> *is guth gadhair fóna cheann,*
> *a chois chladha ní chodlann.*

It is not matched in the translation:

> The hare does not sleep at all,
> point-eared, cunning, tawny-topped.
> When the hound voice is in his ear
> near the ditch he will not sleep.

But the imaginative admonishment is clear in both. At the same time the regularity of stress in the English and its parallel declarations – 'The brown otter does not sleep', 'The hornless doe does not sleep', and so on – reflect the syntactic formality of the Irish and accumulate persuasively and humorously in the drawing up of evidence.

A different tack is taken in poem No. 6, '*A fhir éadmhair 'gá mbí bean,* You that are jealous and have a wife.' Here the poet advises a man to accept that it is the nature of a woman to be flighty. 'She is the serving maid of love/and not herself responsible.' Therefore he must distrust what he sees, ignore what he knows, put up with distress, disregard her moods, feel sympathy for her state; if he cannot do all that, he will 'outclimb all idiots to the peak of madness'. The advice, accumulating to a blunt assertion, is more pragmatic than comforting: accept the woman's inconstancy or be driven crazy.

Kinsella faces some difficult decisions here because of the idiomatic compactness of the original, as in '*ní haici féin a-tá sí*', which literally means 'it is not with herself she is' and which is not caught in his 'and not herself responsible'. On the other hand in stanza three he gets the blunt tone of the advice: '*Ná creid do radharc do shúl,/leath a dtuigfe tú ná tuig.*' 'Don't trust the sight of your own eyes./Half of what you know, know not.' Each of the end-stopped lines captures the epigrammatic force of the original.

The convention of offering advice on outrageous or sarcastic grounds is even more evident in No. 7, '*A fhir do-ní an t-éad,* Sir, so suspicious'. Sometimes, Kinsella improves on the sarcasm in the Irish, as when he translates '*binn an scéal do chor*' (sweet the story in your case) with the realism of 'your case makes fine gossip' but is *ní tuilltear é uait* – 'and all quite uncalled for'. Again, part of the humour arises because of the irony in the advice, which essentially says 'there is no need to be suspicious because nobody would want your wife'. There is nothing worth guarding. 'Not one in a hundred/is safe as you are.'

All these poems are written in syllabic metre which means that there are seven syllables in each line, with the end-rhyme in the second and fourth lines, and rhymes between the final word in the first line and an internal word in the second, and between the final word in the third line and an internal word in the fourth. Usually simple in diction and direct in expression, the poems have an attractive stylistic and syntactical formality. Kinsella respects the intelligence and craft with which they are written but knows there are effects he cannot translate which have to do, as he writes, 'with prosody and technique: the syllabic or accentual rhythm, devices of rhyme, assonance, and so on' (xxxix).

Because the Irish conventions allow for a plentiful use of descriptive adjectives and a rich linguistic music, it is impossible to translate the complex harmony of alliteration, assonance and consonance. Stanza five in '*Tuar guil, a cholaim, do cheol!*, O dove, your song is cause for tears' (No. 11), for example, revels in the initial beat of consonants and the chiming of rhymes, both external and internal, even as it maintains its strict syllabic form.

> *An múr 'na aonar a-nocht*
> *   'na gcluininn gáir chrot is chliar,*
> *gáir na bhfleadh bhfairsing fó fhíon,*
> *   gáir bhrughadh ag díol a bhfiach.*

> [The wall is on its own tonight
>   where we used to hear the sounds of harp and poet,
> the sounds of feasting around the wine,
>   the sounds of hostelers doing their duty.]

The translation does not attempt to reproduce the various kinds of harmony, but does use the seven-syllable line.

> Tonight the walls are lonely
>   where we once heard harps and poets,
> ample feasting round the wine,
>   guestmasters about their duties...

Within this first section of the anthology are also a number of religious lyrics of which '*Truagh mo thuras go Loch Dearg*, Vain my journey to Loch Dearg' (No. 13) is particularly interesting. Saint Patrick's Purgatory in Lough Derg, County Donegal, has been a famous place of pilgrimage since the medieval period. In Kinsella's poem the poet is a failed pilgrim who has been to the lake but who has not felt contrition for his sins.

The Irish has a rhetorical power that the translation finds inappropriate. A line like *'iar ndéanamh gach uilc dar fhéad'* (after doing every evil I could), Kinsella simplifies to 'despite the harm I have done'; and for the line *'mo thruagh, a Rí, créad do-ghéan'* (my sorrow, O King, what can I do), he says, more simply, 'O what can I do, my King?' Throughout the poem Kinsella avoids the tendency towards hyperbole in the Irish in keeping with his own preference for non-emotive language. The language of stanza five is typically excessive.

> *I gcarcair chumhang chruaidh chloch,*
> *d'éis a ndearnas d'olc is d'uaill,*
> *och, is truagh nach bhfaghaim deor,*
> *is mé adhlaicthe beo san uaimh.*

> [In my hard stony narrow prison,
>   after committing evil and pride,
> alas, it is a pity I could not find tears,
>   and I buried alive in the grave.]

> In my narrow hard stone cell
>   after all my proud foul acts
> I can find, for shame, no tear.
>   I am buried in a grave alive.

Kinsella alters the verb *'a ndearnas'* in the second line to a noun 'acts', intensifies the language to 'proud foul acts', and in the process keeps the spirit of the original. The predominant use of monosyllabic words throughout the stanza gives a chiselled effect in keeping with the subject. Placing the key word 'alive' at the end of the line instead of immediately after 'buried' underlines the state of failed contrition.

The address to the body that follows is more intense because the inability to experience remorse for sins committed ensures that the body will go to Hell. The poet has no sympathy for its state – naked, hungry and in pain. Kinsella seems to enjoy the language of rebuke: 'your pains – Hell-bent as you are/mean little to me tonight', is an exact translation of the equally blunt *'go hifreann má tá do thriall/is beag liom do phian a-nocht'*. The choice is stark: the body should find contrition or end up 'in the house of pains'. The Irish also lowers the linguistic pressure in favour of unadorned language as Kinsella does. The vocal register in the translation is the same as in the original. The voice is earnestly contrite and fearful in its dramatization of the poet's endangered state.

That seriousness of tone contrasts with the lightness and good humour in No. 15, '*Mo-chean do theacht, a scadáin*, Hail, herring! You've come!' The herring was the traditional food in Lent, but in place of the penitential earnestness of No. 13, the season of penance is welcomed.

> Hail, herring! You've come!
>   My fine son, come close.

The mode of humorous address carries the poem forward in a kind of mock panegyric. The humour in '*Ní binn do thorann lem thaoibh*, Ugly your uproar at my side' (No. 16) is broader. The poem addresses a 'fine young man' whose snoring disturbs the poet. The essence of the humour comes from the exaggerated comparisons that illustrate the unpleasant noise. The poem's success depends on the accuracy and vividness, as well as the appropriateness, of the successive metaphors. The Irish has a number of striking images: 'The dead would wake in their graves'; 'Pigs' grunts are sweeter'. The tone of comic exaggeration gives force to the complaints. The weightier, adjectival texture of the original contrasts with the simpler diction of the English.

Kinsella includes three examples of poems of the Fianna, Nos. 18–20. Lament for the passing of the Fianna is central to this cycle. Frequently, as in No. 18, Oisín remembers the past in conversation with St Patrick. The coming of Christianity has replaced a heroic past with a less attractive present and its values. In addition these lyrics have a close association with place and the natural world. They are characteristically simple in language, direct in expression, and therefore do not present many difficulties for the translator.

No. 18, '*Binn sin, a luin Doire an Chairn!*', Beautiful – blackbird of Doire an Chairn!', praises the music of the bird and urges Patrick to listen. He narrates the story of the bird's origin: Fionn Mac Cumhaill himself, leader of the Fianna, found it in Doire an Chairn. He associates the bird with places and sounds that Fionn loved. The lines swell and move with the music of the telling.

> *Sgolghaire luin Doire an Chairn*
> *   búithre an daimh ó Aill na gCaor,*
> *ceol le gcodladh Fionn go moch,*
> *   lachain ó Loch na dTrí gCaol.*

> [The clear cry of the blackbird of Doire an Chairn,
>   the bellowing of the stag from Aill na gCaor,
> were music for Fionn sleeping early,
>   and the ducks from Loch na dTrí gCaol.]

> Throat-song of the blackbird of Doire an Chairn,
>   and the stag's call from Aill na gCaor
> were Fionn's music, sleeping at morn,
>   and the ducks from Loch na dTrí gCaol.

These stanzas evoke a pastoral world to which the Fianna related, better by far in Oisín's eyes than the present world of churches.

> When Fionn and the Fianna lived
>   they loved the hills, not hermit-cells.
> Blackbird speech is what they loved
>   – not the sound, unlovely, of your bells.

The contrast between Oisín's love for what has gone, the natural world of beautiful sounds and places, is poignantly present. 'Blackbird speech' in fact becomes symbolic of an entire world that has disappeared; the 'unlovely' sound of the saints' bells is an unpleasant reminder of the present. In '*A Oisín, 's fada do shuan*, Oisín, you sleep too long' (No. 19), the contrast between the pagan past and the Christian present is the substance of a dialogue between the two men, with Patrick's urging Oisín to hear the psalm now that his strength, health and fighting prowess are gone. Although Patrick goes on to praise the music of the church, in a final run of stanzas the dialogue yields to Oisín's threnody of loss, his catalogue of sounds and activities, and the association of place and particular figures. '*Laoi na seilge*, A tale of the chase' (No. 20) is an example of a *lay*, a long verse narrative, in which Fionn pursues a doe that turns into a beautiful girl who weeps because she has lost a ring.

In this first section Kinsella illustrates the poetry of this early period: love poems, religious poems, Fenian poetry, and he includes some satires and epigrams. These, he points out, are transitional poems, echoes of an aristocratic world before Kinsale, 'where love, learning, religion and human behaviour could be contemplated at leisure'. (xxix) The implication is that a more troubled time was to follow.

Part II of the anthology, entitled 'The New Poets', Nos. 22–68, has work by twenty-five poets, each usually represented by one or two poems, but with more generous selections from the major figures, Dáibhí Ó Bruadair and Aogán Ó Rathaille, and extracts from Eibhlín Dhubh Ní Chonaill's 'Lament For Art Ó'Laoghaire' and Brian Merriman's 'The Midnight Court'.

The two poems by Séathrún Céitinn (1580–c.1644) – No. 23, '*Óm sceol ar ardmhagh Fáil*, At the news from Fál's high plain', and No. 24, '*A bhean lán de stuaim*, O lady full of guile' – represent the first important literary figure of the seventeenth century. Better known as the author of *Foras Feasa ar Éirinn*, a history of Ireland, which was popular and stylistically influential for the development of modern Irish, Céitinn's poetry is written mainly in accentual metres, although he appears to have been at home in both types of metre.

The first poem introduces a theme that runs through the seventeenth and much of the eighteenth centuries: the collapse of the old Irish order after the Battle of Kinsale in 1601 and the Flight of the Earls in 1607, when, defeated in the Elizabethan wars, many of the chieftains sailed into exile and the poets were left largely without patrons. Colonial 'upstarts' took over the Big Houses and got possession of great tracts of land. The majestic manner of this poem may be heard in the opening stanza, which has five stresses to each line. Its vowel pattern of *ó á á o í* is followed strictly throughout the seven stanzas, although the natural cadences of the voice transcend the apparent rigidity of the form.

Óm sceol ar ardmhagh Fáil ní chodlaim oíche
's do bhreoigh go bráth mé dála a pobail dílis;
gé rófhada atáid 'na bhfál ré broscar bíobha,
fá dheoidh gur fhás a lán den chogal tríothu.

[Because of the news from the high plain of Fál I do not sleep at night.
I am sickened forever by the plight of its loyal people.
Although long they have been as a hedge against enemy trash,
in the end there has grown up through them a lot of cockle.]

At the news from Fál's high plain I cannot sleep.
I am sick till doom at the plight of its faithful folk.
Long have they stood as a hedge against hostile trash
but a lot of the cockle has grown up through them at last.

Kinsella does not try to repeat the strict vowel system of the Irish, but he achieves a stately formality in his iambic pentameter lines with varying stresses, and matches the verbal directness of the original. The lines move easily; the voice of the speaker laments the disappearance of the old families. Céitinn's language becomes harsh as he rebukes Fódla, that is, Ireland, for allowing the 'hostile trash', 'the cockle', to take the place of the native grain. He imagines the country in her feminine nurturing role, her breast has been 'drained dry by the litter of every alien sow'. The entire poem is a litany of distress for mansions lost, the best land taken, base foreigners in possession with spurious legal entitlements and the inability of the Irish chiefs to resist.

    – Eoghan's seed exhausted, Tál's blood troubled and
        broken,
    and the youth of Bántsrath scattered in foreign lands.

The force of the open vowels and their steady repetition supports the strong
rhythm in the Irish. This inner music cannot be reproduced in English.

    Dá mba beoga ardfhlaith Áine is Droma Daoile
    's na leoghain láidre ón Máigh do bhronnadh maoine,
    dar ndóigh níorbh áit don táinse in oscaill Bhríde
    gan gheoin is gártha os ard dá dtoghaildíbirt.

    [If the great chief of Áine and Druim Daoile lived,
    and the strong lions of the Máigh who bestowed gifts,
    for sure there would be no place for this crowd in the crook of the Bride
    without cries and laments because of their great expulsion.]

    If that high prince lived, of Áine and Drom Daoile,
    or the great gift-generous lions of the Máigh,
    this horde would have no place in the bend of the Bríde
    – smashed, driven out, with outcry and loud wails.

The allusions – mainly to Ireland, Irish families and places – evoke
their traditional resonance. In the final stanza Céitinn raises the lament
to religious fervour, which Kinsella matches in alliteration that bristles
with anger. But the intensity has a desperate edge to it – if God does
not protect Ireland from these enemies, it were better to harvest them
now and send them into safe exile across the ocean.

    If the Craftsman of Stars protect not Ireland's people
    from violent vengeful enemies, bold and ready,
    better gather and winnow them now without delay
    and sail them out wandering safe on the waves of Clíona.

The language of the poem, which is vigorous and forthright, alternates
from a high style of allusions and traditional images for Ireland to
familiar terms and everyday idioms. Its account of Ireland's changed
condition is attested also in the balance in each stanza between statement
and demonstration.
    Although there is some doubt that Séathrún Céitinn wrote No. 24, 'O
lady full of guile', it is usually attributed to him. Written in accented
syllables, five to each line, with end and internal rhyme, and with each
fluent line ending in a monosyllabic word, the poem has a distinct formal

elegance. Kinsella's line has three stresses; the style of spare language and monosyllabic words has a classic simplicity and dignity.

> *A bhean lán de stuaim*
>   *coingibh uaim do lámh:*
> *ní fear gníomha sinn,*
>   *cé taoi tinn dar ngrádh.*

> [O lady full of ingenuity
>   keep your hand from me:
> I am not a man of deeds,
>   even if you are sick for love.]

> O lady full of guile
>   take away your hand.
> Though you sicken for my love,
>   I am not an active man.

There are echoes here of the courtly love tradition in which the man longs for the unattainable lady, but in this case, while her beauties are finely rendered, he declines the opportunity to make love. As in some of the anonymous love lyrics, the manner in which the poet both evokes her beauty, even as he eludes her desire, gives the poem a delicately ironic tone. In a more general sense the conflict between desire and rejection is a felt reality.

On the one hand he asks her to see his wasted condition – grey hair, slack body, tired blood. In the next breath, addressing her as though she were from the spirit world (*a shíodh sheang*: slender spirit), he urges her to love forever without sexual union. Remove your mouth from mine, he tells her, which suggests they have been intimate, but it is possible the poet is merely employing conventions of the *amour courtois*.

> Take your mouth from mine:
>   grave is your condition.

> Touch not skin to skin
>   – the heat leads on to lust.

All her physical attractions 'excite the eye alone'. He advocates an aesthetic of love: prepared to do 'All deeds but that of the flesh'. The word '*gníomh*', often meaning sexual union, is used with some ambivalence in this portrait of a man who tries to pretend that he can enjoy the sensual pleasure of desire without bringing it to its natural consummation. The word '*stuaim*' is also nuanced from something approximating 'ingenuity' in the first line – Kinsella's 'guile' suggests the speaker's fear of her – to its reappearance as the final word of the poem where it has come to mean something more than guile, more than cunning, more like an expression of her desire which has been evident in references to '*thnúth*' (expectation, longing, want), and '*cor*' (state, condition) and various indications of her need.

The placing of '*gníomh*' in the opening stanza affects the tone of the poem and declares the physicality the poet has in mind. The speaker's impotence colours what he says; underlines his regret; makes his refusals less hurtful or demeaning. She may be seductive, he may request her to remove her hand; but the reason is not that he rejects her, not that he finds her unattractive, but that he is unable to respond as he would like. By the end of the poem it is less her seductive ways he has in mind than her love of him and that includes her physical need, her '*thnúth*', with which he sympathizes.

The poem's ironies are both painful and pleasing. The counter-claims, negative and positive, sum up the frustration of the situation. He addresses her as a '*shíodh sheang*', a slender fairywoman, her beauty more than human, but all that he can give her is appreciation. Within this limitation he offers her eternal love – '*go bráth*'. With its language poised between love and denial, the poem trembles with complex emotions, the insoluble dilemma given sensitive artistic expression.

A similar sophistication characterizes poem No. 28, '*Léig dhíot th'airm, a mhacaoimh mná*, Lay your weapons down, young lady', by Piaras Feiritéar (c.1600–53). The resemblance comes in the injunction not to use her charms against him and in the tone of irony with which he speaks.

> *Léig dhíot th'airm, a mhacaoimh mná,*
> *muna fearr leat cách do lot;*
> *muna léige th'airmse dhíot,*
> *cuirfead bannaidhe ón rígh ort.*

> [Put your weapons down, young woman,
>   if you do not want to wound us all;
> if you do not put down your weapons,
>   royal bonds will be placed on you.]

> Lay your weapons down, young lady.
>   Do you want to ruin us all?
> Lay your weapons down, or else
>   I'll have you under royal restraint.

The 'weapons' are her physical beauty of hair, breast, eye, knee, palm and so on. The entire poem is a delightful expression of their wounding capabilities. Its pleasure lies in its delicately humorous handling of the issue, the mock-seriousness, the conceit, in which urgent injunction is also amatory address.

> You may think your knee's not sharp
>   and think your palm is soft:
> to wound a man, believe me,
>   you need no knife or spear!

The first major poet of the period is Dáibhí Ó Bruadair (c.1625–98) whose use of accentual metre is varied and skilful. Although little is known about his background, he had a good education, knew Latin and English, and had an extensive knowledge of Irish literature, history and genealogical lore. His main interest was Ireland and the Catholic religion. He depicted in particular Ireland as he saw it after the Cromwellian wars and confiscations, although he witnessed almost all the upheavals of the time: the Confederation of Kilkenny (1642); the Restoration of Charles II (1660); the Popish Plot (1678–81); the Jacobite wars (1688–91), and the establishment of Ascendancy Ireland. The long decline in his own life into ever deeper poverty epitomizes the fate of the Gaelic population, with the result that his complaints and invective provide a commentary from a Gaelic point of view on the developments of his time. It is not Kinsella's purpose to illustrate this range of material, but the poems he translates reflect its presence.

Often seen as a poet of demanding rhetoric, Ó Bruadair's tender disposition is evident in the religious poem '*Adoramus Te, Christe, Adoramus Te, Christe*' (No. 32), which draws freely from the images of Christ's suffering and man's guilt that made that suffering necessary. Its fervent tone is heard in a succession of active verbs from the direct 'I worship you' in the opening stanza; the metaphors are explicit – Christ as hero, destroyer of evil, man's saviour.

The Irish has a mellifluous flow of internal harmonies. The first two lines of the second stanza are particularly appealing – softly alliterative, the metaphor full of religious association:

> *A choinneall an chuain chuireas chum suain*
>   *siosma na nguas ngáifeach,*

> [O candle of the harbour that soothes to rest
>   dissension of terrible dangers,]

> Harbour-candle that lulls to rest
>   the quarrel of deadly dangers...

The speaker acknowledges that Christ's suffering – the broken side, the three nails – are his fault. Confessing complicity he appeals for clemency.

That directness of response is matched in the bitterly ironic, '*Mairg nach fuil 'na dhubhthuata*, O it's best be a total boor' (No. 34), in which Ó Bruadair asserts that since he is surrounded by boors, it is best to be a boor. The Irish form of the poem is difficult: seven-syllable lines and the end word in each line has to have three syllables; the four stanzas are followed by a fifth in a looser metre. In the first four stanzas the manner is condensed, almost epigrammatic.

> *Mairg nach fuil 'na dhubhthuata,*
> *gé holc duine 'na thuata,*
> *i ndóigh go mbeinn mágcuarda*
> *idir na daoinibh duarca.*

> [It's a pity not to be a complete boor,
>   however bad it is to be one of the boors,
> since I have to be around and
>   among these dismal people.]

> O it's best be a total boor
>   (though it's bad be a boor at all)
> if I'm to go out and about
>   among these stupid people.

His fierce acceptance does not conceal his contempt for the new breed of upstarts:

> It's best to be, good people,
>   a stutterer among you
> since that is what you want,
>   you blind ignorant crew.

They rate one who stutters more than one who speaks well. In bitter abnegation he says he would give his 'lovely skill' away, if he could find someone to take it. In the upside-down world of the new social order clothes are preferred to poetry, so that now, with nothing to show for the years spent on his art, he is the poorer.

> Since a man is respected more
>   for his suit than for his talents
> I regret what I've spent on my art,
>   that I haven't it now in clothes.

In the looser fifth stanza he freely voices his anger and despair, no longer trying to maintain the disciplined and more elegant form of the preceding stanzas.

> Since happy in word and deed is each boorish clod
> without music or metre or motherwit on his tongue,
> I regret what I've wasted struggling with hard print
> since the prime of life – that I might have spent as a boor.

In its use of alliteration and compound words the Irish version is even more gloomy.

> *Ós suairc labhartha is bearta gach buairghiúiste*
> *gan uaim gan aiste 'na theangain ná suanúchas,*
> *mo thrua ar chreanas le ceannaraic cruaphrionta*
> *ó bhuaic mo bheatha nár chaitheas le tuatúlacht.*

> [Since the words and deeds of every boorish clod
> are pleasing without composition, pattern or verbal skill,
> my grief I spent my energy on hard writing,
> since the prime of my life, rather than boorish ways.]

The sarcasm scrapes the bottom of his despair.

In the adjacent '*D'aithle na bhfileadh*, The high poets are gone' (No. 35), the poet moves from invective to lament for the disappearance of the illustrious poets – indeed he mourns 'for the world's waning' – and for the inability of their sons to continue the craft of poetry. He mourns eloquently for the loss of books conceived by those 'drinkers of wisdom'. For them poetry and knowledge were wealth; now their books are turning grey, 'their sons without one syllable of their secret treasure'. These two poems give divergent responses to the same phenomenon: the collapse of the poets' world, the devaluation of their work, and the sad fact that there is no one to succeed them.

The blind poet Séamas Dall Mac Cuarta (1647?–1733) liked to write poems of four stanzas, three in loose syllabic metres and one in the song or *amhrán* [accentual] form. His poems are noted for their feeling for the natural world. In '*Fáilte don éan*, Welcome, sweetest bird' (No. 41), he wishes he could see the elusive cuckoo whose song he enjoys. The poem, which has a lovely simplicity of feeling and expression, begins with words of welcome.

> *Fáilte don éan is binne ar chraoibh,*
> *labhras ar chaoin na dtor le gréin;*

> domhsa is fada tuirse an tsaoil,
>   nach bhfaiceann í le teacht an fhéir.

[Welcome to the bird that is sweetest on the branch,
   that speaks on the top of the bush with the sun;
for me it is a long sorrow of the world
   that I do not see her with the coming of the grass.]

Kinsella keeps the simplicity and naturalness of the original, changing the words slightly to achieve a parallelism between the second and fourth lines; in the process he turns Irish idioms – *'le gréin'*, with the sun, meaning the rising of the sun, and *'le teacht an fhéir'*, meaning with the growth of new grass – into conventional English.

> Welcome, sweetest bird on branch,
>   at the bushes' edge as the sun grows warm.
> The world's long sorrow it is to me
>   I see her not as the grass grows green.

While the poet salutes the bird as the harbinger of summer, he knows that the signs of new life are not matched in his own experience. Seeing the shapes of birds in Ireland, south and north, and the flowers on the hillsides, other people 'love to talk about these things'. But in a quick retreat from these larger perspectives, he says, 'My sharp sorrow I cannot have/a sight of her in the branches' tops.' His appreciation of the music of bird-song is mimicked in the music of the stanzas. Paradoxically and poignantly, he can imagine and render more than he can see and does so without self-pity.

The satirical edge to Mac Cuarta's sensibility may be felt in another poem with the same structure, *'Tithe Chorr an Chait*, The houses of Corr an Chait' (No. 42), a satire on inhospitality, which he sees as a form of spiritual darkness. In a natural metaphor he compares people who do not welcome visitors to badgers whose nature it is to burrow under the earth. It is once again that contrast between generosity of spirit and the blind burrowing which gives the poem its imaginative life. The technical skill is a measure of the poem's quality: line and sound repetitions bind stanzas and create a musical motif inside the stanzas. These and other interlacings and positionings are part of the technical skill that distinguishes Mac Cuarta's poetry.

> *Uaigneach sin, tithe Chorr an Chait,*
>   *is uaigneach a bhfir is a mná;*
> *is dá bhfaighdís ór is fíon*
>   *cha dtig aon díobh i gceann cháich.*

I gceann cháich cha dtig siad
  ar ar cruthaíodh thiar is thoir;
ar ar cruthaíodh ó neamh go lár—
  ionann sin is béasa an bhroic.

Béasa an bhroic bheith ag tochailt faoi
  i ndorchadas oíche is lae;
ar ar cruthaíodh ó neamh go lár,
  i gceann cháich cha dtig sé.

[Lonely are the houses of Corr an Chait,
  lonely are their men and their women;
even if they got gold and wine
  not one of them would come to greet people.

To greet people they would not come
  for the sake of all the created, west and east;
for the sake of all the created from Heaven to Earth.
  that is the habit of the badger.

The habit of the badger is to dig under
  in the darkness night and day;
for the sake of all the created from Heaven to Earth,
  for the sake of anyone he would not come.]

Kinsella matches some of these devices of repetition. His choice of 'cold' instead of lonely makes use of the idiom of coldness of heart, but Mac Cuarta's '*uaigneach*' meaning 'lonely' has the added dimension of isolation – the result of being unwelcoming.

The houses of Corr an Chait are cold
  and cold their men and women.
Not for gold or wine
  would one of them come to greet you.

They wouldn't come to greet you
  for the whole world, East and West,
for the world from Earth to Heaven.
  And that is the badger's habit.

It's the badger's habit to burrow down
  night and day in the dark.
For the world from Earth to Heaven
  he wouldn't come to greet you.

The *amhrán* in its own blunt parallels has an elegiac quality; it describes the inability of the badger people to enjoy life, to take pleasure in wise men, poets and music-makers, to welcome the company of particular friends.

> *Ní hionmhuin leis an ríbhroc aoibhneas, aiteas, ná spórt,*
> *ní hionmhuin leo saoi, ná draoi, ná cumadóir ceoil,*
> *ni hionmhuin leo Séamas caoch ná cuidhiú Néill Óig,*
> *is fanadh gach aon mar a mbíd ag tochailt an phóir.*

[The king-badger does not like pleasure, fun, or sport,
they do not like wise men, druids or music-makers,
they do not like blind Séamas nor the company of Niall Óg,
so let each one remain as they always are digging the soil.]

King-badger loves not gaiety, sport or pleasure;
these love not sage or druid or music-maker,
nor Seamus blind, nor Niall Óg's company.
So let them bide, burrowing in the dirt.

The poet speaks more in pity than in anger, the satirical edge modified by a well-balanced humanity.

Aogán Ó Rathaille (c. 1675–1729) was an educated man who read Latin and Middle Irish prose and verse in manuscript and also some Greek; his poetry, from the point of view of a translator, is challenging.[2] At the forefront of his work is what Kinsella calls 'a heroic desolation and grandeur' as Ó Rathaille tried to come to terms with the chaos in which he and his people found themselves in the later seventeenth and early eighteenth centuries. Regretting the absence of a unifying leader, he identified with those who shared his language, culture, religion and political aspirations. His poetry shows a formidable command of language, which he often uses in a forceful manner, piling on adjectives and compound words. The imagery of poem No. 45, for example, Ó Rathaille's '*Is fada liom oíche fhírfhliuch*, The drenching night drags on', begins with blunt notations of extreme loss.

> *Is fada liom oíche fhírfhliuch gan suan, gan srann,*
> *gan ceathra, gan maoin caoire ná buaibh na mbeann;*
> *anfa ar toinn taoibh liom do bhuair mo cheann,*
> *'s nár chleachtas im naíon fiogaigh ná ruacain abhann.*

[The very wet night is long for me without rest, without snore,
without stock, without the wealth of sheep or horned cattle;
the storm on the wave beside me has disturbed my head,
I was not accustomed as a child to dog-fish or river-cockles.]

The drenching night drags on: no sleep or snore,
no stock, no wealth of sheep, no horned cows.
This storm on the waves nearby has harrowed my head
– I who ate no winkles or dogfish in my youth!

The mood is elegiac and as the poem develops it draws upon traditional
subjects of lament – people and places: his patron, Sir Nicholas Browne,
three great McCarthys from the middle of the century, and the larger
despoliation by foreigners who have ousted the lords of Munster. The
lines accumulate in a tide of invective that bursts forth in the last stanza,
which addresses the wave. External upheaval is fused with, and mirrors,
the poet's internal turmoil.

A thonnsa thíos is airde géim go hard,
meabhair mo chinnse cloíte ód bhéiceach tá;
cabhair dá dtíodh arís ar Éirinn bhán,
do ghlam nach binn do dhingfinn féin id bhráid.

[O wave below, your loud bellowing is highest,
the brain in my head is worn down by your clamour;
if help ever came again to beautiful Ireland,
I myself would wedge your sour howling down your throat.]

You wave down there, lifting your loudest roar,
the wits in my head are worsted by your wails.
If help ever came to lovely Ireland again
I'd wedge your ugly howling down your throat!

An Duanaire has three of Ó Rathaille's *aisling* or vision poems. According
to the conventions of this genre, the poet, who is in a dejected state,
encounters a beautiful woman whose beauty he proceeds to describe in
detail. He asks her who she is. Is she one of the Irish or Greek queens?
She replies that she is Ireland and that she is in the hands of a foreign
boor. The political significance is clear. She is the sovereignty of Ireland
who will be happy when the rightful king comes to marry her.

The *aisling* genre can be traced to a number of sources: an Irish
tradition of vision poems extending back at least to the medieval period,
including the deeply rooted motif of the hag-like creature who is
transformed to a beautiful maiden once she has embraced the rightful
prince; in this tradition the woman is the sovereignty-goddess. After the
Flight of the Earls the image of Ireland as a beautiful woman in distress
awaiting her deliverer became a recurrent feature in the poetry. In
Europe there was the tradition of dream-like visions that poets had of

beautiful women, vision poems of an amatory kind with the result that political allegory and the love-poem overlapped. This also happened in Ireland. In the period represented by *An Duanaire* the *aisling* became the main form of political literature.

In the first poem, '*Gile na Gile*, Brightness most bright' (No. 49), the *spéirbhean* [sky-woman] waits for the return of the Stuart Pretender. Written as a narrative of meeting, pursuit and dismissal, the poem is stylistically ornate. The poet's anxiety is well expressed, but the Irish version with its parallel constructions, intensity, elaborate alliterative embroidery and assertive rhythms is difficult to translate. It relies so much on the internal music – of assonance as well as alliteration, of end rhyme, of an insistent rhythmical pulse and an elevated diction that these elements are difficult to match in English. Within its own conventions it is a fully achieved and resonant dramatic lyric.

> *Gile na gile do chonnarc ar slí in uaigneas,*
> *criostal an chriostail a goirmroisc rinn-uaine,*
> *binneas an bhinnis a friotal nár chríonghruama,*
> *deirge is finne do fionnadh 'na gríosghruannaibh.*

[Brightness of brightness in loneliness I saw on the way,
crystal of crystal her blue eyes tipped with green,
sweetness of sweetness her voice that age had not made dark,
red and white mingled in her glowing cheeks.]

Brightness most bright I beheld on the way, forlorn.
Crystal of crystal her eye, blue touched with green.
Sweetness most sweet her voice, not stern with age.
Colour and pallor appeared in her flushed cheeks.

The poet's sad state is transcended in his spirited description in which a string of superlatives arranged in parallel clauses paints a glowing portrait of the visionary woman. When she relates her story of captivity, he becomes captive to her; and when she disappears, he races after her. The rhythms mimic the sense of speed and urgency:

> *Rithim le rith mire im rithibh go croí-luaimneach,*
> [I ran with a mad speed in my running with leaping heart,]
> Heart pounding, I ran, with a frantic haste in my race...

He follows her through marsh, swamp and moor, by strange paths, until he comes to a strong mansion where he is bound and sees her possessed: 'a lumbering brute took hold of my girl by the breasts': *'s mo bhruinneal ar broinnibh ag broinnire broinnstuacach'*. The mood is dispiriting; his beautiful woman is ravished by a monster, while he himself is put in chains. When he criticized her for being joined to the 'brute' instead of waiting for the rightful king, of Scottish blood, she weeps and arranges for him to be guided out of the house.

In the final stanza he cries out his pain in a succession of fragmented terms, enraged that this beautiful girl is with hateful foreigners and that there will be no redress until the 'lions' come over the water.

> *Mo threighid, mo thubaist, mo thurainn, mo bhrón, mo dhíth!*
> *an soilseach muirneach miochairgheal beoltais caoin*
> *ag adharcach foireanndubh mioscaiseach cóirneach buí,*
> *'s gan leigheas 'na goire go bhfillid na leoin tar toinn.*

> [My pain, my disaster, my collapse, my sorrow, my loss!
> The bright tender kind gentle-voiced girl
> with a horned, spiteful, malicious, hateful, evil band,
> with no cure near until the lions return over the sea.]

> Pain, disaster, downfall, sorrow and loss!
> Our mild, bright, delicate, loving, fresh-lipped girl
> with one of that black, horned, foreign, hate-crested crew
> and no remedy near till our lions come over the sea.

No. 50, '*An Aisling*, The Vision', has a gentler quality. Instead of the bleak landscape of marsh and moor, we have a fertile place, fitting imagery for the idea that the Stuart Pretender will reign over the three kingdoms of Ireland, England and Scotland. The hopeful mood is established from the opening stanza.

> *Maidean sul smaoin Titan a chosa do luaill*
> *ar mhullach cnoic aoird aoibhinn do lodamar suas,*
> *tarrastar linn scaoth bhruinneal soilbhir suairc—*
> *gasra bhí i Sídh Seanadh, solasbhrugh thuaidh.*

> [A morning before Titan thought of moving his feet
> on the top of a beautiful high hill I climbed,
> there met with us a group of pleasant happy girls—
> a band from Sídh Seanadh's bright mansions to the North.]

> One morning ere Titan had thought to stir his feet,
> on the top of a fine high hill I had laboured up,
> I chanced on a pleasant flock of joyous girls,
> a troop from Sídh Seanadh's bright mansions to the North.

After these initial signs of happiness and light the poem progresses through further images of brightness and of a land of fruitfulness. The fairy women light three candles 'of indescribable light' and tell the poet that they do so 'in the name of the faithful king who is soon to come/to rule and defend the triple realm for ever'. But it is only a dream. When he awakens he finds himself 'nerve-shaken, downcast and morose'. Ó Rathaille's sensibility is essentially pessimistic; he is too aware of the predicament of poets in his time to believe in the possibility of the re-emergence of a society in which the poet would have a traditional place. '*The Vision*' speaks of a lost world.

The third of his vision poems, '*Mac an Cheannaí*, The Redeemer's Son' (No. 51), is written in the *amhrán* song-rhythms that were widely popular by the eighteenth century. The 'Son' referred to is the Stuart Pretender. As the previous poem indicates, hopes were strong in 1719 and 1720 that French help for the Jacobite cause would materialize, but they dimmed within a few years. In this *aisling* that loss of expectation is searingly expressed, particularly in the despair of the final stanza. 'The Redeemer's Son' is a sustained lament. Each stanza depicts the 'bitter vision'. The visionary woman (Ireland) may be beautiful in the traditional manner but her state is pitiful: she is crushed by alien flails, her followers hurt and leaderless; she has no music in her life, only tears; she is hungry; she is a dried branch; all her kings have fallen; her Friars are overseas; she has no welcome or love from any quarter. In one poignant stanza she looks in vain for her saviour, the Redeemer's Son.

> *Do-bheir súil ó dheas gach lá fá seach*
> *ar thráigh na mbarc an cailín,*
> *Is súil deas-soir go dlúth tar muir,*
> *mo chumha anois a haicíd,*
> *a súile siar ag súil le Dia,*
> *tar tonntaibh fiara gainmhe;*
> *cloíte lag beidh sí gan phreab*
> *go bhfillfidh Mac an Cheannaí.*

[Her eye looks South day after day
  to the strand of the ships,
an intent eye across the sea to the Southeast,
  my sorrow now her affliction,
her eyes to the West with hope in God,
  across tilting sandy waves;
she will be exhausted, weak without stir
  until he returns, *Mac an Cheannaí*.]

> Her eye looks South day after day
>   to the shore for ships arriving,
> to sea Southeast she gazes long
>   (her troubles are my grief!)
> and a Westward eye, with hope in God,
>   o'er wild and sandy billows
> – defeated, lifeless, powerless,
>   till he come, her *Mac an Cheannaí*.

The Irish has a stately quality arising from its measured movement – the regular stress pattern and the flowing quality in the run-on lines in each stanza. The English cannot always match them or the intensity of the many compound words like '*lagbhríoch*' or '*léirchreach*', for which the English equivalents are 'weary' and 'trouble'. The note of hope in the refrain – 'till he come, her *Mac an Cheannaí*' – is broken in the last stanza when he tells her that her redeemer is dead; there is no one to hear her complaint, no one to rescue her. The news is fatal: she dies before him.

That apocalyptic metaphor merged with Ó Rathaille's personal situation. By the end of his life, as Kinsella remarks in a note to the poem, he despaired not only of a Stuart intervention in Irish affairs but of any restoration of his own status within the community. Written during the poet's final illness, '*Cabhair ní ghairfead*, No help I'll call' (No. 53), begins with a defiant declaration: he will not call upon the McCarthys; even if he did, it would bring no relief; the McCarthys of the seed of the Munster dynasty of Eoghan are withered. There is no going back and it is this uncompromising acceptance of his situation and of conditions in Ireland that gives Ó Rathaille's voice its strength. The lord who might have helped has been destroyed, his veins pierced, his strength decayed. The strength is also felt in the repetition in stanza one between '*ghairfead*' – 'will call' in line one and '*dá ngairinn*' – 'were I to call' in line two. The repetition of sounds also has a further strengthening effect, as do the echoes between *ní ghairfead* – 'No help'; '*dá ngairinn*' – 'it would bring' – and '*ghaire-de*' – 'no nearer'. The placing of '*ár gcodhnach uile*' – 'our total support' – at the beginning of line three calls attention to it and is followed by the identifying 'the strong-handed one of the race of Eoghan'. An interruption of the rhythm in line four gives prominence to the marks of decline – his veins pierced and his strength gone from him. Kinsella translates '*cuisle*' as 'sinews', but the image of veins pierced is also valid since '*cuisle*' normally means veins or pulse.

> *Cabhair ní ghairfead go gcuirthear mé i gcruinn-chomhrainn –*
> *dar an leabhar dá ngairinn níor ghaire-de an ní dhomh-sa;*
> *ár gcodhnach uile, glac-chumasach shíl Eoghain,*
> *is tollta a chuisle, 'gus d'imigh a bhrí ar feochadh.*

[Help I will not call until they put me in the narrow coffin –
by the book if I were to call it would not be the nearer to me;
our main Lord, powerful hand of the seed of Eoghan,
his veins are pierced, his strength has gone to withering.]

No help I'll call till I'm put in the narrow coffin.
By the Book, it would bring it no nearer if I did!
Our prime strong-handed prop, of the seed of Eoghan
– his sinews are pierced and his vigour is withered up.

The language of stanza two, earlier absorbed by Kinsella in his poem 'The Poet Egan O'Rahilly, Homesick in Old Age' (*Nightwalker and Other Poems*), is visceral: 'There's a hole in my gut, there are foul spikes through my bowels', the land has been ravished by a foreigner. The vivid physical images are complemented by the corresponding losses in the land itself, making Ó Rathaille the voice for a whole countryside. These, he says in emphatic identification, are our land, our shelter, our woods, our beautiful places that have been taken by foreigners. The rivers are appropriately 'muffled'; his tears merge with them.

The Sionainn, the Life, the musical Laoi, are muffled
and the Biorra Dubh river, the Bruice, the Bríd, the Bóinn.
Reddened are Loch Dearg's narrows and the Wave of Tóim
since the Knave has skinned the crowned King in the game.

The Knave is William of Orange, the crowned King is James II, who was defeated at the Battle of the Boyne.

In stanza four he declares '*Mo ghlam is minic*' [my howl is frequent]. The word '*ghlam*' is associated more with animals than with humans and its use here is therefore striking. It prepares for the reference to the Pig of death that is invulnerable to archery and the hidden allusion to Torc waterfall in Killarney since '*torc*' means boar, which in turn echoes the story of the death of Diarmaid, who was killed in the Fian story by a boar on the slopes of Ben Bulben in County Sligo. The immediate reference to Goll (Goll mac Morna, another of the Fian) at the beginning of the following stanza, not present in the translation, adds to the literary connection: the local lord is associated with a mythological hero. The play upon '*Gol*' in line one and '*a ghoile*' in line two is also effective: the once strong leader has had his strength stripped from him: the weaker echo of '*cé gaol*' adds to the idea of loss. There may also be a reference to the Hiberno-English barons who were known as *Gall* (plural *Gaill*), although the word also refers to any foreigner. These compressed allusions are part of the force with which Ó Rathaille describes the general weakening.

At the end of the poem, returning to the personal dramatic mode of the first stanza, he bids farewell to himself. Ironically, the only way he can get land is to be buried in it. Proudly arrogant, he rejects the Jacobite cause. Since Ireland has been 'destroyed', his only comfort is to be buried with the Kings his people have always served. He will entrust himself after death, not to a religious salvation which he does not mention, but to the company of those his people have always served.

> I will stop now – my death is hurrying near
> now the dragons of the Leamhan, Loch Léin and
>   the Laoi are destroyed.
> In the grave with this cherished chief I'll join those kings
> my people served before the death of Christ.

While many *aisling* poems are formal and intricate, '*Úr-Chill an Chreagáin*, The Churchyard of Creagán' (No. 57), composed by Art Mac Cumhaigh (1738–73) as a dialogue between the poet and the fairy woman, is simple and unaffected. She invites him to go with her 'to that honey-sweet land still untouched by alien rule', but he is reluctant to desert his friends and to make his wife sorrowful by leaving her. The fairy woman's response goes to the core of his situation.

> '*Cha shaoilim gur caraid duit a maireann de do*
>   *ghaoltaibh beo,*
> *tá tú faofa, gan earra, bocht earraoideach baoth, gan*
>   *dóigh;*
> *nach mb'fhearr dhuitse imeacht le hainnir na*
>   *maothchrobh meor,*
> *ná an tír so bheith ag fonóid faoi gach rabhán dá ndéan tú*
>   *a cheol?*'

> ['I do not think they are your friends those of your relations
>   who survive,
> you are bare, without goods, poor foolish weakling, without
>   hope;
> would it not be better for you to leave with the slender-
>   fingered girl,

than to be mocked in this land for every verse of music you
make?']

'They're no friends, I would think – your relations that still
remain.
You are naked and lost, a poor fool with no hope or goods.
Would you not better leave with this delicate-fingered girl
than be jeered in your home over every ballad you make?'

The honesty of these exchanges brings the participants to life even
though their dialogue is a contest between enticement and loyalty. When
she explains that she is unhappy because the Gaels of Tír Eoghain are
gone and with them the traditional patronage of poets, the political
implications become clear. In turn he is persuaded to leave: 'better come
to our dwellings, and I by your side each noon,/than John Bull's arrows
endlessly riddling your heart'. His only condition, reminiscent of Aogán
Ó Rathaille's, is that, no matter where he may die, 'bury me under this
sod with Creagán's sweet Gaels'.

The last of the *aisling* poems in the anthology is No. 59, '*Ceo
Draíochta*, A Magic Mist' by Eoghan Rua Ó Súilleabháin (1748–84).
Since the conventions of the genre were known, the poet's efforts were
directed at an aesthetic achievement. While '*Ceo Draíochta*' follows the
conventions, it is distinctive for its technical skill – the music of the
lines, the regular end-rhyme, the easy introduction of dialogue, and the
fluency of its imagery.

> *Ceo draíochta i gcoim oíche do sheol mé*
> *trí thíorthaibh mar óinmhid ar strae,*
> *gan príomhcharaid díograis im chóngar*
> *'s mé i gcríochaibh tar m'eolas i gcéin;*
> *do shíneas go fíorthuirseach deorach*
> *i gcoill chluthair chnómhair liom féin,*
> *ag guíochan chun Rí ghil na glóire*
> *'s gan ní ar bith ach trócaire im béal.*

> [A magic mist in the middle of the night guided me
>   Through countries like a fool astray,
> Without a close devoted friend by my side
>   And I in regions beyond my knowledge far off
> I stretched out in true tearful fatigue
>   In a sheltered, nut-laden wood by myself
> Praying to the bright King of Glory
>   With nothing at all but mercy in my mouth.]

The Irish incorporates simplicity of diction with occasional heightened language. Kinsella's lines also have a natural narrative rhythm.

> Through the deep night a magic mist led me
>   like a simpleton roaming the land,
> no friends of my bosom beside me,
>   an outcast in places unknown.
> I stretched out dejected and tearful
>   in a nut-sheltered wood all alone
> and prayed to the bright King of Glory
>   with 'Mercy!' alone on my lips.

This section of the anthology concludes with extracts from two of the greatest poems of the period '*Caoineadh Airt Uí Laoghaire*, The Lament for Art Ó Laoghaire' (No. 62) and '*Cúirt An Mheán Oíche*, The Midnight Court' (No. 63). The 'Lament', spoken by his widow, Eileen Dhubh Ní Chonaill, grieves for the death of her murdered husband. The manner of expression is that of the traditional keen, a ritual incantatory form of expression by the people. It is a dramatic lyric of extraordinary vividness and power. The main qualities are a lively rhythm, a swift descriptive narrative achieved through a succession of active verbs running in parallel declarations or even exclamations. Kinsella matches all these. In the opening section the speaker draws upon the memory of their life together, including a spirited description of her husband's appearance.

> *Mo chara go daingean tu!*
> *is cuimhin lem aigne*
> *an lá breá earraigh úd,*
> *gur bhreá thíodh hata dhuit*
> *faoi bhanda óir tarraingthe;*
> *claíomh cinn airgid,*
> *lámh dheas chalma,*
> *rompsáil bhagarthach*
> *fir-chritheagla*
> *ar námhaid chealgach*
> *tú i gcóir chun falaracht*
> *is each caol ceannann fút.*
> *D'umhlaídís Sasanaigh*
> *síos go talamh duit,*
> *is ní ar mhaite leat*
> *ach le haon-chorp eagla,*
> *cé gur leo a cailleadh tu,*
> *a mhuirnín mh'anama...*

[My firm friend!
my mind recalls
that fine Spring day,
how well your hat suited you
with the taut gold band;
sword silver-hilted,
right hand steady,
threatening gait–
the fearful trembling
of venomous enemies–
you getting ready to ride,
your slender, white-faced horse under you.
The English abased themselves
down to the ground for you,
and not for your good
but out of deadly fear,
although through them you were lost
my soul's beloved...]

My steadfast friend!
It comes to my mind
that fine Spring day
how well your hat looked
with the drawn gold band,
the sword silver-hilted,
your fine brave hand
and menacing prance,
and the fearful tremble
of treacherous enemies.
You were set to ride
your slim white-faced steed
and Saxons saluted
down to the ground,
not from good will
but by dint of fear
– though you died at their hands,
my soul's beloved...

Kinsella's lines capture the haughty aristocratic tone, her contempt for the English, as well as the sprightly and changing rhythms of the original. The poem is wonderfully dynamic with a kind of inner strength in the language that transforms the occasion of grief to one of panegyric and loving recall.

A later section declares in a telling association of man and territory that the district associated with the Ó Laoghaire family will blaze up in grief.

> *Mo chara is mo lao thu!*
> *A Airt Uí Laoghaire*
> *Mhic Conchúir, Mhic Céadaigh,*
> *Mhic Laoisigh Uí Laoghaire,*
> *aniar ón nGaortha*
> *is anoir ón gCaolchnoc,*
> *mar a bhfásaid caora*
> *is cnó buí ar ghéagaibh*
> *is úlla 'na slaodaibh*
> *'na n-am féinig.*
> *Cárbh ionadh le héinne*
> *dá lasadh Uíbh Laoghaire*
> *agus Béal Átha an Ghaorthaigh*
> *is an Gúgán naofa*
> *i ndiaidh mharcaigh na ré-ghlac...*

> [Friend and my calf you are!
> O Art Ó Laoghaire
> son of Conchúr son of Céadach,
> son of Laoiseach Ó Laoghaire,
> West from the Gaortha
> East from Caolchnoc,
> where berries grow
> yellow nuts on branches
> and apples in plenty,
> all in their seasons.
> What wonder to anyone
> should Uíbh Laoghaire alight
> and Ballingeary
> and blessed Gugán
> for the strong-handed rider...]

> My friend and my calf!
> O Art Ó Laoghaire
> son of Conchúr son of Céadach
> son of Laoiseach Ó Laoghaire:
> West from the Gaortha
> and East from the Caolchnoc
> where the berries grow,

> yellow nuts on the branches
> and masses of apples
> in their proper season
> – need anyone wonder
> if Uíbh Laoghaire alight
> and Béal Átha an Ghaorthaigh
> and Gúgán the holy
> for the fine-handed rider...

The main quality of the elegy is dramatic: the drama of changing responses, of a mind and spirit racing through emotions, the expression of heightened memory, the many different feelings all realized with verve and personal passion. The humanity of the poem is evident as are the disciplined language and its stylized achievement. Above all, the characterization of the speaker is vividly realized – proud, independent, histrionic, with passionate urgency in her speech which is delivered with such speed that the normal syntactical transitions are omitted, and spoken with such panache that the dead man becomes an image of Irish heroism that survives deprivation and the English upstarts, their cowed manhood and mean ways. In the process Eileen herself becomes more than ordinary. In a sense she takes over the male role of her husband, stands firm as he had against the English, speaks in a superior manner that matches his proud, even reckless, refusals to yield to their unjust laws. Given his behaviour, his death was always likely and she counters its arrival with a rushing of spirited responses. In the process he is revivified, recreated in her imagination; her words transcend the ugliness of his death and make him live forever. In fact it is a good love poem. Towards the end she declares the power of nature to survive death, but the real transmutation comes in the transforming intensity of her language, where the poem's true originality lies.

Written in 1780, Brian Merriman's '*Cúirt an Mheán Oíche*, The Midnight Court', consisting of a prologue, three dramatic monologues, and an epilogue, is a comic work, bursting with energy. The prologue is a parody of the *aisling*: the poet is visited by a *spéirbhean* (a vision woman) of extraordinary ugliness who drags him off to a midnight Court presided over by *Aoibheall*, a fairy-queen. The issue to be debated is why young men do not marry, since the result is sexual frustration for young women and a decline in population. The debate is conducted in outrageous, vituperative language. The first speaker complains that she has been unable to attract a husband, despite her best efforts to be seen in public and to participate in social gatherings. Furthermore, she has employed all the folk remedies. In her account we hear the rollicking four stressed lines that carry the poem forward.

Níorbh áil liom codladh go socair aon uair díobh
gan lán mo stoca de thorthaibh fém chluasa,
is deimhin nárbh obair liom troscadh le cráifeacht,
is greim ná blogam ní shlogainn trí trátha;
in aghaidh na srotha do thomainn mo léine
ag súil trím chodladh le cogar óm chéile;
is minic do chuaigh mé ag scuabadh ón stáca,
m'ingne is gruaig fán luaithghríos d'fhágainn,
chuirinn an tsúist fá chúl na gaibhle,
chuirinn an ramhan go ciúin fán adhart chúgham...

[I could not settle to sleep at any time
without the full of my stocking of fruit under my ears,
for certain it was no trouble to me to fast with devotion
and bite or mouthful I wouldn't swallow for three days;
in the face of the stream I'd dip my shirt
in the hope in my sleep of a whisper from my spouse;
'tis often I went sweeping from the stack,
my nails and hair I would leave beneath the hot ashes,
I would place the flail back of the fork,
I would place the spade quietly to me under the pillow...]

I never could settle me down to sleep
without fruit in a sock beneath my ear;
I found it no trouble to fast devoutly
three vigils I'd swallow no bite or sup;
I'd rinse my shift against the stream
for a whisper in dream from my future spouse;
many a time I have swept the corn-stack,
I've left my nails and my hair in the ash,
I'd place the flail behind the fork
and peacefully under my pillow, a spade...

But an old man will have none of this. First he belittles her background, parentage, notions of station and sexual innocence, then relates his own unhappy experience of marriage. He was duped by a clever woman who gave birth to a child long before it might be expected and, to add insult to injury, women, aiding and abetting her in deception, pretended to see resemblances to him in the child.

Cheapadar cruinn gur shíolra' an dúchas
maise mo ghnaoi agus íor mo ghnúise,
feilleadh mo shrón is lónradh m'éadain,

deiseacht mo chló, mo shnó is m'fhéachaint,
leagadh mo shúl is fiú mo gháire
is as sin do shiúil ó chúl go sála é!

[They reckoned for sure his heritage grew
from the beauty of my face and the resplendence,
of my forehead, nose and face,
the grace of my form, my complexion and my appearance,
the set of my eyes and even my laugh
in that way from head to heel they traced him!]

They judged for certain his nature sprang
from the cut of my face and handsome features,
the turn of my nose, my gleaming brow,
my elegant mould, my hue and appearance,
the set of my eyes, and my smile, indeed
– from heel to head they traced it all!

In the third monologue, one of the best sections in the poem, a young woman scorns the pitiful sexual performance of the old man. In her view, vigorous young men and well-fed priests in particular should be drafted into marriage. It is the obvious remedy for men failing to marry until they are old and withered and a practical solution to the falling population. Countering the old man's comments on her poor circumstances, she explains that it was the woman he married who was deceived by his promises of 'warmth and shelter'.

cothrom glan is ba le crú dhi
is codladh fada ar leabain chlúimh dhi,
teallaí teo is móin a daoithin,
ballaí fód gan leoithne gaoithe,
fothain is díon ón síon 's ón spéir dhi
is olann is líon le sníomh chun éadaigh.

[fair treatment and cows to be milked
long sleeping on a feather bed,
warm hearths and plenty of turf,
walls of sod without a draught,
shelter and cover from weather and sky
and wool and flax for spinning clothes.]

honest dealing, and cows to milk,
and sleeping late in a feather bed,

      blazing hearths and turf in plenty,
      earthen walls without a draught,
      roof and protection from weather and sky
      and flax and wool to spin for clothing.

But the worst betrayal is his sexual inadequacy. The playful bawdy of the poem is unmistakable in these lines. For the girl is capable of vigorous action

      Ní labharfadh focal dá mb'obair an oíche
      is thabharfadh cothrom do stollaire bríomhar'
      go brách ar siúl nár dhiúltaigh riamh é
      ar chnámh a cúil 's a súile iata.

      [she would not say a word about the work of a night
      and would give equal to a vigorous worker,
      forever as she goes she never refused it
      on the bone of her back with her eyes shut.]

      she'd never complain at a night of work
      but give a brave slasher as good as she got.
      She'd never refuse, any time or place,
      on bone of her back with her eyes shut tight...

The poem is an example of the comic imagination in full flight as it matches one passionate utterance against another and in the process satirizes a community where vigorous sexual pleasure is missing and where the social consequences are considerable. The argument that lusty young men and well-nourished priests ought to be made to marry makes sense in that context and at the same time is a credible thrust against clergy and celibacy. But there are as well notes of let-down and betrayal in the realistic portrait of disappointed partners. One of the achievements of the determined realism and the dramatic presence of particular voices is the sense of personal passion. These, one feels, are not abstract figures but real presences in a community under stress. The attack is spirited, the jaunty pace has a personal sting, and loveless marriages are shown to be a disaster. At the same time, as in many successful works of art, the rage and regret are expressed with such delightful verve and such linguistic play that the aesthetic success of the poem overrides its polemic.

The third section of *An Duanaire* is devoted to 'Filíocht Na
nDaoine/Folk Poetry', which, as Thomas Kinsella points out in a note
in *The New Oxford Book of Irish Verse*, is one of the great riches of Irish
tradition 'in its store of songs of every kind and arising from every
occasion: love-songs and laments, political party-songs and satires,
religious incantations, maledictions, comic narratives...many prayers
and charms, and many great art songs sung in the *sean nós*, or "old-
style"'.³ Unusually, within the contexts of European poetry, men
compose many of the love-songs. They tend to be effusive and eulogistic,
using the rhetoric of praise-poems. "*S í bláth geal na sméar í*, She's the
blackberry-flower' (No. 69), has a simple, unqualified fervour. Kinsella
captures these qualities in a kind of lilting enthusiasm that expresses the
man's declaration of praise in terms of summer-time fecundity.

> 'S í bláth geal na sméar í,
> 's í bláth deas na sú craobh í,
> 's í planda b'fhearr méin mhaith
> le hamharc do shúl;
> 's í mo chuisle, 's í mo rún í,
> 's í bláth na n-úll gcumhra í,
> is samhradh ins an fhuacht í
> idir Nollaig is Cáisc.

> [She is the bright flower of the blackberry,
> she is the lovely flower on the raspberry branch,
> she is the plant of best quality disposition
> to be seen by your eyes;
> she is my beloved, she is my darling,
> she is the flower of the sweet-smelling apple,
> she is summer when it is cold
> between Christmas and Easter.]

> She's the blackberry-flower,
> the fine raspberry-flower,
> she's the plant of best breeding
>   your eyes could behold:
> she's my darling and dear,
> my fresh apple-tree flower,
> she is Summer in the cold
>   between Christmas and Easter.

The uncomplicated feeling is part of the poem's manner. Nature is read as a reflection not only of the woman's beauty but of his feeling for her. '*Nach aoibhinn do na héiníní*, It is well for small birds' (No. 70), has a similar attitude. Its two stanzas again draw upon the natural world, comparing the companionship of the birds with the separation between the man and the woman, praising her beauty because it surpasses the beauty of nature, going on to ever more extravagant idealization, and ending abruptly, as though that expression itself makes him feel anew the pain of the separation.

> *Nach aoibhinn do na héiníní a éiríos go hard*
> *'s bhíos ag ceiliúr lena chéile ar aon chraobh amháin,*
> *ní mar sin dom féin is dom chéad míle grá,*
> *is fada óna chéile bhíos ár n-éirí gach lá.*

> *Is báine í ná an lile, is deise í ná an scéimh,*
> *is binne í ná an veidhlín, 's is soilsí ná an ghréin;*
> *is fearr ná sin uile a huaisleacht 's a méin,*
> *'s a Dhé atá ins na flaitheasaibh, fuascail dom phéin.*

> [It is delightful for the little birds that rise so high
> and are singing together on the one bough,
> it is not like that with me and my hundred thousand love,
> it is far from each other our rising each day.

> She is whiter than the lily, she is more beautiful than Beauty,
> she is sweeter than the violin, she is brighter than the sun;
> better than all these is the nobility of her mind,
> and O God who art in Heaven, deliver me from my pain.]

The music of the Irish cannot be reproduced nor can the easy flow of the voice, but Kinsella gets close to the unforced naturalness of the language and uses the same simple metaphors.

> It is well for small birds that can rise up on high
> and warble away on the one branch together.
> Not so with myself and my millionfold love
> that so far from each other must rise every day.

> She's more white than the lily and lovely past Beauty,
> more sweet than the violin, more bright than the sun,
> with a mind and refinement surpassing all these...
> O God in Your Heaven give ease to my pain!

'*Caiseal Mumhan*, Caiseal in Munster' (No. 72) is a lovely expression of love, passion and grief at separation. Its simplicity and directness is captured well in the translation. Its opening declaration of love is characteristic of the poem's verve and control; the end–rhyme in each stanza and a light-footed liveliness of rhythm accommodate its emotional fluidity.

> *Phósfainn thú gan bha gan phunt gan áireamh spré,*
> *agus phógfainn thú maidin drúchta le bánú an lae.*
> *'S é mo ghalar dubhach gan mé is tú, a dhianghrá mo chléibh,*
> *i gCaiseal Mumhan is gan de leaba fúinn ach clár bog déil.*

> [I would marry you without cattle without pounds without a reckoned dowry,
> and I would kiss you on a dewy morning at the brightening of day.
> It is my dark sickness that you and I are not, steadfast love of my breast,
> in Caiseal of Munster and without a bed under us but a bog-deal board.]

Kinsella is loyal to these values in the language, tone and rhythm.

> I would wed you without cattle, without money or a counted dowry.
> I would kiss you on a dewy morning in the lightening day.
> Sad sickness I am not beside you, dear love of my breast,
> in Caiseal in Munster let our bed be but a bog-deal board.

Stanza two offers a form of earthly paradise, which is appropriate to the couples' non-calculating love: the streams and the birds will be their neighbours. Stanza three promises love and devotion and anticipates their marriage day, ending with the heartfelt declaration that he would die of grief if he saw her with someone else.

The beauty of this and other love-lyrics is that they say so much without refinement or coquetry, without qualification or doubt, without self-consciousness, and in all of that echo the experience of lovers everywhere. Their purity of tone is a testament to the possibility of unambiguous transforming love and the ideals of relationship and circumstance. '*Coillte Glasa an Triúcha*, The Green Woods of Triúcha' (No. 73) issues an invitation to go to a place of love and beauty, an idealized landscape suitable for love, a form of pastoral in which there is neither sin nor death. No. 74, '*Ceann dubh dílis*, 'My own dark head', is a tender expression of deep feeling for his beloved. In No. 76, '*Mo bhrón ar an bhfarraige*, My grief on the ocean', the woman considers the vastness that keeps her lover and herself apart. She must remain at home, forever, but she replaces images of distance and division with images of them together in Ireland or on board ship or in the natural world. That she can create this fiction and its realization makes us appreciate the forlorn state in which she must exist. The poem is beautifully simple and unadorned, with a genuine intimacy in which the woman's plight is brought dramatically alive.

Kinsella feels at home with these folk songs, which are more in tune in their diction with his own unadorned language and his tendency to be restrained in its use. They are closer to his natural manner than the elaborate and exaggerated language of the *aisling* poems. He handles, for example, '*Donall Óg*, Dónall Óg/Young Dónall' (No. 77), with great control; it is a narrative and descriptive poem that uses much of the conventional imagery of the folk poems about love – the appeal to nature, promises made but not fulfilled, seduction and loss, the woman's poignant speech. The last stanza summarizes her state.

Do bhainis soir díom is do bhainis siar díom,
do bhainis romham is do bhainis im dhiaidh díom,
do bhainis gealach is do bhainis grian díom,
's is ro-mhór m'eagla gur bhainis Dia díom.

[You've taken the East from me and you've taken the West from me,
you've taken the before and you've taken the after from me,
you've taken the moon and you've taken the sun from me,
and it is my great fear that you've taken God from me.]

You took my East and you took my West,
you took before and after from me,
you took the moon and you took the sun,
and I greatly fear that you took my God.

The woman's intense feelings of abandonment are conveyed in terms of total loss, including spiritual loss. It is the traditional story of the woman who loved not wisely but too well, and who has been betrayed. The image of the deceived girl appears over and over in these lyrics. Men make extravagant promises, women listen and believe, only to discover the man has gone. In the course of her story, told with specific detail, her character comes through – spirited, trusting, alert to her feelings, one who followed her heart not her mother's advice nor her own conscience. The rhythms of the poem reflect the rhythms of her thought and feeling.

The title, '*Róisín Dubh*, Róisín Dubh/Little Black Rose' (No. 84), is a pseudonym for Ireland; the poem is therefore a political allegory but based, as Kinsella notes, on an older love-lyric. A well-known political song, it remains charged with the intimate tone associated with a more personal poem. The stately quality of the Irish is hard to capture. Kinsella reproduces the rhythms but some of his language lacks the simple strength of the Irish. In the first stanza, for example, '*ná bíodh brón ort*' (do not be sad) is not matched by 'have no sorrow' nor '*fár éirigh duit*' (because of what has happened to you) by 'for all that has happened to you'. There is more movement in '*tá na bráithre ag dul ar sáile is iad ag triall ar muir*' than in 'the Friars are out on the brine, they are travelling the sea'. The archaic 'brine' sounds affected; '*ar sáile*' simply translates as 'on the sea'. The phrase '*ag triall*' means to journey or to travel, but also to proceed to or to attempt. Kinsella's 'travelling' is adequate, but for the purposes of reflecting intention or effort, less effective than it might be. The syntactical awkwardness in the third line removes the more positive effect of the direct statement in the original. Strangely, the fourth line changes the general pronoun of the Irish to the more limited 'we won't spare'.

> *A Róisín ná bíodh brón ort fár éirigh duit—*
> *tá na bráithre ag dul ar sáile is iad ag triall ar muir,*
> *tiocfaidh do phardún ón bPápa is ón Róimh anoir*
> *is ní spáráilfear fion Spáinneach ar mo Róisín Dubh.*

[Róisín, do not be sad for what has happened to you?
the Friars are going on the sea and they are travelling the ocean,
your pardon will come from the Pope and from Rome in the East
and Spanish wine will not be spared for my Róisín Dubh.]

Róisín, have no sorrow for all that has happened you:
the Friars are out on the brine, they are travelling the sea,
your pardon from the Pope will come, from Rome in the East,
and we won't spare the Spanish wine for my Róisín Dubh.

The poem is distinguished by its delicate interface between love and politics, political allegiance and amatory response, the voice of the speaker poised between the two. Kinsella sustains this nicely. The idealizing final stanza alters the earthly paradise of the love poem by making it into a metaphor for revolution.

> *Beidh an Éirne 'na tuilte tréana is réabfar cnoic,*
> *beidh an fharraige 'na tonnta dearga is an spéir 'na fuil,*
> *beidh gach gleann sléibhe ar fud Éireann is móinte ar crith,*
> *lá éigin sul a n-éagfaidh mo Róisín Dubh.*

[The Erne will be in powerful floods and hills will be shattered,
the sea will be in red waves and the sky in blood,
every mountain glen and bog throughout Ireland will tremble
one day before she will die, my Róisín Dubh.]

The Erne will be strong in flood, the hills be torn,
the ocean be all red waves, the sky all blood,
every mountain valley and bog in Ireland will shake
one day, before she shall perish, my Róisín Dubh.

The Irish has a turbulence of sound and rhythm that supports the assertions and is difficult to emulate in English.

'*Droimeann donn dílis*, My dear Droimeann Donn' (No. 85), another pseudonym for Ireland, is less demanding. This time the voice is that of Ireland lamenting her state – bereft of land and home, music, wine, princes, scholars, soldiers. In response the poet begs for the chance to fight and to show his patriotic commitment. In '*Cill Chais*, Cill Chais/ Kilcash' (No. 90), the stately movement of the Irish is repeated in the translation. The poem is a lament for the passing of a house of the Butler family through a succession of images of loss and with a final hapless wish for restoration and has a resonance greater than many other poems in the anthology.

> *Cad a dhéanfaimid feasta gan adhmad?*
> *Tá deireadh na gcoillte ar lár;*
> *níl trácht ar Chill Chais ná ar a teaghlach*
> *is ní bainfear a cling go bráth.*
> *An áit úd a gcónaíodh an deighbhean*
> *fuair gradam is meidhir thar mhnáibh,*
> *bhíodh iarlaí ag tarraingt tar toinn ann*
> *is an t-aifreann binn á rá.*

[What shall we do from now on for timber?
The last of the woods is down;
there's no mention of Cill Chais or of its family
and its bell will not be pulled forever.
That place where lived the good woman
found honour and gaiety over women,
earls used to travel there across the sea
and the sweet Mass was said.]

Now what will we do for timber,
with the last of the woods laid low?
There's no talk of Cill Chais or its household

and its bell will be struck no more.
That dwelling where lived the good lady
most honoured and joyous of women
—earls made their way over wave there
and the sweet Mass once was said.

An Duanaire does not try to illustrate the full range of Irish poetry in
its period. In the seventeenth century alone, despite the unsettled state
of the country, there was a vast amount of literary and scribal activity
and strong links with the European continent. In addition to praise
poems, a survival from the panegyrics of the bardic period, there was an
abundance of moral and religious verse, some of which sprang from the
counter-reformation movement; there were poems in the *amour courtois*
manner, poetical disputations, poems of exile, satires, and a number of
long political poems between 1630 and 1660 that responded to such
matters as the butcheries of Oliver Cromwell's campaign, 1648–53, and
the religious disabilities imposed on Catholics. There is also a large
amount of poetry in manuscript. While the picture of Irish poetry in *An
Duanaire* is partial and incomplete, the anthology in Part I provides
substantial evidence of the nature and quality of the Irish poetic tradition
in its chosen period from the subtle casuistry of the love-poetry, the
fervour of the religious lyrics to the Fenian poetry with its appreciation
of the natural world. Part II illustrates the highly wrought poems of
Séathrún Céitinn and Dáibhí Ó Bruadair, the generous sensibility of the
blind Séamas Dall Mac Cuarta, and the bleak world of Aogán Ó
Rathaille in which two centuries of cultural displacement and personal
dispossession come to a bitter conclusion. In Ó Bruadair and Ó Rathaille,
Art Mac Cumhaigh, and Eoghan Rua Ó Suilleabháin the genre of the
aisling comes to its highest achievement and begins its decline into empty
formulation, but not before its intricate, ornamented techniques could be
deployed and the realities of human decline could be indelibly inscribed
on our minds. No anthology of Irish poetry could omit the contrasting
achievements of 'The Lament for Art Ó Laoghaire' and 'The Midnight
Court', the one a high-spirited elegy for the death of an Irish soldier, the
other with its mocking echoes of the *aisling*, an uproarious comic
response to human disappointment that seems to speak from the
desolation of failed sexual relationships in a community under stress.
While the work of poets like Ó Bruadair and Ó Rathaille is well wrought,
the folk poetry has freshness, simplicity and openness. Throughout the
period, in all three sections of the anthology, the note of lament occurs
so that the lament for Cill Chais echoes across the years to the upheavals
of the sixteenth and seventeenth centuries. Kinsella's translations make
all this, and more, available. He links the present to the past, reaches

across the cultural and linguistic divide, and creates living and vibrant connections between one language and the other. It is a side of his work not always given the credit it merits.

Notes

1   *An Duanaire. 1600–1900: Poems of the Dispossessed*, ed. Seán Ó Tuama, trans. Thomas Kinsella (Dublin: Dolmen Press with Bord na Gaeilge, 1981; reprinted 1994). References are to the number of each poem cited, not page number. The use of capitals in titles cited may often appear inconsistent, but follows the style in *An Duanaire*'s 'Contents'. Unlike the 'Contents', however, titles are given first in Irish, in italics, and then in their English translation. A similar sequence is practised in citing translations: first the Irish text, in italics, then my literal translation placed within square brackets, followed by Thomas Kinsella's translation in *An Duanaire*.
2   In *Repossessions* (Cork: Cork University Press, 1995), Seán Ó Tuama has drawn together the available biographical material about Ó Rathaille and related it to the poetry. See Chapter 7, 'The World of Aogán Ó Rathaille'.
3   (Oxford: Oxford University Press, 1986), p.404.

Part IV
TALES OF THE DISPOSSESSED

One Fond Embrace, 1988
Personal Places, 1990
Poems from Centre City, 1990
Madonna and Other Poems, 1991
Open Court, 1991
The Pen Shop, 1997
The Familiar, 1999
Godhead, 1999
Citizen of the World, 2000
Littlebody, 2000
Marginal Economy, 2006
Man of War, 2007
Belief and Unbelief, 2007

INTRODUCTION

One Fond Embrace together with *Open Court* provides a frame for the reflections on society and the role of the artist that are substantial themes in *Personal Places*, *Poems from Centre City*, and *Madonna and Other Poems*. As *One Fond Embrace* declares, the part of Dublin where Kinsella lives also harbours the 'rodent element'. On the one hand the poem exemplifies his belief that evildoers should be denounced and on the other shows that its satirical edge has been ameliorated by compassion. *Open Court*, a retrospective portrait of the 1950s, is similarly affected.

In *Personal Places*, a mysterious Stranger is a menacing harbinger. Associated with foreboding, ill luck and death, he haunts the environs of Percy Place where Kinsella lives, and subsumes all the other threatening figures in this collection and the following one. The threat, which is subliminal in some poems and embodied in administrator, priest and speculator, culminates in *Personal Places* but is more clearly focused in the figure of Aogán Ó Rathaille, who stands at the ocean's edge looking out into the ultimate point of meaninglessness. The transition from the dark stranger with his Jungian connotations to this declaration defines the bleakness of Kinsella's outlook. In the past he gave limited credence to Teilhard de Chardin's concept of evolution towards an Omega point, later he derived support from Jung's theories, now he contemplates the idea of nothingness in its fullest significance.

The idea, already identified in *Her Vertical Smile*, pertains with particular force to the modern artist. Alienated from Church and State, where he finds no system of supportive beliefs, and socially disaffected, he has to discover values that work for him. Since, Kinsella believes, we exist in isolation and do not communicate with one another, he speaks to a projection of himself, as in 'At the Head Table', or through the voices of others, who include Aogán Ó Rathaille, Oliver Goldsmith, St Augustine and Marcus Aurelius. The scales of justice weigh the value of the good man: Valentin Iremonger, who suffered personal tragedy, and Aogán Ó Rathaille, who matched personal chaos with the external turmoil of the ocean, a feat of compelling imaginative achievement.

How the poet conducts himself is crucial. When in 'The Back Lane' (*Poems from Centre City*) he goes from his workroom to the place of impoverishment and death, he prays for the right tools so that he can engage with the particulars of place. The analogy is with Dante, the chosen model, whose condemnation of the citizens of Florence parallels Kinsella's response to the inhabitants of his native city. The evidence of barbarous mentality and aesthetic indifference surrounds him. Even more fundamental is his own opinion of human beings who are, he says, 'a worthless and objectionable form of life. I don't see that it is possible, or even desirable, to redeem such a thing.'¹ Nevertheless, beauty may be found in even these unlikely contexts. 'At the Head Table' (*Madonna and Other Poems*) describes the perfect work of art and the ideal audience.

In her various roles the woman companion is the necessary presence. The idea animates *Madonna and Other Poems* where the union of husband and wife is celebrated in a modest ritual. The appraisal includes not only social irritations but the momentous meeting with Eleanor Walsh which *The Familiar* celebrates for its sexual, mythological and personal associations. At the heart of this analysis is the acknowledgement of initial difficulties because of their different temperaments and personalities, but they find a closeness that absorbs and transcends differences. Their breakfast ritual affirms an enduring flexibility.

That human ceremony contrasts with the appraisal of *Godhead*. Whereas the human relationship is imbued with feeling, the Divine is cold. God the Father is passive, His work finished but inadequate. Far from being a guarantee of Redemption, the Incarnation is a violation of the woman, an experience of meaninglessness akin to Ó Rahaille's. The absence of a Divine power, while depriving the poet of a central faith, is no excuse for defeatism. Both the human and the Divine are alike in that both know what it is 'to grasp completely/while remaining partly incapable'. Inadequacy characterizes both of them. Redemption has failed. Christ on the Cross is a figure of abandonment. In the poem's dialogue between the poet and the Father, God insists that the poet should proclaim the inescapable reality that people die, death being the ultimate inadequacy.

Nevertheless, the poet has to cope not only with isolation and mortality but with public misunderstanding and indifference. Oliver Goldsmith's concern in *Citizen of the World* with the neglect of Alexander Pope, who was refused burial in Poets' Corner, mirrors his own feeling of isolation. In *The London Journal*, Boswell wavers between optimism and depression. These usages are exemplary. A writer has to contend with disabling forces in the world; he may be neglected and reviled but that is no excuse for failing to deal with what he observes. In *The Pen Shop* the poet walks through the place of the dead, and, as he records what he sees, the city comes to life. *Littlebody* discloses the poet's delight in the natural world. He accepts nothingness, faces the void and celebrates what can be celebrated. The flight of midges suggests the possibilities of the imagination.

In a nightmare situation Kinsella turns to allegory in *Marginal Economy* to illustrate his philosophical position. There must be no complacent trust in the 'Word', no wishy-washy feeling that redemption will come from outside ourselves. The world is a comfortless place; it is not going to be made better through Divine intervention. Made inadequate by a baffled view of life, a temperamental division between military engagement and philosophical reflection, Marcus Aurelius floundered between action and inaction. Conor Cruise O'Brien could not comprehend that Irish poetic tradition is made up of work in two languages. The quality of Kinsella's position may be gauged in the exact manner of observation in 'Wedding Scrvicc', as in the deliberate excess of 'Blood of the Innocent'. Being on the margin has an aesthetic and a psychological aspect, which concerns the use of language and the capacity of the individual to cope with life. Man is inadequate. We live in 'soiled survival', in a state of minimal expectancy, doing the best we can. The poet's responsibility is to write on the basis of truth perceived and to do so without distortion or self-deception. People work with increasing difficulty at the outer edge; their meagre achievement exactly measured.

Man of War reflects on man's capacity for self-annihilation. It alternates between graphic depictions of violence, ironic argument and disappointment that man's advance from primitive forms of society to sophisticated systems of government did not result in humane and rational ways in which to deal with the causes of war.

Belief and Unbelief, on the other hand, returns to measured assessment in which the aptitudes of the death moth in 'Novice' – 'Designed for its exact needs' – is an aesthetic manifested through the entire collection.

The tenor of Kinsella's appraisal is heard in epigraphs, injunctions, definitions and careful organization – the pairing of collections, the examination and re-examination of basic issues, and the presence of a key poem in each collection. There are pairs of butterflies, ravens and crows; a figure at the ocean's edge in Ireland and a figure at the ocean's edge in America; the poet's workroom and the world of waste; the poet and the mysterious other; greedy speculators and rapacious women; Divine and human imperfection; the ugliness of the city and the beauty of nature; the breakfast ritual in one collection and the same ritual in another. Pairing is endemic.

Note

1   Badin, *Thomas Kinsella*, p.191.

8

A LOCAL WATCHFULNESS

In the omission of Jesus Christ and his beloved disciple John from Michelangelo's 'The Last Supper', which he chose as a cover illustration for *One Fond Embrace*, Kinsella signals the failings that underlie modern Irish life. A version of the poem was published in 1981 in a limited edition, its time of composition indicated by the quotation from Diderot's letter to Voltaire quoted in the introduction to *A Technical Supplement*. *One Fond Embrace* begins in a relaxed and appreciative mood, seasoned with humour, including the play on affectionate and foolish in 'Fond', as Kinsella takes time off from more serious work, and embraces his home in Percy Place. It is a personal place, 'hearth and home', where children have grown and he is content. However, the circumstances are inauspicious. The district is 'sagging'; it has its faded colonials, upstarts, Catholic Actionists, smug do–gooders and the 'rodent element', speculators, irresponsible architects and Corporation officials who have turned Dublin into a zoo.

> Invisible speculators, urinal architects,
> and the Corporation flourishing their approvals
> in potent compliant dance;
>
> planners of the wiped slate
> labouring painstaking over a bungled city
> to turn it into a zoo...(274)

They have built 'twinned experimental/concrete piss-towers for the underprivileged'. The reference is to apartment towers erected at Ballymun to house the poor whom they have moved out to the margin, to an alien environment, away from their personal places; but the apartment towers are unsuitable and so neglected that they have deteriorated into slums. The City Fathers, in their ignorance, have also destroyed a Viking site to make room for an office block and car park. As this evidence accumulates the poet's mood changes, his enjoyment so soured by what has been done to his city that he lashes out at the officials – 'May their sewers blast under them!' – and is disgusted by the presence of sleaze – 'Dirty money gives dirty access.'

He wants to throw down his pen in disgust but in a change of rhythm and tone salutes the world of nature with lyrical enthusiasm – bright gulls, magpie, maggot, the fat spider, the ash tree – 'Fellow citizens!' whom he embraces for their 'natural behaviour!' He then invites 'friends and others' to his table for a last supper, a secular communion. Appraising them in a mock epic catalogue, he evaluates each in turn: you 'employing tedium to persuade', you 'the loser in every struggle', you 'silenced us with your skills in analysis/excited us with your direct methods'. Except for speculators, city officials and gutless clerics, these are minor instances of human behaviour; association and compassion soften the satire: they and the poet 'are all participants/in a process that requires waste'.

Sometimes the details, although scrambled to avoid identification, reveal recognizable people: Seán Ó Riada, because Kinsella uses language already associated with him; Edna Longley, who failed to appreciate the organic nature of his poetry; Charles Haughey, who reappears in the language of 'Nightwalker'; John Hewitt, for his adherence to pentameter; or Conor Cruise O'Brien for his 'Redmonite bafflement' at what was happening in Northern Ireland. The poet takes a swipe at a critic who operates within the bounds of particular approaches. 'Work not amenable to those procedures/does not call for consideration.' That leaves Kinsella out of the reckoning. In its earlier version the language was more vitriolic, the anger more splenetic, particularly when the poem took in the polluting effects of industrialization on the countryside. Ireland had become 'the latrine of the western world'. It is an easy transition from that echo of J.M. Synge's *The Playboy of the Western World* to a Swiftian proposal for the extermination of 'Everything West of the Shannon'. Behind this sarcasm lies the fact that Irish culture, which Kinsella has valued and which had endured in the western regions, has been allowed to deteriorate. He pretends to excuse what politicians have done with the reminder that 'we are dealing with the slow to learn' whose fathers 'fought the wrong civil war', attacking one another when they should have combined to fight the British in Northern Ireland. The prayer to a Church positioned between compliant Catholics and intractable Protestants is equally ironic, piety in both taking the place of religious integrity. Kinsella's portrait of his contemporaries, while often critical, views them within time's consuming advance and within the unavoidable presence of waste.

Through its metaphor of stone absorbing the heat of the sun, the epigraph to *Personal Places* affirms the interactive relationship between place and person.

> There are established personal places
> that receive our lives' heat
> and adapt in their mass, like stone.
>
> These absorb in their changes
> the radiance of change in us,
> and give it back
>
> to the darkness of our understanding,
> directionless
> into the returning cold. (283)

The kind of intense interchange that Kinsella defines is a recurrent trope in these two collections – in his response to social injustice or moral weakness, in the reaction of Aogán Ó Rathaille to internal chaos, in the required response of the ideal reader to the ideal work of art, or in the incestuous fantasies in a hospital. It is present in a more relaxed form in the portraits of contemporaries in *One Fond Embrace* and *Open Court*. The brooding observer is another aspect of this two-way assimilative process.

Although not situated in Dublin 'Apostle of Hope', the introductory poem, depicts a symbolic 'sick place'. The town is Wilkes Barre, Pennsylvania, but with images drawn from the presence of British troops in Northern Ireland. Peopled by waifs 'in the silence of the stunned' and characterized by 'waste', it represents the moral vacuum of urban life. The figure elevated above it by 'local enterprise' is the defining, tasteless metaphor for these poems about the ugliness and moral decline in urban life.

> Above all, lifted on high,
> enlarged by local enterprise,
> Man the Measure cruciforked
> upon His wheel, jacked up erect,
> splayed like a target against the grey,
> smooth as an ad. Grossness uprisen.
> Godforsaken.
>   Forgive. Forgive. (284)

The violence of the language – 'lifted', 'enlarged', 'cruciforked', 'jacked up', 'splayed like a target' – highlights the violation. The poem is outspoken, its title fiercely ironic: an advertising hoarding that abuses Leonardo da Vinci's idealized drawing of the human figure proclaims the new religion. The god of commerce is the false redeemer. The fifteen-foot-high figure above the rooftops, bolted like a target to a frame of girders, demeans the redemptive message of Christ on the Cross. It replaces the Vitruvian/Renaissance ideal in which Man was indeed the Measure. The appropriate response, Kinsella insists, to such a distortion of values is hatred, not the forgiveness that Christ prayed for.

In the background of several of these poems lie immediate issues – two plans by Dublin Corporation, one to build social housing to the rear of Percy Place and to expand the roadway along the front. The Kinsellas and others formed the Huband Bridge Neighbourhood Association to resist the scheme. The Corporation's other plan to build an office block on a Viking site resulted in the formation of the Friends of Medieval Dublin to which Kinsella belonged. In October 1978, 20,000 protesters challenged that decision; they seized Wood Quay and for a month prevented the bulldozers from entering. Their aim was to delay construction so that archaeologists could do their work. In opposing the mechanical power of the crane with the mental force of those who are protesting, Kinsella in 'Night Conference, Wood Quay: 6 June 1979', encapsulates his opposition to such practices. Its closing lines equate what officials are doing with what Viking plunderers have done: 'Visages of rapine . . . white-cuffed marauders'. The mood of the poem is angry and outspoken.

'In Memory', the key poem of the collection and its moral centre, considers the significance of Valentin Iremonger, who as Civil Servant and poet managed two careers. He was, for Kinsella, a figure of authority and the first of the new generation of poets. But he did not fulfil his potential and in time his early influence waned. In his notes Kinsella summarizes the forces that worked against him: 'ill luck, the terrible mishaps, willed and unwilled, misfortunes to self and family, all your talents ruined in remote isolation, posted where you would suffer most from your own enemies' (box 29, folder 15). It is a classic Kinsella situation: the man, bayed about by enemies, suffers, loses authority, but has an inviolable integrity. Kinsella writes about the 'miserable occasion' of the funeral and about the changes that have taken place in a generation Iremonger once inspired.

The 'You' is 'silver-quiffed' in the first line; everybody is white-haired in the last. In between are various indications of change: the break-up of 'Our group', their regrouping at the funeral, and Kinsella's assessment of them. The end sympathetically reveals the dead man and his suffering – in his own life and in the violent death of a daughter. The violence done to this good man confirms Kinsella's inalterable view of the 'irreducible/malice and greed' of the human species. That assessment is poignantly offset by memory.

> ...The memory
> of a gentle self, affronted
> by the unmanageable,
> aroused and self-devouring. (289)

The final embodiment of waste and pain and the most complete statement of the situation in which the poet finds himself come in the last poem – 'At the Western Ocean's Edge' – which, as it positions another poet in the context of extreme suffering and distress, summarizes the collection. Heroic figures deal with forces outside them – Fate in the case of Cú Cuchullain, the middle classes in the case of Yeats – but Aogán Ó Rathaille deals with forces inside himself. Two lines in the first stanza – 'And one, finding the foe inside his head,/who turned the struggle outward, against the sea' – are taken up in 'Any force remaining/held on waves of threat inside the mind' (*Collected Poems*, 1996, 303), in the fourth, changed in *Collected Poems* (2001) to 'storming back at the waves', as quoted below. Balancing one against the other, 'in a posture of refusal', Ó Rathaille uses the force of the ocean to represent the violence in himself and, as Kinsella notes, the 'power in the image is in the waves' attack from within' (box 25, folder 10).

> – the energy of chaos and a shaping
> counter-energy in throes of balance;
> the gale wailing inland off the water
> arousing a voice responding in his head,
>
> storming back at the waves with their own force
> in a posture of refusal... (292)

The poet at the ocean's edge stands for the ego at the boundary of the psyche. He sets his face into the dead calm of the unconscious and stares into the totally unknown and negative milieu, beyond death. In this unequal conflict he meets force with force, matches chaos with chaos, and discovers an alien steel kind of order whose synonyms are 'cold', 'black' and 'unfeeling'. 'Dame Kindness' – muse, mother, beloved, displaced by the new social order – has suffered, her bowels 'torn'. Here, too, decent values have been abused. These lines are omitted in *Collected Poems* (2001). In an earlier version Kinsella wrote more explicitly.

Aogán Ó Rathaille defined his art
At the ocean's edge, a beggarman converting
The gale wailing inward off the water
Into a voice responding in his head,
Cursing back at the waves on their own terms
– energy of chaos and a shaping
counter-energy in throes of balance;
solitary response, eliciting
order from the uproar of particulars,
struggling toward a posture of refusal
on the basis of some kind of understanding,
Man's beggar rags in tatters in the tempest. (box 25, folder 10)

In *An Duanaire*, Kinsella writes of Ó Rathaille: 'His poetry, the best of which has a heroic desolation and grandeur, is in many ways a result of his effort to come to terms with the chaos in which he and his people found themselves.' (139) Ó Rathaille is the isolated artist who has nowhere to turn for support. His only response, steely in its determination, is to meet the energy of chaos with counter-energy, a moral and artistic force found internally and not to be silenced by the vision of a meaningless void. As Kinsella insists here and elsewhere, the circumstances may be damaging and uncongenial, but the poet's duty is to write.

'At the Western Ocean's Edge' is a concentrated statement, placed at the conclusion of the collection and foreshadowing *Poems from Centre City*. It clarifies the contextual implications of the stranger who appears in that collection. It is no longer a question of evolutionary advance, psychological descent, or even of Dantesque engagement with social, political and moral issues, but a metaphor of interlocking and engaged forces. Its account of an individual's force battling against an extreme force is the enabling metaphor. In a physical and spiritual landscape deprived of moral and integrating principles, life succumbs to the threat embodied in the stranger. Individuals yield to evil, to greed, to spinelessness, and are blind to aesthetic values. Life becomes intolerably bland. It is the responsibility of the poet to maintain his integrity and to remain alert. The idea of meaninglessness threatens creativity, making it difficult for him to continue. In Kinsella's case it leads him to question basic issues, to appraise the values that operate in society, to assess the purpose of art, and to question the effectiveness of Divinity.

How the poet conducts himself is fundamental. The issue is taken up in 'A Portrait of the Artist', the opening poem in *Poems from Centre City*, and later in 'The Back Lane'. Against the background of the discussion in James Joyce's *A Portrait of the Artist as a Young Man*, it begins with an argument about beauty. Kinsella's definition of beauty – 'A jewel of process/The fugitive held fast in its accident' – is Joycean. It affirms that beauty is drawn from flux and defined in and through its particulars. Raised in the opening section, defined in the second, and illustrated in the third through the images of the car, its 'pulsing rose' a distant echo of Joyce and Dante and the prostitutes, beauty, will be defined further in 'At the Head Table' in the next collection; but in 'The Back Lane', the key poem in *Poems from Centre City*, Kinsella places the artist amid signs of official barbarism and hits sarcastically at man's culpable ignorance.

> A black stain of new tar on the ground
>   – shade that in the beginning
> moved on the concrete.
>
> And the remains of a cement mash
>   emptied direct on the clay; betraying
> the carelessness of the telephone people,
>
> the slovenliness of the City and its lesser works.
>   Culpable ignorance, distinguishing Man
> from the cat and the other animals. (298)

He moves from the 'long workroom', place of creative effort, into the world of raw material. The book he takes with him is *The Divine Comedy*, the 'profile' that of Dante, the three lamps an echo of the three books of the *Comedy*. Surrounded by the evidence of what he has to cope with, 'waste', 'ruin' and 'exit', he addresses Dante, deliberately associating him with the smell of death. Given the evidence, Kinsella prays for the right skills.

> Lord, grant us a local watchfulness.
>   Accept us into that minority
> driven toward a totality of response,
>
> and I will lower these arms
>   and embrace what I find. (300)

The terms – 'local watchfulness', 'totality of response', 'embrace what I find' – reaffirm Kinsella's guiding principles. Like Joyce he embraces what he defines – waste, death and barrenness in modern society. He will deal with all that can happen – rapacity, the failed Catholic Church and total meaninglessness. The brother figure who briefly appears represents what one might meet when least expected and foreshadows the appearance of the stranger in the following poem.

The questionable figure in 'The Stranger' embodies Kinsella's sense of the menace that dogs his days, always hovering and by now virtually a curse because of the ill-effects of his presence. The poem relates a series of sightings in areas close to Percy Place. Now on 'night patrol', inhabiting the darkness, he represents the Jungian shadow, the dark brother, the animal side of the psyche, and has transfixed the poet by his presence. Already evident in priests and speculators, he is the appropriate presence as Kinsella writes *Butcher's Dozen* where he deals 'with troubles any Stranger might desire'. The troubles include the killing of protesters on Bloody Sunday 1972, which were considered by the Lord Widgery tribunal. That poem reacts to the injustice and dishonesty of the tribunal's report. The stranger, however, is not meant to be clearly identified. In his notes Kinsella thinks about him in language that connects him with the priest-administrator. Under the heading 'Death: Disease', he remarks that in the olden days the Stranger would have been identified with 'Death, Ill-luck, the Curse; placed in his parable, analogue, invoked and distanced'. Kinsella associates him with the meaningless, one of many:

> Busy, but elsewhere. Passing, close, toward the other. The profile pale and bare, an eye-socket; that standard dread grin...Or fixed in a stare upward. Or looking, this way, and that, for any change/alteration in anything. (box 27, folder 10)

He represents 'a possible Fate, not yet selected, a curse not yet uttered, the fact of death'.

References in 'The Back Lane' to Dante and *The Divine Comedy* establish a context for the poems in these two collections. It is clear from many longer drafts that Kinsella thinks of the area around Percy Place in a way that is comparable to Dante's view of Florence. 'Social Work' identifies some who threaten the area – Corporation officials, a Catholic doctor, a house agent, the parish priest who emerges as the central figure. As Kinsella's notes reveal, 'Friends and Neighbours', a longer version of 'The Back Lane', describes neighbours and their homes. 'The Bell' is part of a much longer poem, as are the brief portraits of Jack B. Yeats and Eamon de Valera in 'The Last', all of which pay attention to the locality. Kinsella broods over the significance of priest, priest-administrator, the mysterious stranger, the dark brother, social injustice, and greed in a manner reminiscent of Dante's reflections on the inhabitants of Florence.

Although it is possible to detect the main concerns of these two collections, they are not as integrated or as fluent as those that follow. There are strong poems – 'Apostle of Hope', 'Night Conference at Wood Quay: 6 June 1979' – in *Personal Places*, but others are less fully achieved. 'Seven' follows a dream pattern in which images of urgency, flight and weightlessness convey the female nature of the voice as one butterfly addresses another. Male response comes in images of darkness and predatory claws gripping a stone head.

> Steel carrion eyes
> stared from a sharp midnight road
> above the empty square.
>
> The leather claws
> tightened on a stone face,
> strengthening their hold with black nails. (285)

The nature of the meeting of the lovers is indicated through suggestions of crudity, uneasiness and the brainless murmur of a pigeon. Appropriately, the prayer 'In the name of the Father' is a litany of the physical. The illicit nature of the relationship becomes clearer in references to advancing shadow and their cars 'ill-matched in the yard'. While one can follow the plot, the poem does not provide sufficient detail for full understanding. On the other hand 'Brothers in the Craft', which comments on the relationship between one generation of writers and the next, is needlessly explicit.

> In the elder, an impulse against that settled state
> when the elements work in balance against each other
> in worn stability, no longer questioned;
>
> to borrow something out of the restlessness
> of the half ready, confide an ethereal itch
> into new, committed fingers. (287)

In *Poems from Centre City*, 'The Bell', 'Household Spirits', 'Departure Platform', and 'The Last' read like notations, rather than fully articulated poems.

> Standing stone still on the path, with long pale chin
> under a broad-rimmed hat, and aged eyes
> staring down Baggot Street across his stick.
> Jack Yeats. The last.

> Upright, stately and blind, and hesitating
> > solitary on the lavatory floor
> after the Government meeting down the hall.
> > De Valera. The last. (303)

Poems in the following collection *Madonna and Other Poems* are better integrated.

Madonna and Other Poems, which has four poems and an epigraph, focuses on the woman companion as wife, queen, beloved, wise old woman and mediator in important matters – artistic creativity, the creativity of the earth, and the movement of the tides and the seasons. 'Madonna' deals with involvement from the first appearance of the chosen woman to a mature and quiet union. She is associated with the mother figure, in part with the Muse whose 'tender, deliberate incursion' is recalled from *A Technical Supplement*. In the language of closeness and sexual intensity their separate 'awarenesses' are joined, their 'piercing presences exchanged'; but the poem exists in a shadowy area between the subconscious and the conscious before opening at the end to a sacramental description of breakfast. The cutting, opening and eating of a blood orange, associated with Persephone, affirm physical closeness. The kitchen, not the church, is the place of communion.

In the obscurely reflective 'Visiting Hour' the poet/narrator is in a drugged dream-state, a 'brother' appears, his belated arrived noted and dismissed, but it is the woman, part mother, part seductress, part Muse, who receives closest interpretation. The setting is a hospital, the atmosphere one of sickness in which the incestuous phantasies are not out of place. The woman is the seductive Muse, source of creativity, mother of his imagination, her temptation part reverie, part hallucination.

> I turned away, toward the tall Victorian window.
> And she was there, against the crimson drape.
> > One thin hand out, denying,
>
> the other pulling the lace back from her thigh
> and the dark stocking with the darker border
> > toward the pale motherly places:
>
> the sac of flesh and fervour where we met
> and nourished each other for a while.
> > Mother, in your faded folds,
>
> taking refreshment at my well of illness,
> fragile in the smell of woodbine,
> > take my love back, into the medicine dark. (309–10)

They have 'nourished each other in the past'. Now she takes 'refreshment' from his 'well of illness'; he counters her 'taking' with a prayer for the curative power of love. It is a state of fruitful, psychic interaction.

Moving away from these introspective self-assessments, Kinsella appraises his situation in 'At the Head Table' in an objective biographical manner, summing up the principles of behaviour that have guided him.

> ...I have devoted
> my life, my entire career,
> to the avoidance of affectation,
> the way of entertainment
>
> or the specialist response.
> With always the same outcome.
> Dislike. Misunderstanding.
> But I will do what I can. (310)

He then explains his view on art and its correct direction, speaking at first to an audience who are incapable of understanding because they have fixed ideas and expect to be entertained. Then he addresses an ideal audience, partly the Muse, who are capable of responding to the perfect work of art with an intense and total awareness that perceives its complexity, coherence and unity. The process is as rigorous in its demands on the reader as it is on the poet. The poem itself defines his comprehensive engagement with the process of creativity.

Behind the poem lies the parallel story of Hephaestus, the lame god, who mediated when a row broke out between his parents, Zeus and Hera. Appealing to his mother not to quarrel, he hurries forward with a two-handled cup, which he places in her hand. He offers her a toast, brings back her smile and then serves the other gods in turn, beginning from the left. Good humour is restored, they eat, Apollo plays, and the Muse sings delightfully. What Kinsella/Hephaestus offers – this 'lovely beaker/with the slim amphibian handle' – is an abstract equation of an ideal work of art: 'gave me the greatest trouble'... 'Yet proved the most rewarding'.

> A fit vessel also
> for vital decoration.
> These marks of waves and footsteps
> somewhere by the sea

> – in fact a web of order,
> each mark accommodating
> the shapes of all the others
> with none at fault, or false;
>
> a system of live images
> making increased response
> to each increased demand
> in the eye of the beholder,
>
> with a final full response
> over the whole surface
> – a total theme – presented
> to a full intense regard... (311–12)

A defence of Kinsella's work and poetic methods, the poem answers more fully the question raised in 'A Portrait of the Artist' as to the nature of beauty.

The marks of waves and footsteps on the cup introduce the poet and seer Amergin, whose ship shows the signs of 'perils past' and whose 'few firm footprints' signal the new beginning, with 'perils still to come'. These signs the poet offers to the Muse for whom he pours a libation 'of the best blood brandy' and raises the 'brimming beaker/to her motherly regard'. Kinsella/Hephaestus, the artist-son offers a prayer to the Father who holds a place between him and the Muse, who is also mother and companion, close to the Father.

> 'Remembering the Father,
> His insult when offended,
> our proneness to offend,
> we will drink to His absent shade.' (312)

She has been charmed and softened, her 'furious arms' open to acknowledge him. Kinsella is a human being, limping like Hephaestus, but doing the best he can: he has satisfied the woman, has drunk to her remembering the Father, and now fills the glasses of each member of the audience, thereby communicating with 'everyone in turn'.

The toast to the Madonna-Muse recalls Amergin's appeasement of the female divinities in the *Book of Invasions*. Associated here with Ó Rathaille in 'At the Western Ocean's Edge' through references to the ninth wave and nine steps, he is the poet-seer who gave the first judgement in Ireland just past the magic boundary of the ninth wave. By calming the wind that drove his people off, he ensured their safe arrival.

Like Kinsella he is associated with appraisal, definition and poetic
power.

The companion collection, *Open Court*, another descent into the
crowded and contentious Dublin underworld, considers an assembly of
literary figures who are still 'here in Hell' marked by the restrictive and
wasteful conditions of the 1950s. The setting is depressing, 'an over-
crowded sty', but the portraits are lively – the 'ruined' poets, the
might-have-been Arnold, Auden, Wilde, one 'snarling', one 'sunken in
defeat', the other 'doomed'; the self-important 'ageing author'; the
absurd topics of discussion, the out-of-place provincial and, finally and
most fully, Patrick Kavanagh, the 'ruined Anonymous': 'Accursed pity/I
ever came to Dublin City...'. Behind the satire lies sympathy for those
who found no exit. The vitality of the poem arises from its ability to
record in lively rhyming couplets amid dispiriting circumstances.

> 'When I was a growing boy
> and bent my back in ditch and dung
> it wasn't mockery that flung
> my holy body down one day
> in ecstasy upon the clay,
> but Truth that ne'er obeyed the call
> with witty intellectual
> – the tragic thing that shames the jiber
> and monthly magazine subscriber!' (318)

The Pen Shop achieves a similar transmutation. In this poem, Kinsella,
the reflective walker, portrays himself in particular places, with his own
memories and associations. Motivated by the need to get refills for his
pen, he moves through the centre of Dublin from the General Post
Office to Bewley's Cafe in Part I, from there to Hely's Pen Shop in Part
II. He observes his surroundings – the inside of the GPO, the colonnade
outside, the statues in O'Connell Street, the bridge across the Liffey, the
statues near Trinity College, directions west, east and south from there,
remembers the river's associations with his family, and refers to places
associated with himself and his work: 'I circled among my reflections/
out under the colonnade'.

> Our souls passing among each other
> under the cathedral ceiling. Around the bronze hero
> sagging half covered off his upright,
> looking down over one shoulder at his feet.
> The harpy perched on his neck. (323)

Cú Cuchullain may be a mythic hero, evoked in 'At the Western Ocean's Edge', but what Kinsella perceives is the 'sagging', the downward gaze and the Morrígan, bird of death. The statues along O'Connell Street – of Jim Larkin, John Gray, William Smith O'Brien and Daniel O'Connell – are observed with partly critical, partly humorous comments. He recalls Leopold Bloom clasping and unclasping his hands in the vicinity of Gray's statue: 'About here'. What he notes often corresponds to what Bloom sees, such as O'Connell Bridge and the Guinness barge passing underneath. The river Liffey is the dividing line of the poem.

> The river poured in dirty and disturbed.
> …
> From Islandbridge. Under Kingsbridge,
> with the black currents turning among each other
> in among the black piles at the lower Brewery gates:
>
> the hogsheads, swinging high up off the jetty,
> delivered down in their chains
> to a deaf ghost directing them to their places… (324)

When he stands on O'Connell Bridge he suffers a slight epileptic seizure – 'Cold absence under the heart' – with a *déjà vu* distinctness in which he remembers his grandfather, the barge captain, at the lower brewery gates loading the barrels and then the barge sliding in 'under my feet'. Because of the seizure, he needs a drink and has to take the two tablets. As the barge passes beneath him with its Charon-figure, he recalls the dead men in his family and acknowledges their 'capacity' – skill, craft, a heritage modified from generation to generation, 'Measured to the need'.

The physical and mental movements of the walker carry the poem forward. When he enters Bewley's Café, the momentum is maintained in parallel sentences, participial verbs, specific actions and the arrival into the 'fellowship' of male elders. The constant ingredient is concrete detail: 'grinder', 'bins', 'shelves', 'shoppers', 'scales'.

> I crossed over
> and as far as Bewleys'.
> By the great grinder, into the front shop;
>
> by the bins of coffee in their dark sorts
> on the high shelves; passing among the shoppers
> gathered at the scales, precise in their needs;

> to the women and the urns at the back counter.
> Carried my coffee among the tables
> through the inner room murmuring with crockery
>
> toward the elders seated along the far wall.
> Set my tray down on the wiped marble
> with a nod of fellowship.
>
> And sat back against the plush.
> We were all males. There was no distraction.
> Speechless, ordering our cares. (325)

He passes the hags and the urns to the old men, takes the two tablets and the curative drink under the care of the not quite adequate, the 'Partly informed', Muse.

At the same time *The Pen Shop* opens outwards beyond the immediate scenes. When he directs our attention to the Number 21 bus moving westwards, all the place-names – the Fountain, the Forty Steps, Kilmainham, Inchicore – have associations with his family, his school and the autobiographical poetry. His mind advances 'Toward the thought of places/beyond your terminus' to the west 'where I have seen/the light of cities under the far horizon'. The reference to the New World recalls people in the *Book of Invasions* led westwards by a speck of light on the horizon. That, too, connects powerfully with a large part of Kinsella's work. Indeed this section associates with so much of his work that it is impossible to make a full list; it includes many of the poems in *New Poems*, most of *One*, *The Messenger*, all the 'Settings' in *Songs of the Psyche*, all *St Catherine's Clock*, and many of the early poems which have settings in the Basin Lane region.

He fixes his personal data against the cardinal points. The allusions are threefold: to the western shore and the New World beyond, to the southern shore and the eastern shore. When he looks south he draws in ancestors in County Wicklow, present in 'His Father's Hands', his connections with County Wexford through marriage, and previous poems; beyond Wicklow lies 'Finistère', the place of Irish beginnings and a reference to his poem of the same title. When he looks eastwards he salutes 'voices' in Europe and first peoples beyond Jerusalem, somewhere in place and time.

Each part of the poem ends on a note of satisfaction; in each the walker arrives at a destination. In Part I, he enters the coffee shop. At the back counter are the symbolic urns and the women dispensing the satisfying draft. In a distant echo of Aeneas' meeting his elders in the Otherworld, he enters in 'fellowship' a community of male elders and equals and experiences order, composure and the sensual taste of the black drink.

> And the black draft
> entered the system direct,
> foreign and clay sharp. (326)

In Part II in another ritual, he arrives at the 'cell', obtains the black refills, and is confirmed in his sense of where he is and who he is. At the same time *The Pen Shop* has a personal plot centred on mortality, present in the crow/harpy reference, his presence as one of the 'souls', the crossing of the Liffey/Styx, the *petit mal* attack, Charon, Bloom the dark stranger, the cauldron/grinder/scales/women, acceptance among the elders, the black draft that has the savour of death, the ill-tempered personal detail about an 'enemy', the summing up against the cardinal points, the man in the Pen Shop who is there for one last duty.

But the poem has a larger significance. As the spiritual 'cell' from which Kinsella has always bought refills, the shop itself is the source of his work. The specific allusions to different poems and the use of such metaphors and images as walker, woman, grill, black, river, cell, kiss, counter, journey reinforce its function as an echo-chamber for the work. A poet who has achieved so much can reject the Morrígan, can oppose her negative power with the creative force of this poem. The ending brings us back to the beginning, which identifies the harpy as the Morrígan, the 'she' to whom he has written. With a 'final' kiss the walker rejects her 'fierce forecasts'. The poem itself counters them in its measured rhythm, civilized responses, imaginative extensions, and the purposeful and confirming nature of the walker's journey. A work of art or an entire *oeuvre* is a victory over impermanence, waste, death and the dark stranger. The poet is shown to exist in a world of flux and to record. He is an artist and we are aware of his work: he is doing what he should do.

In a further enlargement *The Pen Shop* evokes a subliminal, archetypal myth. This, too, is the land of the dead, a descent into the lower regions past the bird of death. The souls in the GPO have come 'out of the light'; all those recalled are dead. The statues are from the past; the city is devoid of people; black is the dominant colour, in the crow, the brewery, the coffee bins, the coffee, the flats of the river, even in Bloom. Crossing the Liffey with the boatman underneath takes its place in the iconography of a journey to the Otherworld where the *Lady Patricia* is queen. Within the coffee shop the walker has the confirming contact with the elders and the coffee is appropriately 'foreign and clay sharp'. In Part II the poem lifts towards what has been confirmed – Kinsella's own work, its sources, and lights on the horizon. Bloom, too, went from Glasnevin cemetery towards its glimmering gates.

9

GNATS OUT OF NOTHING

The significance of Thomas Kinsella's meeting with Eleanor Walsh is well attested. In its progression from church to bedroom to kitchen, from the spiritual to the physical, 'Madonna' outlined the experience, but the title poem in *The Familiar*, in its published form and in its manuscript drafts, focuses on the event in illuminating detail. Its seven-part narrative affirms a maturing process in which the poet moves from the loneliness he experienced prior to Eleanor's arrival to the complex emotions that ensued – from initial disagreement, anger, hatred and separation – they were 'Mismatched' – to the closeness of their sexual union and a ritual of togetherness.

On her arrival, allegorical demons above his door recall the struggle he had dramatized in 'Baggot Street Deserta'. They enter 'together', united in their 'animal thoughts'. Sensual and seductive, the Muse-woman attends to him; his mind is 'black' with physical desire. He reacts intensely, incarnating a future through her, that is, the work he will create with her indispensable support. The motif of the demons contrasts with the picture of the three graces whose assistance he needs. Copied from Picasso's painting of Chastity, Sensuality and Beauty, they introduce a mood of release and peace. He searches 'for the lost well-head' in a romantic context of the joy and blossoming associated with the enabling graces and the blessing of Persephone:

> slanting down golden
> glistening with seeds,
> in a glade humming with pleasure. (331)

In these reassessments Kinsella intensifies, deepens and mythologizes the significance of his meeting with Eleanor. The description of the advancing nymph continues the images of romantic pastoral and highlights her seductive power. Her hair transforms to 'floral tresses' that 'lifted and swayed,/whispering: *Come*'. The poem then returns to reality and plain speech. What was expressed through half-dream in 'Madonna' becomes actual, the breakfast ceremony in the former confirming its liberating reprise in the latter.

'Active Blessedness', an expanded, unpublished version, connects the experience with his room in Baggot Street. Its exclamatory style and feeding metaphor emphasize love and sensuality. The poem is a tribute to Eleanor, the Persephone figure, whom he runs to meet. Its celebratory images, mockingly ironic in their excess, include limbs moving, golden light, a fragrant nymph, dew, dancing, poppies, red blossom, a spring, cells of ruby blood, pink tongues, expectant questions ('What bright being?'), and invitations ('whispering: *Come*').

> – But dearest, how *you* still dance
> in the red blossom! How they spring
> spontaneously and paint your path
> like magic! How you choose
> among them, tear them out of the earth
> and lay them in the crook of your arm
> with long grasses, nurse them
> against your cheek, with your hair
> falling all over them,
> mixed with the remains
> of the morning's floral crown.[1]

The consummation is mysterious and reassuring.

> And I felt Love
> in the likeness of some dark body
> sink down on me, closer
> than a mother. The darkness parted
> and I heard a voice at my ear
> say:
>   *It is all*
> *right. It is all right.*[2]

Another draft called 'Calypso', with its Joycean associations, and addressed to the 'Nymph', is explicitly sexual, referring to 'The wet of our (love)-nest/her sighs and her body liquids', and oral sex:

> readying herself frankly
> her eyes into his eyes
> lowering her (yr) mouth onto his manhood
>
> swallowing his aching flesh
> in the cool oils of her thirst
> her busy neck beaded/with the sweat of her dark hair.
> (box 84, folder 2)

The 'friendliness' of their locked legs, found in the published version, is defined in a manuscript.

> There is a friendliness
> related to wisdom, where differences are welcomed
> as an enrichment. I cannot initiate it
> but I could respond so that it can last a lifetime.
> You have come; wilful under your clothes. I held the door open.
> (box 82, folder 2)

He responds to her 'wilful' sensuality. Conscious initially of their being mismatched, they are now able to welcome differences, independence and mutual respect – an enrichment that can last a lifetime

The Muse/Nymph/Calypso/Eleanor figure represents love and creativity. In 'Close of Day', also in manuscript, Kinsella affirms their total communion. They went from 'our last furious farewell', their state of 'never to be seen again' to the blessedness of their reunion. 'We had been singled out and knew we were blessed.' The progression is defined and the significance of their union more comprehensively raised and affirmed. Again the emphasis is on their ability to absorb differences.

> But we had not learned
> to adapt to/our differences/different expectations/needs/wants
> had not yet found in the radiant friendliness
> where differences enrich and increase a lifelove
> with a wanton flesh
> embracing/finding/holding onto our differences/separate flesh
> differences
> and resumed/gone back into our original separate normalities.
> (box 84, folder 2)

The real progression is from limited understanding to a more comprehensive recognition of individuality and the ability to adapt to that as a strength. The affirmation of a willingly accepted closeness and of union within separateness, further expressed in a less heightened style through the ironic account of breakfasting together, offsets the perception of meaninglessness elsewhere and of the poet's fundamental isolation. The contrast is dramatic between the voice of personal bonding and the voice of existential loss.

If 'The Familiar' reminds us of the marriage relationship in the 'Wormwood' poems, it does so by virtue of the contrast between the pain there and love's ardour here with its promise of creativity. Presiding priest-like over their morning ceremony, the poet relishes the 'chilled grapefruit', even while he notes the companionable crows that climb the air beyond the waterfall. The 'sacrifice' is treated in a lightly humorous manner: he arranges the pieces of grapefruit 'in slight disorder', stands in his dressing gown with arms extended while she blandly observes, 'You are very good. You always made it nice.' Nevertheless, it is ceremony; it endures, satisfies and takes place in the real world. That modestly expressed claim to the importance of ceremony contrasts with what happens when, in the companion collection, *Godhead*, he moves from the sustaining force of love to the diminished power of religion and looks critically at the role of Divinity.

Godhead, a sequence of engaged reflections, scrutinizes the divine at a time when religion has lost much of its authority. We always live, Kinsella believes, in a dark time.

> There were no lighter times. Ever. The records are there. We are not communicating with each other, across the heads of the unworthy or the evil. We are looking into our hearts & finding the inadequacy there, recognising that we are an inadequate species in an inadequate place. And only raising our voices. We are talking to a projection of ourselves, putting it as clearly as we can. And it doesn't matter. We cd. stay quiet. Or take part. It makes no difference. (box 85, folder 2)

These bleak conclusions, reminiscent of the previous reflections on meaninglessness, underlie *The Familiar*, *Godhead*, *Citizen of the World*, *Littlebody* and *Marginal Economy*. They describe the isolation of the artist, the failure to communicate, and the sense of human inadequacy. In these circumstances artists can only talk to 'a projection of ourselves'. That conclusion helps to explain some of the directions found in these poems – the preoccupation with inner states, the use of exemplary figures, such as Dante, Ó Rathaille, Augustine, Goldsmith or Boswell. The state of frozen feeling that appears in 'Dura Mater' and elsewhere defines the paralysis. The hard mother, the dark brother, the stone faces, the grin of the goddess, the Gorgon Medusa, all express emotional barrenness. Now the descent to the underworld has a grim outcome – dry, stony, no longer saturated with potential. The question Kinsella asks is what can the artist do to counter these negative realities. He can create the well-wrought cup, can attest to the value of ceremony, can celebrate love and the natural world.

The connection between Kinsella and the early Irish poet Amergin, the priest-figure at the ocean's edge already present in 'Nightwalker' and 'Finistère', prepares for the introduction of 'Godhead'. Virtually a prose poem at first, its long descriptive line was shortened in successive revisions. In its contemplation of the three Divine Persons 'Godhead' is austere and dryly critical. 'Trinity' portrays the Father in terms of passive virtues: absolute beauty and stillness, but shows His limitations. 'He has done everything in His power' but it is not enough. The Son, 'hanging on high', attempts to make up for the Father's shortcomings, 'reconciling the Father's requirements/with His capacity', has done 'all that the Father required of Him'. An exact image of the Father, He supplies what the Father lacks. The basis for Kinsella's interpretation is the idea that the Father's work was inadequate. In his notes Kinsella considers a range of synonyms to describe this: 'not answerable/ unaccountable/unamenable/exempt from, incapable of responsibility'. Their association with the poem indicates his thinking. Ironically, having completed the task of Creation, the Father is fulfilled despite the botched nature of His achievement. The Third Person, 'holding Its breath', merely hopes it works, and is therefore irrelevant.

The poet-persona prays to the Father who, inert and motionless, and 'Lost in the work', is still trying to understand. Imploring Him to be 'mindful of us', he identifies the Father's shortcomings. The Father, like the poet, he points out, also knows 'how it is possible to grasp completely/while remaining partly incapable'. The Divine and the human are therefore alike in that both understand the impossibility of achieving perfection in their creations. That He responds 'bodily, but with a palpable tongue/trafficking in carnal things', confirms this perception.

The Father insists that the poet must declare the corruptibility of flesh. Although the poet, in response, expresses fear that people will not believe him, will not accept his word, the Father asks in rhetorical anger '*Who hath made thy mouth?*' The poet, He insists, must tell the truth: all men die. This dialogue, phrased in language drawn from Exodus 4, approves what Kinsella has been doing. Accepting the Divine injunction, he asks, '*Proclaim Our incompleteness, only begotten.*' That is the main point. Inadequacy pertains to both the Divine and the human and like death is part of the essential truth. The allusion to Exodus brings in the very different relationship between Israel and Yahweh. Israel's faith was not based on the notion of a God who was remote from the human struggle, nor did it question his omnipotence. It depended upon the response of a God who was active within the human story, guiding and shaping the course of human affairs in accordance with His sovereign purpose.

Inadequacy is part of life. In His role as proclaimer of truth about waste, the Father verifies the menace in the waiting stranger. In 'Son', the Father in the form of the 'Stranger', incarnates the Son in the woman who has 'two memories in her flesh': the Stranger who united with her, 'without love' and 'the Adjustment in her body', mechanistic

and without feeling, to the conception. Mary encounters the stranger
waiting, with disappointing consequences.

> A Stranger fallen across her
> in fierce relief, without love.
> And the Adjustment in her body. (338)

Drained of Divinity, the baby that results behaves like any mortal child,
crying and whinging, 'the little face wrinkled back in hatred'. Kinsella's
description of the baby being handled has its comic side. The
Incarnation itself is at the heart of Christian belief. Behind it lies the
mystery of the Holy Trinity. *Godhead* is a devastating devaluation of that
mystery and its associated beliefs in the love of the Father who sent His
only-begotten Son to redeem mankind through death on the Cross.

The manuscript versions of this section are more explicit about the
violation that occurs and about Mary's reaction. The Stranger has made
'animal use of her flesh'. She was at 'His mercy'. Under the title 'The
Christface', she is described as pale with rage, 'Her lips pulled back from
Her thin teeth.' The 'enterprise' had 'evolved out of control'.

> The outcome
> – a narrowing of Her options
> and a Christface lifted over the horizon. (box 85, folder 2)

In another version, it is 'a confrontation' beyond her control, fixed in
black and white. She is 'maimed/at the unmanageable margin', at the
edge of meaninglessness in a situation that echoes Ó Rathaille at the
shore. She has risen with rage, her mouth pulled back lipless from her
thin teeth. The various revisions probe at the human side of the incident,
on a woman's sense of rage as her privacy is invaded, her will denied,
her future determined by an event not of her choosing. In a testing of
possible words to describe the incident, Kinsella considers 'ignorant/
brutal/merciless/pitiless/blunt/cruel/ungracious' (box 85, folder 2).
From his point of view, they all fit. These versions are less restrained
than the published one which portrays her in more passive mode,
prepared to endure. They therefore provide a more explicit meaning.
The incarnation is 'without love'; her body adjusts to it like a
mathematical instrument; heart and mind have no part in it. In the final
version it is her frozen feeling that is emphasized. The event hardly
registers with her. It is imposed; her body adjusts. It denies the principle
of accepted difference found in poems about the poet's relationship with
his wife. That in turn has moved on from the assumption of identical
reactions in the 'Wormwood' sequence.

The same kind of language is used to describe the Crucifixion. The Son's head on the Cross signifies 'abandonment' by the Father and 'acceptance'. The first line of the 'Spirit' echoes St Augustine, who described Divinity as 'a wind that passes and does not return'.[3] Similarly, Kinsella says that when man has come to the end of his process, there is nothing but 'desert' and 'dust'. Redemption does not work. Christ has failed. The Father does not respond, the Muse does.

Kinsella's attraction to Augustine is many-sided. He, too, was concerned with the nature of evil, the conflict between good and evil, and the search for understanding or wisdom. His concept of the primal fall corresponds to Kinsella's sense of the reality of evil, but where Augustine sees the world moving toward a divine goal, Kinsella sees an evolutionary advance to 'the dust of our last born'. For Augustine, the Divine was a living force in the world; for Kinsella it is manifested in the ocean's power. In that perception he differs from Augustine, who sees God as independent of creation, complete and fulfilled in Himself. It is again a measure of the loss in the power of religion that this should be so. Augustine's *The City of God* vindicated Christianity and the Christian Church; its function here underlines how much the power of the Church has declined. His *De Trinitate* expounded the true relations between the divine and the human. In *Godhead*, Kinsella sees the divine as merely a reflection of the other. Divinity is made human, mirrors the human, with imperfection and mortality. In Augustine's view, man has fallen from his Earthly Paradise. Those in *The City of God* who have turned from the desire for God's love find themselves in hell; so in Kinsella's poetry Dublin has become an underworld of loss and death. His earthly city has its false gods, its speculators, and their clerical associates.

Two framing poems in *Godhead* comment on the 'unearthly power' of the ocean. The first, 'High Tide, Amagansett', is richly descriptive: its visual images, rhythms and syntax mimic the movements of water, the waves coming in and breaking noisily along the shore, one wave as it withdraws meeting the next as it advances. Set on the east coast of America, it deals with cosmic force, as it is perceived directly by the poet in exile, from its furthest beginning to its closest manifestation. The first of the two tercets is shaped through a succession of active verbs – 'mounted', 'folded', 'dismantled' – each supported by participial verbs that enact the motion of the water – 'approaching', 'whitening', 'delivering', 'returning', 'overhanging'. The waves are 'alive', 'arguing', hurrying in disorder between two stillnesses: one far out 'at a depth without light', the other stopped at his foot, 'discovering the first thought of withdrawal'. Set on the west coast, '*Midnight, San Clemente: a gloss*' deals with the same 'unearthly power', earthed and deified in Irish tradition, and calling from his distant home. The natural world manifests the Lord's creation; the thunder of waves is a metaphor for the Holy Spirit, whose 'black breath' it is.

But like the ocean, poetry expresses the Divine, as '*Midnight, San Clemente*', the concluding poem says, quoting Giolla Brighde Mac Con Midhe, the thirteenth-century poet.

> *All metre and mystery*
> *touch on the Lord at last.*
> *The tide thunders ashore*
> *in praise of the High King* ... (340)

The absolute stillness of the Godhead, its sealed feelings that include the Virgin Mother's response, contrasts with the fluid interactive power of the ocean that swells with movement, is filled with 'unrest', capable of disorder and disarray, 'in praise of the High King'. In the end, when religion loses its authority, poetry may be a substitute.

Kinsella at the ocean's edge recalls the liminal encounter of Ó Rathaille in 'At the Western Ocean's Edge'. Echoing its images the scene resonates powerfully with the description of Amergin's ship in 'At the Head Table', with the Kinsella family at the seaside in 'Carraroe', with 'the silt of the sea floor' in 'Worker in Mirror at His Bench' where the conclusion

> Blackness – all matter
> in one polished cliff face
> hurtling rigid from zenith to pit
> through dead

is replicated in the 'mass', which in turn recalls the similar conclusion to 'Nightwalker' and other rocky encounters and conclusions. Pondering in his notes on the significance of the waves at Amagansett, Kinsella compares their progress to the ways in which memory assembles material, the present path traversing a path out of the past. Poetry and the natural world are expressions of God's work (box 85, folder 20). The poet's window is 'open'.

But it is not plain sailing. He has to live in a real and transient world where there are few consolations and religion provides little comfort. It is one thing to be true to one's convictions and to write with as much integrity as one can, it is another to experience indifference and misunderstanding. A sense of public disregard expressed in 'At the Head Table' is articulated metaphorically through the figure of Oliver Goldsmith (1730–74) in the title poem of *Citizen of the World*, with the explicit identification: '(*words: Goldsmith*)'. Four preceding poems reflect on the position of the writer. 'The Design', taking up an idea declared already in 'Apostle of Hope', insists that good and bad are aspects of the same reality; there is no choice but to accept. However, they must be identified honestly for what they are. In 'Apostle of Hope' the given reality includes violence, brutality, injustice; which results in the waste of effort and significant matter. The system is imperfect, with waste as a component. We can condemn brutality and injustice, but the given reality is not subject to criticism. It is a negative time, and we must accept. We can only label it for what it is. 'Complaint' states that in bad times the poet can only record. 'Echo' defines how ideally he should conduct himself and gives a few 'rules' for the labelling: in general, label it exactly for what it is, not considering any outside requirements or expectations, and applying no fixed requirement of our own.

> Thou shalt not entertain,
>   charm or impress;
> consider the response
>   or the work of others;
> confirm viewpoints,
>   satisfy expectations,
> leave crucial issues confused,
>   or impose order. (342)

'Migrants', an allegory about two butterflies, represents two different kinds of poetic response to the data – one unmethodical and impulsive, the other dogged and persistent, neither fully adequate.

> Voluptas: stinging and sweet,
> starting to die already, exposed to the air.
> Vulgaris: restless and sullen.
> Lasting a little longer.
>
> Migrants. Of limited distribution. (343)

The ideal response was expressed in 'At the Head Table' (*Madonna and Other Poems*).

Kinsella externalizes the issues by dramatizing them through Goldsmith's views on the treatment and response of the writer in *Citizen of the World or Letters from a Chinese Philosopher, residing in London, to a Friend in the East*[4] and through the views James Boswell (1740–95) expressed in *The London Journal, 1762–1763*.[5] The identification of section I with Goldsmith and of section II '*(words: Johnson)*' with Samuel Johnson is misleading. The first fourteen lines of section 1, dialogue enclosed with quotation marks, are taken from Goldsmith's *The Citizen of the World* (Letter XII). The remaining six lines of section I and all of section II are drawn not from Johnson's words or from Boswell's *The Life of [Samuel] Johnson* but from James Boswell's *London Journal* (mainly 29 December 1762; 20 January, 25 January, 8 February, 10 March, 12 March, 1763). Kinsella has rearranged the lines and omitted an occasional word but essentially the original prose passages have been altered to give them the appearance of poetry. Section III, which describes Goldsmith's death, has been taken from Boswell's *The Life of [Samuel] Johnson*.[6]

The poem begins with Goldsmith's question in relation to the treatment of Alexander Pope, the brilliant seventeenth-century poet, critic and satirist who was refused burial in the Poets' Corner at Westminster Abbey. Through this dialogue a century later, Goldsmith objectifies his feelings about public neglect of, and antagonism to, poets, and also his own experience. On being told that people have not done hating Pope, Goldsmith asks rhetorically:

> ... 'can any be found
> to hate a man whose life was wholly spent
> in entertaining and instructing his fellow creatures?'
>
> 'Yes,' says my guide, 'they hate him for that very reason.
> There are a set of men
> who take upon them to watch the republic of letters...' (343)

They are, he says, in a bitter simile, like eunuchs in a seraglio, incapable of giving pleasure themselves and hindering those who would. Furthermore, they are without literary gifts. All they need to achieve their aims is 'to be very abusive and very dull'. It is, he believes a general truth: 'Poets of any genius/are sure to find such enemies.' Pope had behaved in accordance with the contemporary view that it was the duty of the poet to follow the Aristotelian maxim to instruct and entertain; he defined the moral values behind his satires in the *Moral Essays* (1731–35) and *An Essay on Man* (1733–34). Pope's attacks on his fellow writers, notably in *The Dunciad* (1728, 1742) earned him the title 'The Wasp of Twickenham'.

At that point, while keeping the apparent connection with Goldsmith through the continuation of the 'I' persona, the poem draws upon Boswell's *London Journal*.

> During this conversation I behaved
> with a manly composure and polite dignity
> that could not fail to inspire an awe.
>
> For really, to speak seriously,
> I think there is a blossom about me
> more distinguished than the generality of mankind. (344)

The youthful Boswell, newly arrived in the big city, had such occasional highs but suffered, as *The London Journal* makes clear, from a radical sense of insecurity and a fundamental lack of confidence, perhaps even more frequently from depression, as did Samuel Johnson. Section II, attributed mistakenly to Johnson, reflects Boswell's oscillations between optimistic determination to follow 'a scheme of sober regularity' and despair when, once again, he fell into excessive expenditure and dissipation.

> I sat in close. I hated all things.
> I could see nothing in a good light. I was quite sunk.
> I looked with a degree of horror upon death. (344)

Two events in particular at this time had upset Boswell. One was that he would not get a commission in the Footguards. Owing to his circumstances – lack of funds and lack of 'pull', since his father, Laird of Auchinleck and a judge in Scotland, would not back him – it was always unlikely that he would get into the army. The other, and more immediate, was the discovery that Louisa, the actress with whom he was having an affair, had given him gonorrhoea. In other words, the specific reasons for his depression are not literary, but Kinsella adapts Boswell's feelings as a factual account of depression. Unable to enjoy life and looking 'with a degree of horror upon death', Boswell thinks of hiding from the world, even of living abroad, but remembers that he needs money. He considers taking obscure lodgings but concludes sensibly that for a man to think 'he will vex the world' by hiding from it is 'absurd': 'the world/are too busy about themselves to think of him.' He determines to follow a dignified course.

> I have resolved to preserve my own dignity;
> pay court to nobody; keep my own counsel;
> proceed consistently and resolutely,
> moving like clockwork, my affairs conducted
> with the greatest regularity and exactness;
> and follow the dictates of my own good sense,
> than which I can see no better monitor. (345)

Ideal though his resolve may be, it is not without its touch of vanity and impracticality. Boswell's purposes of amendment were temporary; the lines have a dual purpose: they express an ideal while implying that it cannot be attained. At the same time *The London Journal* is an imaginative history of his own mind and record of his life written with detachment, candour and stylistic brilliance.

Goldsmith's final words, reported in section III, cast a poignantly ironic tone over his principles articulated in the first two sections. When Goldsmith was dying, his doctor, noting that the disorder of his pulse exceeded what might be expected from his degree of fever, asked 'is your mind at ease?' 'Goldsmith answered it was not.' His ending, as Kinsella noted, was not peaceful: '3rd April 1774 ... he wakened from a deep sleep and fell into strong convulsions until he died.' (box 86, folder 1).

At the time of his death Goldsmith suffered from Bright's Disease and was seriously in debt. In fact his life was irregular and the above description of desirable behaviour, drawn from Boswell but applied to Goldsmith and couched in eighteenth-century terms, is contradicted on virtually every point by what is known of his life. He frittered away his talents, lacked discipline and had little of the self-confidence claimed in these lines. Far from paying court to nobody, he sought company, was ingratiating, played the fool, was envious of Samuel Johnson and disturbed by the success of others. He did have a fundamental integrity and was a generous, good-natured man; but his work is often careless and inconsistent, as was his life. Nevertheless, he is, for Kinsella, an example of a writer who persisted with his work despite personal and societal difficulties.

The disabling forces the writer has to contend with run through 'Theme and Variations' where they are represented in the rapacious female who is another aspect of the greedy predators. Appearing allegorically in different guises – instinctive cunning, natural hunger, selfish exhibitionism, desire for adulation, determination to be the centre of attention, in 'Coffee Shop' she is the dark temptress. Her snake image appeared in a drawing by Anne Yeats in *One*. In another context, as Kinsella records in his notes, she is the Terrible Mother, the Dura Mater, Lamia, who is also the snake and the shark, whose gaping mouth equals the abyss, who eats men, consuming flesh. In her negative aspect, Lamia, part woman, part snake, seen in a tree with writhing branches and roots, and with a spring at its root, equals waste, sterility, spiritual blockage or death; she is unseeded (box 25, folder 33). This poem brings together the daylight world of Bewley's Café where men are drinking and the dark world of the psyche represented by the snake-woman. The arrangement of stanzas illustrates this division: stanzas on the left relate to the former, three inset stanzas to the latter. Seductively 'whispering her needs', the woman represents creative absorption, mental needs and subconscious impulses. Responding sexually, the man who has been here in *The Pen Shop* drinks his 'black drink' to her. She is a darker version of the nymph in 'The Familiar'.

In 'Virgin', which deals with the same situation, both sun and moon are rapacious. In 'Undine', a female water-spirit representing death invites the passers-by to come closer '...and we will dispute together/ the detail and the whole...'. She resembles Rusalka in Slavonic myth that was regarded as the spirits of drowned girls who bewitch and drown passing men. The invitation is worded in terms that appeal exactly to Kinsella's approach to poetry. His answer – 'Womanbody/I will be passing closer on the return' – points towards the ending of *Littlebody*, where he anticipates their next meeting.

Littlebody is made up of three introductory poems with a personal and psychic setting, the title poem, and four poems in 'Cul de Sac' that focus on disappointments in family life. In the epigraph, from William Petty's *Down Survey* (1655–57), young men 'chanted beside the public way':

> *Is there any sorrow like ours*
> *who have forfeited our possessions*
> *and all respect?*

> And the virgins of the Parrish of Killmainham
> hung down their heads. (351)

The analogy between material dispossession and emotional loss is clinically defined in 'Breakdown' where the persona, experiencing the disruptions of dementia, is beset by restlessness, confusion, a 'coarsening of the personality', childish stubbornness, self-centredness, irritation and 'ceaseless indiscriminate demands on others'. 'Shop Shut', where the 'I' persona locks the door on his 'den of images', also deals with dispossession, but then opens to the attractions of the natural world:

> Summer night, Percy Lane.
> The last light full of midges.
>   Gnats out of nothing. (352)

'Gnats out of nothing' foreshadows images to come. This is the choice, the alternative to the failed system and lost beliefs. It is firmly positive in the midst of encompassing negatives, but the stoic acceptance is hard-won.

Notes made at the time of writing 'Shop Shut' and related poems, such as 'The Stable', 'Household Spirits', and some unpublished work, provide a context of ideas. In relation to images found in 'Household Spirits', Kinsella refers to nocturnal creatures that emerge: Comer's cat, the New Guinea pieces, mongrel images hanging from their hooks, half-finished things, things abandoned that included 'the dream/scheme, also abandoned'. The door has been slammed on 'the debris of system'. The squat [ape-] figures and goblins out of the Pacific, all God's and Jung's creatures, represent 'the surface inhabitants of the mind'. He imagines himself 'stooped in invocation, speechless in private, urging, asking, invoking, easing the possible and the necessary into organic existence: all those circling the correct moment in the ever-particularised saturated context' (box 87, folder 2). All this, Kinsella tells himself, may be meaningless but has to be accepted. The selection is random, the congruence is random – it may be utterly pointless, and it does not matter whether it is accessible or not. Nevertheless, he will accept and maximize it all in a long act of thanksgiving and gratitude to nothing and to a random nothing in the no-mind of a Prince of Zero, the squat sparrow-corpse up against the rusted gate panel (box 87, folder 2). The reference is to the image of a dead sparrow in an earlier draft of the poem. But tone and syntax show a kind of desperation. The reflections circle back upon themselves in frustration. Zero is no longer a place of becoming. Like Ó Rathaille on the edge, Kinsella contemplates the void, the nothingness from which things come, the nothingness towards which they go. We are back in the imagery of *Notes From the Land of the Dead*; the significant iron key, once the means of access and transformation, turns the lock on his 'den of images', moving from the unconscious, the dark underside of the mind, into the possibilities of the light which is 'full of midges'.

Rearranging some stanzas from *Madonna and Other Poems*, with slight revisions, Kinsella in 'Glenmacnass', the key poem, develops these attractions of natural beauty which replace false attachments to 'hissing assemblies', the comforts of the 'spurious' and duplicitous responses. When he holds the handful of high grass 'on a fragrant slope' above 'our foul ascending city', he chooses between urban ugliness and natural beauty.

> I turned away in refusal,
> holding a handful of high grass
> sweet and grey to my face. (352)

A deer 'sailing back and forth', looking back at the 'mess/scattered at our back door' celebrates lightness, freedom and precision in movement. The 'ribs frail/silk paw/pearl fang' of Pet, the playful cat, furthers the representation of beauty.

The poem moves simply and naturally from one set of associated images to another. The stiff and abstract language of 'Godhead' is replaced by fluency and grace. Again a ceremony that might be associated with religion takes place in the human world. When the couple sits at the kitchen table with their cups empty, they hear the voices of the crows, mates for life, flying in an orderly way 'to their place'. In each section natural images serve as emblems of beauty, freedom, fidelity and orderliness. In the final section, the narrator enters 'the quiet wood' where trees stand in order in their own grain, an image of rightness and fullness that offsets the images of unease and division in 'Breakdown'. The mysterious bat, like the snake-woman, is that part of the natural world humans cannot fully discern, but its movements echo the image of movement and flight elsewhere in Kinsella's poetry, particularly in the 'Prologue' to *One*, an 'angel' feeding, reaching out to the invisible.

> Meant only to be half seen
> quick in the half light: little leather angel
> falling everywhere, snapping at the invisible. (354)

At this point Littlebody appears in the context of black turf, white cottonheads, old cuttings, the old stony marker, the prow of rock: 'the music of pipes, distant and clear'. It is a visionary moment: a pagan shape in the air, a guttural dance, then the figure hugging his uileann pipes, playing in the open air. Tradition says, if you find the leprechaun, he has to hand over his purse of gold. Challenged to do so, Littlebody hands over his purse with a warning, in keeping with his association with death, the ultimate rapacity, and the dark stranger, 'when I dance on your ashes'. He thought he was 'safe' on the hillside: 'You have to give the music a while to itself sometimes,/up out of the huckstering'. Huckstering – showing off, prostituting your art – is not acceptable; it relates to Kinsella's dislike of poetic ornamentation. The speaker has identified this temptation in the poem's opening: 'the hissing assemblies./The...ease of the spurious'. Littlebody's 'slow air/out across the valley' is a lament for this waste. The speaker understands and respects this need to be alone, playing for the music's own sweet sake. Not accepting the Faustian bargain, unlike the magician self in *New Poems*, he refuses the purse, so can meet Littlebody on his own, uncompromising terms.

The collection concludes with negative material in the 'Cul de Sac' sequence in which 'Going Home' returns to family matters – quarrel, argument and prolonged hatred; the opposite of what was presented in 'Glenmacnass'. These, too, are part of the human context. In 'Holy Well' boys drink the water, but it tastes like a 'stale kiss', it has the taste of death. In 'Cul de Sac' the poet sees a clerical figure lying on the steps 'with his arm across his face', both school and cleric seen in a context of disuse and a dead end, whereas Littlebody was found on the heights, in images of flight, openness, old cuttings, music. The series ends with the rituals and disappointments of a family funeral in 'The Body Brought to the Church'. The notion of loss enlarges here to include the family brought momentarily together by death, but a sense of hollowness and loss pervades the poem, which ends with false promises. The service has none of the lightness, sensory pleasure or the moral and imaginative satisfactions of 'Glenmacnass'.

In 'The Body Brought to the Church' Kinsella places himself at the centre of a descriptive narrative poem. It is his observing and reflective consciousness that records the setting, the incidents and tells the story. The notes he made on the occasion provide an insight into his mood and attitude. The occasion is, he thinks, 'a pointless exercise of guilt and grief' by a family of strangers. He hardly remembers the cousin who has died, although they were born in the same year. He dislikes having to be part of 'the melody of common tedious belief', sharing a half-hour of curiosity in a vault of cement, aged and without character, where he may one day sit on his own and 'let the whole meaning and meaninglessness assemble and disassemble as it will around my tired being'. The families have lived apart. 'I know nothing about any of their lives or loves or disappointments' (box 87, folder 2). He has no sense of loss.

The poem conveys these feelings of estrangement and separation in its detached and unemotional manner. In the opening line, the woman's voice inviting him to the funeral is 'remote' and that remoteness persists through the momentary exchanges, the voice of a son who speaks with directness and love, people assembling around the coffin, communion, the sign of peace, the procession in which they join. Concealing his indifference, Kinsella goes through the motions and departs, allowing the style to express what he thinks and how he feels. This final poem has the veneer of a communal occasion, while implying the observer-participant's complex sense of separation so that what the poem does not contain is more important than what it does.

Notes

1   'Invocation', *Notes from the Land of the Dead* (Dublin: Cuala Press, 1972), p.9. The text is not included in *Collected Poems* (2001).

2   Ibid., p.15.

3   Echoing Psalm 77.39, Augustine in his *Confessions*, 1. xi. 17 – 1. xiii. 21, refers to himself as 'mere flesh and wind going on its way and not returning'.

4   Oliver Goldsmith, *The Citizen of the World or Letters from a Chinese Philosopher, residing in London, to a Friend in the East* (London: Folio Society, 1969).

5   James Boswell, *The London Journal, 1762–1763*, ed. Frederick A. Pottle (New York: McGraw-Hill, 1950).

6   Quoted by James Boswell in *The Life of Johnson*, ed. George Birkbeck Hill, rev. edn L.F. Powell, vol. 3 (Oxford: Clarendon Press, 1934), p.164.

10

THE INADEQUATE MAN

*M**arginal Economy* begins in nightmare.

> *Wandering alone*
> *from abandoned room to room*
> *down the corridors of a derelict hotel,*
> *searching for the lost urinal*...(9)

Key words carry the motif of isolation – 'alone', 'abandoned', 'derelict', and 'lost' – while the participial verbs, 'Wandering' and 'searching', emphatically placed – describe the dreamer's distress. When he awakes, he identifies those images of dereliction as 'the night facts', that is, things around him in the dark replacing the dream images. His address to 'Nightwomen,/picking the works of my days apart' echoes Hesiod, who inspected a dangerous world. Inspectors of the dreamer's achievements, the Nightwomen, hag-Muses, attend not only to what he has done but 'work' yet to come. They are looking for something in all art and may not find it here. Placing them between past and present sets the paradigm that runs through the collection.

Each of the ten poems in the collection is a narrative, its language simple and economical, unless heightened for the purpose of deflation. While being economical has a stylistic significance, it also has moral and philosophical implications. In their position between past and present, individuals interpret or relate to what has gone before with varying degrees of reliability. In effect the poems are allegories of behaviour. The first four are realistic; those that follow have looser settings.

'First Night', a colloquial narrative that relies on descriptive particulars, concentrates on that period in the early 1950s when the poet had left home after disagreement with the 'woman' there, and had begun his new life in Baggot Street. He is open to experience, determined to learn from the stranger who talks obsessively about 'the early days,/and the way everything went wrong', that is, about 1916 and the setting up of the new Irish State, but who fails to connect what went wrong with 'the realities of the past forty years'. The stranger's closed mind makes it impossible for him to adapt to change. The narrator on the other hand is open to experience. Both are in a marginal position. A 'footstep, stopped at the corner' refers to an anonymous unknown figure. An unnamed figure in the form of a grandson talking to his girl cousins, practicing his technique, is there again in the following poem, deceptively charming. The girls are in a period between innocence and experience. For them life is still a game.

Readers who investigate the incidents behind 'The Affair' discover that the figures meeting at the grave of Valentin Iremonger are identifiable, although the poem itself is careful not to be explicit about the identity of the stranger. The poem relates a series of events to account for the mutual dislike between the poet persona and the other man: early contacts when they responded to each other's work: 'My picking on one of his/self-admiring tropes./His fastening on/something slack of mine in return'; a deeper dislike when they had sharply different views on the matter of Yeats and Fascism with the result that a 'lifelong animus' developed between them. At that point the poem goes back again to their proximity in the Civil Service – 'his initials, like insects – /earlier all over my files' – before returning to a more recent event that sharpened this 'exchange across the grave', when they 'exchanged nods, in old dislike'. What follows is an angry portrait of the unnamed adversary, almost as murderous in its verbal barbs as the 'murderous review' it mentions.

The poem does not require specific identification for its particular purposes, its narrative of growing antagonism, but internal evidence relates to Conor Cruise O'Brien. The 'lifelong animus' began when they participated in a conference held at Northwestern University to commemorate the Yeats centenary in 1965. In an *ad hominem* argument O'Brien maintained that Yeats in maturity and old age was generally pro-Fascist. Because Yeats admired Kevin O'Higgins, strong man of the government who had ordered the execution of seventy-seven Republicans, and also admired Mussolini and the rise of Fascism in Europe, he was, O'Brien claimed, as near to being a Fascist as the conditions of his country permitted.[1] Kinsella strongly objected to this view of Yeats as a right-wing, Fascist thinker.

O'Brien's dismissive review of Kinsella's *New Oxford Book of Irish Verse*,[2] two years before the Iremonger funeral, had sharpened the acrimony:

> – debating his fixed viewpoints
> in a three-piece colonial accent –
> for a murderous review:
> a flow of acid colloquialisms
> dismissing a main thesis
> based on a misreading
> of the images off the cover... (15)

The illustrations showed on the front cover a view of Upper Mount Street in an aristocratic, Georgian area of Dublin and on the back a view of Grianan Ailigh, a stone-built hill fort near the Donegal and Derry border, once a stronghold of the Northern Uí Néill. O'Brien dismissed the anthology as a failed attempt to establish continuity from Irish to English in the tradition, as though the illustrations were meant to express that idea, whereas the book itself, in its subtitle, introduction, and contents, demonstrated the effects of disruption and defeat on poetry in Irish. Thereafter, there is the transition to Anglo-Irish poetry in the English language. 'It should be clear at least,' Kinsella writes in his Introduction, 'that the Irish tradition is a matter of two linguistic entities in dynamic interaction, of two major bodies of poetry asking to be understood together as functions of a shared and painful history.'[3]

O'Brien, who is portrayed as a type of faded colonial, dismisses this notion of continuity. To him 'Irish verse' can refer only to poetry in English written by Irish men and women. More than half of the collection, he points out, consists of translations from 'the Gaelic', almost all of which are by Kinsella himself, a fact he deplores, ignoring Kinsella's explanation that he did not use existing translations because of the great unevenness in the range covered and the lack of agreement on their accuracy. O'Brien also fails to comment on the quality of the translations or on the anthology's contribution to Irish culture. In Kinsella's view, his closed mind makes it impossible for him to respond with the openness that is required to appreciate the evidence that Irish tradition is made up of two strands, the Irish and the Anglo-Irish. In the former, poetry is written in the Irish language; in the latter it is written in English; in each case those who write are Irish.

As for the 'flow of acid colloquialisms', O'Brien sneers at the 'folly' of Kinsella's concept of there being such a 'thing' as an Irish poetry in two languages. Irish poetry, he says, 'turns out to be a cultural Siamese twin'. He belittles Kinsella's 'pushfulness' in using only his own translations. 'I wonder that Oxford didn't blow the whistle on that one' and adds, 'Continuity my eye!' He scoffs at the 'nonsense' about 'a bicorporate bilingual entity called Irish poetry'. Kinsella has, he concluded, 'a good, hard neck'.

'The Affair' concludes with the lowering of the coffin and with O'Brien moving off 'Under a shadow'. Implicit is a contrast between the virtues of 'our gentle mutual friend./Goldenhaired. Spent in the service', in an echo of Apuleius's Cupid, and the 'thick back' of an enemy. In the next poem, 'Wedding Service', Tom and Eleanor Kinsella attend a wedding in the 'protected world' of Trinity College. The poem has a leisurely narrative pace, with the poet as outsider, taking note of external details and in the process emphasizing the pagan reality underlying the ceremony. The meaning is in the mannered formality and the quiet registering of differences. The poet/observer, open to differences, transcends religious antagonisms. Like other figures in the collection he is on the margin between two traditions.

A Catholic service takes place in a Protestant chapel. All the details quietly support the idea that the Kinsellas are outsiders. Marginalized by religious differences, they look about at the 'avenue of old trees', 'a quiet walk', and at the bridegroom who attends to them because they are 'her' guests. Inside, the over-curious poet – 'I looked about me.' – remarks the antiquity in the wood panelling and 'ill-fitting particulars' – no statues, no Stations of the Cross, no holy water font, and people facing one another rather than the altar. With the help of a single server the priest has to carry in everything he needs to say Mass. In this place 'purged of sacrifice', the atmosphere is unlike that in a Catholic Church. There is 'No muttering over body and blood', that is, no transubstantiation, the event, central to the sacrifice of the Mass, that separates Protestants from Catholics. Nevertheless, it is ceremony as this quietly formal epithalamium affirms.

> All their hands primal.
> The Bride comely.
> The Groom steadfast.
>
> The ring fixed on her thin finger
> in loving kindness
> and firm succession of the flesh. (18)

The love that joins them is stronger than artificial differences. The poem rises above historical antagonisms between landlords and peasants and more recent sectarian prohibition by the Catholic Archbishop of Dublin against Catholic students in his diocese entering Trinity College.

Inadequate understanding and a fixed intention also characterize the allegorical 'Blood of the Innocent', which also deals with sacrifice and matches 'Wedding Service' with the special victim, unnamed, recognized and treasured from the beginning. She is destined for sacrifice by a priest-like figure who 'stands at the block/in the place of praise'. The event is rare. The last time was when a revolutionary Christ-like 'young local genius/tried to get them to change the system':

> persuading the Authorities
> that making an offering back to the source
> with an act of thanks
> is an interruption of the process.

That the life-form as we have it
is inadequate in itself; but that
having discovered the compensatory devices

of Love and the creative and religious imaginations
we should gather in each generation
all the good we can from the past,

add our own best and,
advancing in our turn
                    outward into the dark,

leave to those behind us,
with Acts of Hope and Encouragement,
a growing total of Good (adequately recorded),

the Arts and the Sciences,
with their abstractions and techniques
– all of human endeavour –

in a flexible and elaborating
time-resisting fabric
of practical and moral beauty...(22)

The revolutionary advocates a re-examination of tradition, but the executioners will not be deterred from their sacrifice of the innocent. His argument sounds persuasive in its fluency, as though the inadequacy that is inherent in the 'life form' could be replaced by an idealized, impractical proposal. In his pivotal position the young revolutionary overrates what happens, much as Conor Cruise O'Brien failed to deal with the dual tradition.

The key poem, 'Marcus Aurelius', is in three parts. '*On the Ego*' is an account of birth from an unknown source into a sensation of loss, with the mind, the *nous* or ego of Aurelius's threefold division of man, in control. To be born is to suffer 'the gasp of loss'; it is creation 'Out of nowhere' and another example of the trope of expectation followed by disappointment. Positioned at a time of transition, the Emperor is inherently incapable of dealing with some of the tasks he faces.

In Part II, Aurelius is 'in a false position' at a troubled time characterized by 'over-confidence and ignorance everywhere'. He is an observer rather than a man of action:

> cast in a main role,
> while fitted with the instincts of an observer;
> contending throughout his life with violent forces
> that were to him mainly irrelevant. (25)

He fought off the German and other tribesmen who swarmed across the Danube but cannot overcome the 'contagion' from the East 'that led to the break-up of the Western Empire'. This might seem to refer to the plague that Roman soldiers brought back from the Parthian campaign – the most destructive plague in Roman history – but actually refers to the coming of Christianity from the near East, undermining the citizens' 'depths of will', their dealings with one another, and cannot be resisted since it exists 'in the movement and nature of things'. It includes a historical process that eats away at the foundations of the Empire.

Kinsella portrays Aurelius as a gifted man in the wrong job whose duties as Emperor conflicted with his preference for philosophy. Judged to be one of the great Emperors, he is remembered best for a secondary achievement – *Meditations*, a highly personal document charged with self-scrutiny and self-admonition, which in Kinsella's view reflected the 'baffled humane' in him. Life, Aurelius observed, expanding and humanizing Stoic teaching and revealing the vein of sadness that runs through his work, is short and transient, a temporary visit to an alien land. Men must endure as best they can, must strive onward, but also turn inward to draw from their inner resources. He has the modern qualities of being both alienated and involved at the same time. The portrait develops a series of contradictions – 'accepting...but not believing', 'proposing...while pausing', 'life' and 'death':

> accepting established notions of a cosmos
> created and governed by a divine intelligence
> – while not believing in an afterlife;
>
> proposing exacting moral goals, with man
> an element in that divine intelligence
> – while pausing frequently to contemplate
>
> the transient brutishness of earthly life,
> our best experience of which concludes
> with death, unaccountable and blank. (26)

He appears as the voice of an era of tremendous change, much like the present, with the disappearance of religion, total changes in communication and the keeping of records, and Islamism, that other new force, coming from the East.

Part III shows the brutalities of life – his wife's passion for a gladiator, Aurelius having the gladiator killed and his wife bathed in his blood. Their son Commodus ruled with his father and then became sole ruler. A voluptuary who dressed up like Hercules, his megalomania led to his downfall; and after his death the 'civic affluence and stability' that characterized his father's reign turned to 'chaos and civil war'. The possibility of civilized and humane existence is destroyed. In an almost comic conclusion the son embodies the forces of dissolution.

> His plan to appear for an Imperial function
> in the arena, dressed as a gladiator,
> led to public outcry, and his assassination,
> strangled in private among his close advisors. (27)

The following poem, 'Songs of Exile', is an allegory of waiting. In a state of exclusion a tired tribe, a primitive, desert-dwelling people, await 'the Word'. They indulge in barren debate, asking which causes greater pain:

> fade and exit
> pure and faithful,
> or soiled survival
> dispersed on the world. (29)

It is a major moral choice – whether to opt for excellence, with certain extinction, or compromise, with possible survival. They decide for the latter with the result that 'we', the whole human race, are soiled and wandering, exiled from excellence. The pattern is repeated. In a different setting women are wordless and veiled, while men sing in unison, their song a sterile solo 'up to the Father'.

In Part II a closed community of slum-dwellers is trapped – 'revelling in noise and gang,/Spitting irresponsible'. They are shut in, the young dissatisfied, the soul, seat of impulse, according to Marcus Aurelius, confined behind a lattice that separates 'her' from the beauty outside.

> Looking out at the day and the bright details
> descending everywhere, selecting themselves
> and settling in their own light. (30)

Sterile confinement contrasts with those natural processes. The community waits passively for 'the Word', which never comes, their inactivity indicative of their state of exile from life. Here the allegory is intensified to a state of total exclusion; victims of, as Kinsella points out, the 'wrong' choice are looking out at natural excellence, in a 'good' world.

In 'Marginal Economy' the 'We', in a particular instance in the 'wrong' (or real) world, have a bleak existence as they work out towards 'the edge' but find little, their search requiring more and more care, their reward growing less and less until they have to move on again.

> We accepted things as they were,
> with no thought of change.
> The only change was in ourselves:
> moving onward, leaving
> something more behind each time. (31)

They manage as well as conditions permit. It is a modest achievement, but it is achievement, positive, exactly measured and gained within a limited time, which is also accepted. They make no great claims for what they do and realistically do not wait for 'the Word' to change their lot.

'Songs of Understanding', a philosophical statement about the conditions of existence and humanity's role, generalizes about the real, or 'wrong' conditions. In Kinsella's view, reality includes 'waste', 'process', 'excess', and 'inadequacy' which seem to have no function, yet are essential and must be accepted:

> ... the waste and the excess,
> and a fundamental inadequacy
> in the structure as a whole
> and in each individual part,
> there is still an ongoing dynamic
> in the parts as they succeed each other,
> and in the assembling record,
> that registers as positive. (32)

There is a dynamic that can be taken as purpose. Through waste, excess and inadequacy comes an 'ongoing', 'dynamic', 'positive' effect. The following stanza entertains the illusion, once articulated by Augustine, of advance toward a 'final meaningful goal', 'of advancement toward the End', a belief Kinsella does not share. Section III, a recipe for the well-intentioned individual, reduces the illusion to a four-line summary:

> Reclaiming out of the past
> all the good you can use,
> add all the good that you can
> and offer it all onward. (33)

Section IV adjusts the perspective as it takes in a 'fault on the outermost rim', on the edge of existence, there for an entire lifetime, 'a glimpse of preoccupied purpose' so compelling in its cold indifference to man that it 'chilled the blood in my face'. The section warns the well-intentioned individual that he will not (or may not) matter.

The poem is virtually a manifesto of these elements that are substantial in Kinsella's work, an act of faith that the positive ones can offset the negative forces; but he does not exaggerate. A 'self-selective few' may interpret this balance of opposites as 'purposeful', a matter of communal endeavour towards a meaningful goal. Section III sums up in a tone of ironic resignation, but his vision of the fault is chilling, a modification of any tendency to be optimistic. This idea is taken up in the concluding poem, 'Rhetoric of Natural Beauty', which is connected with the mathematical cover design of two almost complete half-domes divided from each other by a horizontal bar. This resembles the crimson sunset 'halved' in 'seeming fullness' before night falls; the speaker's doubts fall silent: 'fulfilled in acceptance,/reflect, and disappear'. Man's doubts are momentarily stilled by the beauty of God's creation seen in the apparent fullness of the sunset before 'the dark embrace' of night.

> In the face of God's creation
> our last doubts fall silent.
>
> fulfilled in acceptance,
> reflect, and disappear. (34)

They who wait for a sign in the Heavens or a Word will wait in vain. The poet has no such illusion. The 'preoccupied purpose', mentioned in 'Songs of Understanding', is indifferent to the individual and to a people. This final poem, together with the image on the cover, dramatizes the self-reflecting meaninglessness – a seeming whole, actually on the verge of vanishing.

Marginal Economy is a lucid and coherent collection, subtly developed and unified through recurrent issues that are taken up successively, expanded from simple exposition to more complex illustration, and defined in the end in realistic terms. Its portrayal of inevitable historical decline is also fundamental to the next collection, *Man of War*, which returns to one of Kinsella's fundamental beliefs: man is prone to war.

This long poem reflects on man's capacity for violence. Two epigraphs – 'On being asked to sign/an appeal for the abolition of war' and 'an epistle to the hopeful in heart' – explain the work's origin and purpose. The poem itself is divided into three sections entitled 'Argument', 'Retrospect' and 'A Proposal', followed by 'Notes' which contains seven footnotes and is about the same length as the other three. The interaction between text and footnote creates an unusual tension, since the footnotes not only support what is being said in the body of the text but do so in different ways – by illustration, simile, analogy, confirming, extending or providing specific evidence. They both disrupt and arrest, making it necessary in the course of reading, or subsequently, to move from text to footnote in order to respond as required to the dynamic between the two.

The entire work reiterates in more extended and detailed fashion what Kinsella has often made the informing idea of his poetry: man has a propensity for violence. The evil that men do is fundamental and has been revealed and examined in successive poems. *Man of War* is a conclusive measuring *sub specie aeternitatis*, with and through the perspectives of evolution, civilized advance and historical time of man's destructive proclivity, recurrently and variously made manifest. Within the main text and also in the footnotes there is an accumulating, selective use of literary and historical examples from history, the Old Testament, the Dead Sea Scrolls, Homer, and various later sources. At the heart of the poem, hidden within its eloquent demonstrations that war is inevitable, is a lament for the waste of human resources, for the loss of 'profound potential', because by his very nature man is compelled to engage in self-destructive activity. Thereby he negates his finest achievements, his capacity for rational engagement, for orderly arrangements, and for civilized procedures.

'Argument' outlines the evidence in history, in evolution, in biblical narratives, in civilized advance. It sets down the 'brutal basis' on which the subject has to be considered. Throughout the section the deployment of evidence is compelling, the illustrations of combat vigorous, the language blunt and realistic. Historical evidence shows that rational behaviour and achievement are undermined by war. Man is distinguished from animals by 'the willed, and mass, occasional destruction/of others, face to face, of the same kind'. The 'mark' of Cain is ineradicable.

We would be startled and transfixed were we to see 'other living creatures' behave as man does:

> —employing every means at their disposal
> and draining their essential life resources
>
> to the detriment of every other need,
> with prodigies of gallantry and skill
> beyond exhaustion, reason and despair—...(9)

The enormity is in the emphatic language – 'every means', 'essential', 'every other need' 'prodigies', 'beyond' and 'organised for self-extermination'. This is what sets man apart. The simile of the ants in footnote 1, '*An insect analogue*', illustrates cold and methodical destruction; they too, 'organised for self-extermination', 'destroy their own kind'. Text and footnote make the same point.

So extreme is human behaviour, Kinsella argues, that a 'just Observer' would, as Moses did, introduce the virtues of 'Mercy. Love. Control.' to stop the madness. That effort failed and the Old Testament God punished the people, as footnote 2, '*By the Dead Sea*', points out in plain, apocalyptic language.

> Then the rains of Hell will descend
> on every part of the earth.
> The rivers will flood with fire
> so the trees on their banks will burn
> from the sources out to the sea.
>
> Tongues of flame will discover
> the fault in the world's foundations
> and all in the land of the living
> at the hour of the final judgment
> will wail as they cease to be. (22)

The 'chosen species' are set apart by the mark of Cain. This is the 'Curse' they must bear. Their accomplishments are perverted to military uses for which they have an irrational proclivity. The evidence of the butchery that accompanied the First Crusade, cited in footnote 3, '*A sleeping cancer*', demonstrates how even a 'holy call' can be deflected into a self-renewing brutality:

> —the taste of vengeance. Drunk on Jewish blood,
> they wiped their swords, and crossed the Rhine, renewed,
> raping onward toward Jerusalem. (23)

Changing to a more regular rhythm, 'Retrospect' describes ceremony, picturesque panoply, and apparently honourable exchanges that seem to elevate military action to an acceptable kind of behaviour but juxtaposes them with horrific illustrations of butchery and mayhem that destroy all notions of the picturesque, all grandeur, all pretensions to civilized behaviour. In its jaunty rhythm the style upholds the notion of honourable procedures but at the same time exposes its hollowness in excessive alliteration:

> Then the reality, the raw disorder
> —discipline and breeding to the winds:
> howling and rioting in all directions;
> spears and rapiers into breasts and bowels;
> axes hacking heads and necks asunder;
> swords and sabers slicing arms and faces;
> blades and barbs buried in body parts. (12)

The tangle of horses, frequently depicted in Renaissance and other paintings to express the pain and 'bedlam' of battle, is the ultimate metaphor.

> lost in the bedlam: legs in disarray,
> blood and entrails, heads flung up, jaws open,
> whinnying and staring like mad fruit. (12)

Footnote 4, '*The War Horse*', sees the 'bedlam' from the perspective of cavalry horses. The rhetoric of acclamation, taken from the Book of Job, celebrates the horse who disdains fear, exults in his strength, faces weapons, becomes weapons, and responds eagerly to the sounds of battle.

> He gallops in the valley, loving his strength,
> laughing at fear. He attacks armies!
>
> He does not avoid weapons: he wears weapons
> —a shield, a sharp spear and a lance—...(24)

In the main text, terms and syntax seem to praise improvements in weapons of destruction – 'arms evolving', 'maturer methods', 'could be inflicted', 'could penetrate', 'increased in skill', 'restoring the precision while/maintaining the choice' – but conclude in the oxymoron of 'shining showers of death'. Civilized advance results in more specialized weapons, more efficient means of mutual slaughter.

In grotesque ceremony, one side would surrender to the other, the honourable sword of one commander presented to the other. Self-deceiving ceremony does not alter the fact that 'Self-annihilation' is still a 'given'. The section ends with the absurd ceremony of judgement, punishment and execution. The analogies from *The Iliad* and other classic texts in footnote 5, '*Instances from the Greek*', provide the matching evidence. Naval battles reveal a chaos similar to what has been described in land engagements:

would the triremes bear down upon each other,
ranked poles beating the salt surface,
in battle order to the point of contact.

Then the confusion. Multiple collisions.
Oars let fall and weapons seized in riot,
the sailors leap from ship to ship, transformed,

coming at each other in the chaos...(26)

Meanwhile the common man, no longer excluded, is given 'an equal role in serious affairs'. The sentimental *'Old Soldier'* in footnote 6 prolongs the notion of inclusiveness; he is the deceiving and self-deceived voice of these 'brothers in arms'. Finally, the poem describes modern warfare, bombing raids and atomic destruction; human advance through scientific discovery results in even greater carnage.

'A Proposal' presents reasonably argued but unsustainable solutions. Adopting the role of man of reason, in a voice of controlling irony, Kinsella says, he would sign, 'all protests and appeals' for the abolition of warfare, if he could see 'where to send them that would have effect'. There is, he acknowledges, no prospect that any solution, no matter how reasonable or high-minded, is going to succeed. To limit battle to oral conflict, as he proposes, or to put leaders in a pit to fight to the death will not work. Given that impossibility he proposes acceptance of the 'Curse' but with control so that violence may take place only between professionals in a closed space.

His third proposal made with Augustan detachment and Swiftian irony advocates the establishment of a policy in which heads of state and all those responsible should be allowed to face each other in a carnal public rite:

...sending the leaders
and all responsible for the decisions
and free from body contact until now,
naked against each other in a pit...(17)

Heads of state, however, are unlikely to arrange for their own deaths.

'Irresponsible Leadership—a particular case', footnote 7, muses in apparent puzzlement why some are chosen for total power. Possible explanations – family background, the right connections, social manners – are not persuasive. The individual portrait resembles the leader he had described in 'Tyrant Dying', the inflexible man who unleashed his huge forces, 'with simple rhetoric and a lack of feeling', 'careless of the carnage'

he caused. Continuing in his role, the poet offers himself as willing assistant in the arbitration of cases of dispute 'at mortal chess', although not 'with hangings or decapitations', since he dislikes bloodshed. But he would, if needed, help with the 'administration': 'preparing the site; preparing the instruments;/consoling the victim on the night before', even assisting on the day as though participating in the celebration of a 'sacrifice'. In these final lines the irony that has permeated the proposal becomes exquisite.

The ultimate irony is that a poem which in its immediate origins began as a refusal to sign an appeal for the abolition of war became in the course of composition, arising from psychic depths and conducted in an eighteenth-century rationalist manner, a powerful exposition of man's self-corrupting addiction to violence and in tandem with that a lament that his potential for fine achievement is so irretrievably blunted by that addiction. Written as an occasional poem, *Man of War* advances a series of reasons to support the premise that people are prone to violence, ridicules the ceremonial trappings that disguise this reality, and provides a set of apparent, but absurd solutions. In effect the suggestions are just as sensible as, or even a distillation of, the reality of opposing masses of individuals slaughtering one another without any personal reason. The poem's argument is circular, moving from the position that war is inevitable to its conclusion that war is inevitable.

Continuing the examination of abstract issues from *Godhead* and *Marginal Economy*, the poems in the companion collection, *Belief and Unbelief*, are characterized by delicate relationships between phrase, line and line units, and by their adapting elements within the poem for an overall purpose. 'Novice', the opening poem, clarifies a process of learning in which the alert 'I' speaker is defined through a method of inspection, in particular his precise description of the death moth:

> the jointed gut pointed back straight;
> the little stick legs angled
> > up off the back and forward off the neck ... (7)

His conclusion that it resembles 'Exactly' its illustration in the animal book he examined as a child in 'Bow Lane', confirms his ability to inspect closely and to reach a conclusion:

> the species that sucks and swallows
>
> only while it is growing; that cannot eat
> once it reaches maturity.
> > Designed for its exact needs. (7)

'Designed for its exact needs': the physical definition has an aesthetic application. It reaffirms the trust in data that has been at the heart of Kinsella's work from the beginning and which he advocated as a critical procedure in *Readings in Poetry*. The observing novice is 'alive' to the rhythms of the world, past and present: the flowing river, the memory of the smell of old clothes and of his name in the book – as in 'Bow Lane' – the 'dry ancient smell off the death moth' which, in a wanton act of rejection/refusal, reminiscent of the child's refusal of a generous little gift in 'The High Road', he squeezes into the moss on a stone.

'Delirium', which deals initially with electro-shock treatment, moves from images of violence – 'Uproar', 'strapped', 'straining', 'jerking, 'wired', 'drained', medical attendants like 'masked assassins', the healer 'distant' – to recovery and a prayer for release from the treatment and from inquisitive 'familiars' whom he dismisses: 'Come to see us sick/that would not see us well.'

'Superfresh' relates a chance meeting in a supermarket with a Russian woman who asks where he came from. Two strangers, both old, both far from home, experience a moment of intimacy. The clarification emerges from small details and perceptions.

> I touched the backs of my fingers
>
> against her cheek, abstract-intimate,
> in a fragrance off the shelves
> of Italian loaves and French boule. (11)

The bread's fragrance intimates the ability to appreciate sensory pleasures of all kinds.

That belief recurs. In 'A Morsel of Choice', in another encounter, it is the woman who is animated and alert. Imagining 'plucking something wet off her tongue', he catches 'a distant taste of the raw random'. He interprets randomness as a positive force preventing us from becoming hardened and keeping us alert, even in old age. In the following poem 'Echo', the deliberate return to the place of first love fulfils an old promise:

> They revealed their names
> and told their tales
> as they said they would
> on that distant day
> when their love began. (13)

The process seems complete, yet the woman whispers 'a final secret/

down to the water', thereby intimating the incompleteness of even the happiest and most lasting of relationships.

In the allegorical 'Art Object' a predator, totally committed and fulfilled in the act, sinks her fangs into a 'young prey'. The scene, depicted on the cover of the collection, illustrates the relationship between the artist/creator and raw material. Her victim, understanding her need, accepts his part: 'Another's need fulfilled.' The interpretation is clear: 'his lot/to be selected at random, and stopped'. Later, others consume what is left in a process that is 'moderate and methodical – and also necessary–'. The poem illustrates the paradigm of random selection, acceptance, understanding and fulfilment, which is central to the relationship between the artist and his material.

The concept of randomness itself echoes through Kinsella's work from 'An Old Atheist Pauses by the Sea' (*Moralities*) to the fortuitous conjunction of 'Cover Her Face' (*Downstream*), the search through the 'shambles' of 'Nightwalker', 'the noble accident' in 'St Paul's Rocks: 16 February 1832' (*New Poems*), and his ideas about the processes of creativity. 'A Selected Life' insisted that each new beginning is as 'random' as any that preceded it.

The second section of the collection entitled 'Belief and Unbelief' begins with related parables. In 'Legendary Figures, in Old Age' old women retain 'without shame' their capacity for 'intimate companion-ship' and play; their sexual relationship – 'with all that remained/of the barbed shafts', of Cupid's dart – diminished but not impeded by age; their sense of themselves affirmative. 'We cannot renew the Gift/but we can drain it to the last drop.' The contrasting poem 'Lost Cause' exemplifies superficiality and self-delusion. Instead of inspection, these 'others', 'grey-featured and slow-moving', deal 'only with the sympt-oms,/endlessly'. Because of their inadequacy, they are aging into eternity, failing to bring the process of understanding, 'the causes of their complaints', to its conclusion.

In 'Ceremony' he describes a return visit to a church – 'the great black door', 'high darkness', 'pious presences', 'the hidden Host'. The cere-mony is the solitary sacrament/celebration of the loss of faith. The poem's matter-of-fact tone conveys the lack of response. Instead of a spiritual experience, he finds himself, 'considering/the detail of the cold stone' and being aware of his own physical nature – the 'breath warm on my fingers', 'knees damp and chill'. The narrative concludes,

> I will return through the high dark
> among the shadowy believers
> to the orderly interests of the day. (19)

Life and love are found not in the darkness of the building, but in the orderly processes of the world outside its walls. 'Foetus of Saint Augustine' also affirms the value of the non-religious world. It takes place after the loving interplay of his parents. In a humorous conceit the future theologian/philosopher, is imagined in embryo:

> as though examining the terms offered,
>
> or examining the carnal basis
> for issues of such spiritual complexity,
>
> or as if listening for a breath of wind
> that has passed, and might return. (20)

The 'terms' include the sexual or carnal but the lines refer to the entire bodily/worldly basis of his boundless spiritual speculations. Physicality, as each of these poems insists, is primary, even to someone noted for his power of reasoning. In images taken from Augustine's *Confessions* he will see both flesh and Divinity as something that passes and does not return.

'Genesis' describes life among a primitive people in Ireland and then compares their experiences to those of people in our present world. Their stories, plainly listed – 'of exile and dispossession,/family division, fatal women, honour and shame/rivalry, wrath, alien kings, births foretold or exchanged' – resemble those of people in our time. They too, live under the sign of death, of Morrígan.

> And Fate took shape once and settled among them.
> On a great stone, as a bird with black wings. (21)

These certainties are assessed further in another statement of values in 'Prayer I' and 'Prayer II'. In the modern world, where the community is 'disordered and misguided', the more accomplished and more fulfilled people stand aside 'unwilling to take part'. He prays that the 'minds and hearts' of the main body may heal and fulfil and that redemption will follow. Redemption is

> a turning away
> from regard beyond proper merit,
> or reward beyond real need,
> toward the essence and the source. (22)

He proposes in 'Prayer II' that the cardinal humours may not become hardened but remain capable of the fluidity of understanding.

> That the rough course
> > of the way forward
> may keep us alert
> > for the while remaining. (23)

The final poem, 'Addendum', offers reassurance. The speaker –
Whoever or Whatever started and is responsible for existence – asks that
we remember that 'My ways', which may seem to be 'mysterious and
unfair/and punishing to the innocent',

> will justify in the end
> the seeker after justice
> and not the power seeker
> crumpled in his corner. (24)

The lines are ambiguous: they promise reconciliation and a time when
'the seeker after justice' will be rewarded, but those who do not seek
after justice have to endure baffling uncertainty. The situation resembles
the Christian message of ultimate redemption and understanding, but
only after one has lived through a lifetime of injustice. This leads to
unbelief. The idea that life on earth is merely a preparation for life after
death is a gamble too far. The black bird is more real, the gifts of earthly
love and of the raw random are more attractive. The readiness is all.

Just as each poem in *Belief and Unbelief* is finely tuned technically, so
the collection is orchestrated about its subject matter. It states Kinsella's
belief in the physical and in sensory apprehension. Love, personal
engagement and death are real, demonstrably part of human experience.
At the same time he expresses his disbelief in concepts of Divinity and
the idea of supernatural redemption.

In the first section the death moth is perfectly adapted for its needs,
the poet makes contact with the woman from Russia and tastes invigor-
ating life on another's tongue. The animal feeds deep in emblematic
figuration of the necessity to do so. These are allegories of belief. The
theme continues in the next section: the love-play of the old affirms their
commitment to sensuous feeling; not to dig deep, not to examine, to
refuse, as the 'Novice' does is a form of failure in 'Lost Cause'. The
religious institution fails in 'Ceremony', whereas life triumphs. Saint
Augustine will learn the physical basis of existence. For all its adum-
bration of evolutionary time, 'Genesis' concludes with death, the
ultimate reality, as present now as it was in 'Landscape and Figure'. In
a misguided age the better people stand apart, in unbelief, and wait for
'the first sign of redemption'. If what 'Addendum' offers sounds like
Christianity, what the poet defines is at least based on what he has

actually experienced. In these later collections Kinsella enters a period of detached reflection in which there is little evidence of the harried self.

Notes

1   O'Brien's talk was subsequently published in the *TriQuarterly* (Fall 1965) and included as 'Passion and Cunning; An Essay on the Politics of W.B. Yeats', *In Excited Reverie*, eds. A. Norman Jeffares and K.G.W. Cross (London: Macmillan, 1965).
2   *The Observer*, 8 June 1986, p.25.
3   'Introduction', *The New Oxford Book of Irish Verse*, p.xxvii.

CONCLUSION

It is not because of anything he has done that Thomas Kinsella lives on the margin of society. If he sees the world as flawed, that is because his perception never allows him to forget the forces that take away innocence. If his awareness of evil is grievous, his response is potent; the dynamic between what sours and what saves hard-won and enduring. Out of an unendurable reality, out of erosion, waste and bitter experience, he seeks to create lasting beauty.

Initially he faced the threat with panache, executing stylish poems in conventional forms but, while he articulates his sense of threat, he also dramatizes it as a shocking awakening. The poems themselves are manifestations of order. To be able to shape experience into lyric form is a victory over mutability. To be able to write exploratory narratives that absorb particular surroundings and historical events is to clarify his relationship with the outside world.

Recognizing that evil has a human origin, he explored its manifestations in the world that produced him. 'Nightwalker' merged public and private experience; in its double vision he found a means to establish a wide focus through which to perceive himself and what shaped him. What he observes in the Ireland of the time not only corresponds to how he feels, but by coming under the management of the critical intelligence, also demonstrates both the possibilities of the creative process and the ordering process of the poetic intelligence. In its imagined drama of self and society it finds the structure the questing self needs, creating out of multiple voices and forms a complex portrait of what it was like to be Thomas Kinsella, who has been shaped by various forms of violence, political, religious, cultural, educational.

A portrait of the isolated artist thrown back upon his own resources, 'Nightwalker's central premise is that he is part of what depresses. He will not deny who and what he is. In many ways the poem foreshadows what will occupy Kinsella's attention in later collections. All the autobiographical poems are grounded on the premise that he will accept himself as he is and will explore the self and its familial contexts without distortion. 'Nightwalker' is the poem in which acceptance, hitherto taken for granted, becomes an article of faith.

The order perceived in 'A Country Walk' and 'Downstream' is balanced, one set of experience countered by another. But he will distort that symmetry to find a form that draws them into closer involvement, one with the other. The 'Wormwood' poems illustrate the idea that life is a bitter drink. This is a darker idea of the self's situation. It is a truer reflection of how he feels about the world and about the conditions in which man exists. Because of the way in which the world is – contaminated by the star that fell – man may become embittered, and this is a form of death. The solution is to accept the tainted cup and to find in that acceptance the only individual joy. Instead of being shocked by evil, as he had been in 'Downstream' and 'Nightwalker', he deals with it, creates scenarios that demonstrate its presence and effects. In the past, love was an essential reassuring presence: now it is part of a new paradigm, a dialogue of lovers in which the woman is the strong, silent partner. Life is a bitter business, a daily nightmare that must not be overlooked, but absorbed. That is the only way to turn adversity into something positive. Nature is dying, day is unbearable, but paradoxically the lovers will endure only if they drink the bitterness. There is nothing starry-eyed about this love. What the 'Wormwood' poems stubbornly affirm in tone, texture, and theatricality, is that love persists, no matter how aggressive the destructive forces may be. Deprived of peace, denied redemption, excluded from the secret garden, the marriage partners do not give way to despair. This is a moral position.

The ethic of suffering also has an aesthetic component. This is ultimately the theme of the 'Wormwood' poems. Out of nightmare comes the poetry that describes it. Agony so endured results in the poetry that illuminates it without reservation. In these grim encounters the poet has to rely on himself – there is no appeal to God or philosophy but to his beloved to get him through it. 'Nightwalker' is another example. Kinsella will absorb its depressing scenario and out of its unattractive reality make his poetry. To confront suffering is to be energized enough to recover from it, temporarily.

A self-dramatizing mode runs through the early work – in lyrics, longer narratives, poetic sequence and psychodrama. It identifies, lays out for analysis, broods over, pulls apart, pursues in different linguistic terms. If it eventually fragments poetic structure, it also achieves a new coherence. If it voices fear, anger, love or determination, it also overcomes bewilderment by survival techniques. 'Phoenix Park' has its philosophical reassessments, 'Wormwood' its handicapped protagonist, 'Nightwalker' its multiples presences, 'Cover Her Face' its numbed witness, 'The Laundress' its harmonious relationships. These are many-faceted illustrations of, and responses to, life's exigencies. They speak of an intelligence and imagination that are irrepressible, successively rise above trauma and anguish to deal with experience. In 'Nightwalker' the perplexed self knows that there is a gap between the way things seem and the way things are. In 'Phoenix Park' the poet creates a coherent reflection in which there is no disjunction between appearance and reality. Art can transcend division even as it incorporates it. It can both reflect and readjust. At the basis of the poetic vision is strength of purpose won out of adversity that makes adversity itself the basis of strength. In a sense Kinsella adapts to hardship. It fits his sensibility, excites his imagination, challenges him deeply, for out of conflict he creates his versions of truth. The options are failure and death.

The true journey is evolution. In its unappeasable life-hunger, the self advances through a succession of experiences. Everything is linked. What went before connects with what follows, in life as in art. There is a plenitude of implication in 'From the Land of the Dead'. The plunge into the abyss, a deliberate fall out of consciousness, is another metaphor. The path of individuation results in a more complete understanding. The paradigm of child and grandmother says it all; the vegetation myth and the archetypal journey lead to renewal. Aeneas went into the underworld, Dante descended through the circles – both come back reconfirmed. Once again the poems enact the drama of individual encounter, deepened and more comprehensive, in the knowledge that the outcome is ordained, verified in the archetypes.

What Kinsella learned from Jung confirmed what he had intuited through experience and reflection. Entering the psychic treasure house of mankind, he found there validating analogies in myth. Furthermore, if myth helps him to understand his own experience, it also improves communication with the reader who completes the circle of understanding because he, too, connects with mythic experience. What is most striking about 'From the Land of the Dead' are the interconnections between the poems and the confirming presence of myth and the transforming use of language. The poet's associative intelligence now comes into its own.

Thomas Kinsella's interest in the artist – his duties towards himself, subject and audience – is constant. The more he learned about the creative process and its psychic sources, the more he thought about the position of the artist. The death of Seán Ó Riada brought these concerns into immediate focus. Kinsella's sense of loss, largely implicit, is nevertheless a constant presence. Through their mournful particulars, the elegies raise the issues of art and the artist into pressing imaginative reality. By means of their austere discipline, style and structure he gathered his powers to meet the challenge of a death that was overwhelming and insistent. Death's hunger had surfaced throughout the early collections, blending with universal instances of violence and decay. But this death touched him where it mattered – at the heart of his preoccupation with what was most important to him. In the Ó Riada poems Kinsella entered the land of the dead, its landscape and monuments, its legacy and ghostly presence, its losses and emotional pressures. More than that, he thought about promise and failure, the optimism of untried youth, the power of the artist to transform a cultural heritage, to speak to a whole people, to reflect their deepest feelings, to be fulfilled temporarily as a result. But, he knew that what was gained in one engagement left the artist exposed to the demands of the next subject, the gap between what might be achieved and the difficulty of making it happen. He imagined the beam of light coruscating down the sky as confirmation of what might be possible but then countered it by the facts of pain and darkness.

These mysteries of choice and potential entail the evaluation of achievement and personal worth. Other poems range out from the individual instance of Ó Riada or the poet's father. *The Good Fight* concerns itself with the examination of character, the nature of leadership, the qualities required, and the way they are used. Weighed in the balance between Kennedy's confidence and Oswald's repression, it concerns itself with motivating forces. Plato and Frost are also balanced in scales that tip in favour of the poet, who has the better measure of what may happen to individual hopes. All unreasonable things may happen. To be 'unillusioned' is better than to be disillusioned; it is closer to reality and less likely to be shocked by experience. 'Nightwalker' had its harrowed victim, who had his season in hell. He did not shirk reality then, he does not shirk it now. He does not succumb to the tragic vision, but works through it.

The power of the artist is real, expressed in the idea of a concentration so powerful that it becomes transformative. The metaphor is central; it is the paradigm of the union of the male principle with its destined other. Creative engagement expresses the primary hunger: in *One* a people settle in, engage with the land, discover its saturated depth, its responsiveness. The voyagers in 'Finistère' arrive and recreate in the cycle of advance and failure. The carpenter's bench yields its spermatozoa. They enact the process of consumption, satiation and renewed need. Even the shock contact between child and grandmother has its rewarding insight.

Poems salute intensity as well as persistence. Despite setbacks, such as the death of Ó Riada, struggles in his personal life or the disappointment when the numerological system fails, Kinsella did not turn away from his task. He had always believed in the presence of change and erosion and disappointment. Philosophical and religious ideas did not provide answers to his uncompromising questions. The collapse of system also had to be absorbed and made part of the poetry. As explanations of experience the archetypes turn out to be inadequate. The issue of causation persists, without resolution. A new realism emerges in the later books, a cool appraisal and reappraisal of politics, philosophy, religion and the way in which the artist is treated. At the same time Kinsella continues to delve into psychic material, the love relationship, children, family, Dublin, philosophy, religion and the nature of art itself.

In the aftermath of his loss of faith in the numerological design and his trust in Jung's theories, there is a harder edge to Kinsella's approach. In a succession of defining positions, he moves away from the orchestrated lyricism of *Her Vertical Smile* and the integrated complexity of individual points of view to an engagement with specific topics – society, business-men, women, religion, public response, personal values and the role of the artist. The artist on the margin takes a critical look at basic issues. In his own state of strain and disappointment, he returns to what has made him, determined to clarify issues once again. The Stranger is the embodiment of danger associated with corruption in Church and State, associated also with Fate and the menace of meaninglessness that presses in upon the poet, a chameleon figure, his presence suspected even when not seen. Through his reflections on Ó Riada's death and the engagement with Mahler came the realization of nothingness, of meaninglessness at the heart of things. This is the belief that underlies later collections. It underpins his feelings about the Stranger. It is caught in the figure of Ó Rathaille trapped between powerful opposing forces. He is on the margin, on the edge, as figures will be in *Marginal Economy*. The concept underlies all these later collections, propelling their no-holds-barred evaluations, their occasional angry outbursts. Appraisal, assessment, judgement, condemnation, praise, selection are the terms that function and are enacted in an orderly approach, a clipped diction, a determination not to exaggerate. The style refuses ornamentation. It avoids lyricism, at times is cryptic and tight-lipped.

The systematic evaluations are carried out without flourish or fanfare. If society as a whole is wishy-washy when it comes to exact accountancy of values that should operate, the strict assessment of the role of religion in our lives, or strict assessment of the value of beauty, then the poet will take on the responsibility, his duty being to condemn where condemnation is merited and praise where praise is due. This clears the air, strips away dishonesty, muddled thinking and passivity. If he is isolated and out of touch, at least he will know where he stands, will define himself in relation to major topics, even the most major of all – the power of Divinity in the modern world.

In the past men turned to Divinity, but for Kinsella this is no longer possible. *Godhead* analyses received wisdom about the Trinity, does not shirk the task of measuring the Divine, of trying to extract whatever sign of goodness or helpful connection he can. The diminution in God's power is starkly imagined in the contrast between Saint Augustine's confidence and Kinsella's questioning. But, he concludes, the Divine and the human are alike. Both can conceive a possible creation, but the result is less than that envisioned. Both are inadequate. It is a further stark delimitation of possibility. There is no outside Being or power that might help. We are on our own. *Marginal Economy* subtly develops this belief further. It defines his position with an exact measuring, each poem working within a simple language to a modest assessment but a crystal clear outlook: there is no redemption from outside, no Word that will affect human existence, no magnificence on the horizon. The analogy with Christianity is unmistakable. Nevertheless, he will carry on, doing what he does. *Man of War* is a dynamic demonstration of man's destructive appetite for self-annihilation. *Belief and Unbelief* has a greater serenity and detachment. If there is no expectation, there is less disappointment. This form of self-criticism insists on absolute clarity and honesty. There is at the heart of Kinsella's sensibility a yearning for harmony and completion. His empathetic nature suffers from his bleak assessment of existence. The terms that expressed his earlier perception – ignominy, mutilation, brute necessities – have been replaced by excess, waste and process. If the voice of the Almighty, like God speaking to Moses, commands him to proclaim the fact of mortality, that injunction conveniently approves in any case what Kinsella has been doing for years. In a more general assertion, implicit in several poems, the Irish are like the Israelites, awaiting a Redeemer who will take them out of exile, but like the Israelites they have given in to evil ways. They worship the false Gods of Commerce and Greed. Nevertheless, they, and their traditions, are marginal survivors, custodians of 'something'. At times Kinsella is like Bloom, a wanderer among an exiled people, at times like Moses to whom God speaks but who is unable to bring his people into the Promised Land.

Death is a reality, connected with the Stranger, the context of all Kinsella does and of all relationships. It sets limits that he never ignores and determines the toughness of his perception of life. Other people may choose to ignore that looming fact, but for him it is a kind of personal nemesis stalking everything he does and affecting his thinking. It underlies all experience, is part of the nothingness, part of the 'meaningless'; dampens down false enthusiasm and requires absolute honesty in the assessments of life's reality and possibilities.

When he was working on 'From the Land of the Dead', he recorded his appreciation of Darwin's belief in organic order. It is, he wrote, something we do not and never will fully understand, but we must not conclude from that it is beyond understanding, that is, meaningless: a realization of meaninglessness at the heart of things (box 25, folder 33). Darwin's conclusion became an article of faith for Thomas Kinsella:

When we no longer look at an organic being as a savage looks
at a ship, as something wholly beyond his comprehension;
when we regard every production of nature *as one which has had
a long history*; when we contemplate every complex structure
and instinct as the summing up of many contrivances, each
useful to the possessor, in the same way as any great
mechanical invention is the summing up of the labour, the
experience, the reason, *and even the blunders* of numerous
workmen; when we thus view each organic being, how far more
interesting – *I speak from experience* – does the study of natural
history become![1] (quoted in box 25, folder 33)

In the margin he approved of all the italicized words: every production
of nature is the result of significant experience; blunders are part of
waste; and of the final affirmation. He quotes his own lines from
'Wormwood' on 'the restored necessity to learn': 'the only individual
joy'. (62) There is, as Darwin believed, an order at work.

   In his bleaker moods Kinsella puts down a depressing marker. Nothing
matters. What the artist does makes no difference. In a less pessimistic
mood he identifies what is valuable – certain people and events, the
possibility of an aesthetic order, the discovery of beauty among the debris
of modern life. Instead of the idea of a rational God, he accepts the given
situation, past and future, substituting something like 'accident'. In the
absence of a Divinity, Eleanor is the Muse-goddess, source of creativity
who opens her arms to him, understanding and embracing his inadequacy.
He is not Zeus but Hephaestus, who carries a handicap. Although he is
not unique in his inadequacy, the artist is on the margin, isolated,
neglected by an indifferent public, his work misunderstood, unable to
communicate. So he speaks to projections of himself – historical figures
like Ó Riada, Diderot, Goldsmith, St Augustine, Marcus Aurelius, and
many others, voicing opinions and values through them. It is a fascinating
imaginative landscape, peopled by historical figures, a personal pantheon
to which he can relate. He worked this method of dramatic externalizing
in *Out of Ireland*, *The Good Fight* and *Her Vertical Smile*, but it has been
developing. From the start he has been a poet of many voices. In a sea of
indifference and false expectations of art, in an almost valueless world,
how should the artist conduct himself? As Dante's example confirms, he
should denounce evil and discover beauty.

Note

1   Philip Appleman, ed., *Darwin. Selected and Edited* (New York: W.W. Norton & Co.,
    1970), p.196.

SELECT BIBLIOGRAPHY

Primary Sources

Poetry

Poems (Dublin: Dolmen Press, 1956).

Another September (Dublin: Dolmen Press, 1958).

Moralities (Dublin: Dolmen Press, 1960).

Poems & Translations (New York: Atheneum, 1961).

Downstream (Dublin: Dolmen Press; London: Oxford University Press, 1962).

Wormwood (Dublin: Dolmen Press 1966).

Nightwalker (Dublin: Dolmen Press, 1967).

Nightwalker and Other Poems (Dublin: Dolmen Press; London: Oxford University Press, 1968).

Nightwalker and Other Poems (New York: Knopf, 1968).

Tear (Cambridge, MA: Pym-Randall Press, 1969).

Butcher's Dozen. Peppercanister 1 (Dublin: Peppercanister Press, 1972).

A Selected Life. Peppercanister 2 (Dublin: Peppercanister Press, 1972).

Finistère (Dublin: Dolmen, 1972).

Notes from the Land of the Dead (Dublin: The Cuala Press, 1972).

Notes from the Land of the Dead and Other Poems (New York: Knopf, 1973).

Selected Poems: 1956–1968 (Dublin: Dolmen Press; London: Oxford University Press, 1973).

New Poems 1973 (Dublin: Dolmen Press, 1973).

Vertical Man. Peppercanister 3 (Dublin: Peppercanister Press, 1973).

The Good Fight. Peppercanister 4 (Dublin: Peppercanister Press, 1973).

One. Peppercanister 5 (Dublin: Peppercanister Press, 1974).

A Technical Supplement. Peppercanister 6 (Dublin: Peppercanister Press, 1976).

Song of the Night and Other Poems. Peppercanister 7 (Dublin: Peppercanister Press, 1978).

The Messenger. Peppercanister 8 (Dublin: Peppercanister Press, 1978).

Fifteen Dead. Peppercanister Pamphlets, 1–4 (Dublin: Dolmen Press, 1978; London: Oxford University Press, 1979).

One and Other Poems. Peppercanister Pamplets, 5–7 (Dublin: Dolmen Press; London: Oxford University Press, 1979).

Poems 1956–1973 (Winston-Salem, NC: Wake Forest University Press; Mountrath, Portlaoise: Dolmen Press, 1979).

Peppercanister Poems 1972–1978 (Winston-Salem, NC: Wake Forest University Press, 1980).

Poems 1956–1973 (Winston-Salem, NC: Wake Forest University Press, 1979; Dublin: Dolmen Press, 1980).

Songs of the Psyche. Peppercanister 9 (Dublin: Peppercanister Press, 1985).

Her Vertical Smile. Peppercanister 10 (Dublin: Peppercanister Press, 1985).

Out of Ireland. Peppercanister 11 (Dublin: Peppercanister Press, 1987).

St Catherine's Clock. Peppercanister 12 (Dublin: Peppercanister Press, 1987).

One Fond Embrace. Peppercanister 13 (Dublin: Peppercanister Press, 1988).

Blood and Family. Peppercanister Pamphlets, 8–12 (London: Oxford University Press, 1988).

Selected Poems 1962–1989 (Helsinki: Eurographica, 1989).

Personal Places. Peppercanister 14 (Dublin: Peppercanister Press, 1990).

Poems from Centre City. Peppercanister 15 (Dublin: Peppercanister Press, 1990).

Madonna and Other Poems. Peppercanister 16 (Dublin: Peppercanister Press, 1991).

Open Court. Peppercanister 17 (Dublin: Peppercanister Press, 1991).

From Centre City. Peppercanister Pamphlets, 13–17 (Oxford: Oxford University Press, 1994).

Collected Poems 1956–1994 (Oxford: Oxford University Press, 1996).

The Pen Shop. Peppercanister 19 (Dublin: Peppercanister Press, 1997).

The Familiar. Peppercanister 20 (Dublin: Peppercanister Press, 1999).

Godhead. Peppercanister 21 (Dublin: Peppercanister Press. 1999).

Citizen of the World. Peppercanister 22 (Dublin: Peppercanister Press, 2000).

Littlebody. Peppercanister 23 (Dublin: Peppercanister Press Press, 2000).

Collected Poems 1956–2001 (Manchester: Carcanet Press, 2001).

Marginal Economy. Peppercanister 24 (Dublin: Dedalus Press; Manchester: Carcanet Press, 2006).

A Dublin Documentary (Dublin: The O'Brien Press, 2006).

Man of War. Peppercanister 26 (Dublin: Dedalus Press; Manchester: Carcanet Press, 2007).

Belief and Unbelief. Peppercanister 27 (Dublin: Dedalus Press; Manchester: Carcanet Press, 2007).

Selected Poems (Manchester: Carcanet Press, 2007).

Thomas Kinsella Poems 1956–2006 (Claddagh Records Limited, 2007)

Translations

Longes Mac Unsnig: Being the Exile and Death of the Sons of Usnech (Dublin: Dolmen Press, 1954).

Thirty-three Triads. Translated from the XII Century Irish (Dublin: Dolmen Press, 1955).

The Breastplate of St Patrick (Dublin: Dolmen Press, 1954; rev. as *Faeth Fiadha: The Breastplate of St Patrick* (Dublin: Dolmen Press, 1957).

The Táin. Táin Bó Cuailnge (Dublin: Dolmen Press, 1969, 1982; London and New York: Oxford University Press, 1969).

An Duanaire. 1600–1900: Poems of the Dispossessed. Trans. Thomas Kinsella. Ed. Seán Ó Tuama (Dublin: Dolmen Press with Bord na Gaeilge, 1981, reprinted 1994).

The New Oxford Book of Irish Verse (Oxford: Oxford University Press, 1986).

Essays, Notes and Anthologies

'Note on *Another September*', *Poetry Book Society Bulletin*, 17 (March 1958).

The Dolmen Miscellany of Irish Writing. Ed. with John Montague (Dublin: Dolmen Press, 1962).

'Note on *Downstream*', *Poetry Book Society Bulletin*, 34 (September 1962).

'Poetry and Man', *Art: The Measure of Man, Directions*, Judith Hall (ed.) (Springfield, IL: Illinois Art Education Association, 1966–1967), pp.7–8.

'Poetry Since Yeats: An Exchange of Views', *Tri-Quarterly*, 4 (1965), pp.100–11.

'Note on *Nightwalker and Other Poems*', *Poetry Book Society Bulletin*, 55 (December 1967).

'The Irish Writer', in W.B. Yeats and T. Kinsella, *Davis Mangan Ferguson? Tradition and the Irish Writer*, ed. Roger McHugh (Dublin: Dolmen Press, 1970). Reprinted in *Éire-Ireland*, 2, 2 (1967), pp.8–15.

'The Divided Mind', in Seán Lucy (ed.), *Irish Poets in English, The Thomas Davis Lectures on Anglo-Irish Poetry* (Dublin and Cork: Mercier, 1972).

Statement, in James Vinson (ed.), *Contemporary Poets* (London: St. James; New York: St. Martin's Press, 1975).

Statement, in *Contemporary Authors: A Bio-Biographical Guide to Current Authors and Their Works*, James Vinson (ed.), Vols. 17–18 (Detroit: Gale Research Co., 1976), pp.263–4.

'Ancient Myth and Poetry: A Panel Discussion', David Greene, Thomas Kinsella, Jay Macpherson, Kevin B. Nowlan, and Ann Saddlemyer, Moderator, in Joseph Ronsley (ed.), *Myth and Reality in Irish*

Literature (Waterloo, Ontario: Wilfrid Laurier University Press, 1977), pp.1–16.

'Preface', in Seán Ó Riada, *Our Musical Heritage*, ed. Thomas Kinsella. Music Ed. Tomás Ó Canainn (Dublin: Dolmen Press, 1982).

'W.B. Yeats, the British Empire, James Joyce and Mother Grogan', *Irish University Review*, 22 (Spring–Summer 1992), pp.69–79.

'Origins of Ancient Irish', *PN Review*, 20, 1 (1993), pp.20–8.

The Dual Tradition: An Essay on Poetry and Politics in Ireland. Peppercanister 18 (Manchester: Carcanet Press, 1995).

'A Note on Irish Publishing', *The Southern Review*, 31, 3 (1995), pp.633–8.

'Preface', in Stephen Enniss (comp.), *Peppercanister 1972–1997. Twenty-Five Years of Poetry* (Emory University Archives and Libraries Series, No. 3, 1997).

'The Dolmen Press', in Maurice Harmon (ed.) with introd. in *The Dolmen Press: A Celebration* (Dublin: The Lilliput Press, 2001), pp.133–55.

Readings in Poetry. Peppercanister 25 (Dublin: Dedalus Press; Manchester: Carcanet Press, 2006).

Interviews

Orr, Peter. 'Thomas Kinsella'. *The Poet Speaks: Interviews with Contemporary Poets* (London: Routledge & Kegan Paul, 1966).

Haffenden, John. 'Thomas Kinsella'. *Viewpoints: Poets in Conversation with John Haffenden* (London: Faber and Faber, 1981), pp.100–13.

O'Hara, Daniel. 'An Interview with Thomas Kinsella', *Contemporary Poetry: A Journal of Criticism*, 4 (1981), pp.1–18.

Deane, John F. '*A Conversation*', *Tracks*, 7 (1987), pp.86–91.

Fried, Philip. 'Omphalos of Scraps', *Manhattan Review*, 4 (Spring 1988), pp.3–25.

O'Driscoll, Dennis. 'Interview with Thomas Kinsella', *Poetry Ireland Review* 25 (Spring 1989), pp.57–65.

Badin, Donatella Abbate. 'Excerpts from 14–15 August 1993 Interview'. *Thomas Kinsella* (New York: Twayne, 1996), pp.193–201.

Secondary Sources

Appleman, Philip, (ed.), *Darwin. Selected and Edited* (New York: W.W. Norton & Co., 1970).

Augustine, *Confessions* (Oxford: Clarendon Press, 1992).

Badin, Donatella Abbate, *Thomas Kinsella* (New York: Twayne, 1996).

Bethge, Hans, *Die chinesische Flöte: Nachdichtungen* (Leipzig: Insel Verlag, 1907).

Boswell, James, *The London Journal, 1762–63*. (The Yale Editions of the Private Papers of James Boswell). Ed. with introduction and notes by Frederick A. Pottle (New York: McGraw-Hill, 1950).

— *The Life of [Samuel] Johnson*. George Birkbeck Hill (ed.). L.F. Powell (Rev. edn). Vol. 3 (Oxford: Clarendon Press, 1934–50, 6 vols).

Brown, Terence, *Ireland: A Social and Cultural History 1922–2002* (London: Harper Perennial, 2004).

Dante, Alighieri, *The Divine Comedy*. Charles S. Singleton (trans.) (Princeton, NJ: Princeton University Press, 1970).

Diderot, Denis, *Selected Writings*. Lester G. Crocker (ed.) (London: Collier-Macmillan, 1966).

Goethe, Johann Wolfgang von, *Faust*. Stuart Atkins (trans.) (Cambridge, MA: Suhrkanl/Insel, 1984).

Goldsmith, Oliver, *The Citizen of the World or Letters from a Chinese Philosopher, residing in London, to a Friend in the East* (London: Folio Society, 1969).

Haffenden, John, 'Thomas Kinsella'. *Viewpoints: Poets in Conversation with John Haffenden* (London: Faber and Faber, 1981).

Harmon, Maurice, 'By Memory Inspired: Themes and Forces in Recent Irish Writing', *Éire-Ireland*, 8 (1973), pp.3–19.

— *The Poetry of Thomas Kinsella: With Darkness for a Nest* (Dublin: Wolfhound, 1974).

— 'Nutrient Waters', *Poetry Ireland Review*, 21 (Spring 1988), pp.20–4.

— '"Move, if you move, like water": The Poetry of Thomas Kinsella, 1972–88', in Elmer Andrews (ed.), *Contemporary Irish Poetry: A Collection of Critical Essays* (London: Macmillan, 1992).

— 'Ancient Lights in the Poetry of Austin Clarke and Thomas Kinsella', *Éire-Ireland*, 29, 1 (1994), pp.123–40.

— 'The Dolmen Miscellany', in Maurice Harmon (ed. with introd.), *The Dolmen Press: A Celebration* (Dublin: Lilliput Press, 2001), pp.92–8.

— 'Thomas Kinsella: Poet of Many Voices', in Barbara Brown (ed.), *Selected Essays* (Dublin: Irish Academic Press, 2006).

Jackson, Thomas H., *The Whole Matter: The Poetic Evolution of Thomas Kinsella*. (New York: Syracuse University Press; Dublin: Lilliput Press, 1995).

Jacobi, Jolande, *The Psychology of C.G. Jung* (London: Routledge & Kegan Paul, 1942).

John, Brian, *Reading the Ground: The Poetry of Thomas Kinsella* (Washington, DC: Catholic University Press, 1996).

Joyce, James, *A Portrait of the Artist as a Young Man* (London: Jonathan Cape, 1916).

— *Ulysses* (New York: The Modern Library, 1934).

— *Dubliners* (London: Jonathan Cape, 1950).

— *Finnegans Wake* (New York: The Viking Press, 1947).

Jung, C.G., *Memories, Dreams, Reflections*. Richard and Clara Winston (trans.). Aniela Jaffé (ed.) (London: Collins, 1963).

Macalister, R.A., (ed. and trans.), *Lebor Gabála Érenn: The Book of the Taking of Ireland (Book of Invasions)*, 5 vols (Dublin: Irish Texts Society, 1938–1956).

O'Brien, Conor Cruise, 'Passion and Cunning: An Essay on the Politics of W.B. Yeats', in A. Norman Jeffares and K.G.W. Cross (eds), *In Excited Reverie* (London: Macmillan, 1965).

— Review of Thomas Kinsella's *The New Oxford Book of Irish Verse. The Observer*, 8 June 1986, p.25.

Ó Tuama, Seán, 'The World of Aogán Ó Rathaille'. *Repossessions* (Cork: Cork University Press, 1995).

Rees, Alwyn and Brinley Rees, *Celtic Heritage: Ancient Tradition in Ireland and Wales* (London and New York: Thames & Hudson, 1961).

Ronsley, Joseph (ed.), *Myth and Reality in Irish Literature*. (Waterloo, Ontario: Wilfrid Laurier University Press, 1977).

Synge, John Millington, 'The Playboy of the Western World', in Ann Saddlemyer (ed.), *Collected Works. Plays* (Toronto: Oxford University Press, 1968), pp.51–175.

Tubridy, Derval, *Thomas Kinsella: The Peppercanister Poems* (Dublin: University College Dublin Press, 2001).

Yeats, William Butler, *Responsibilities: Poems and A Play* (Churchtown, Dundrum: The Cuala Press, 1914).

— *The Poems: A New Edition*. Richard J. Finneran (ed.) (Dublin: Gill and Macmillan, 1983).

INDEX

Abbey Theatre, 28
accentual form, 124, 137,
  see *amhrán*
Adler, Alfred, 84
Aeneas, 184–5, 224
allegory, 26, 50, 68, 80, 142, 159, 169, 194, 209
alliterative, 125–26, 135, 142
Amergin, first poet of Ireland, 28, 69, 91, 181, 189
amhrán, 137, 140, 144
amour courtois, 120–21, 124, 133, 162
'Ancient Myth and Poetry: A Panel Discussion' (1977), 34–5
Anglo-Irish War of 1919–21, xi, 16
Another September (1958), ix, xiii, xvi, 1, 3, 10, 11, 53
Auden, W.H., xviii, xx, 182
Augustine, 50, 167, 189, 192, 210, 219, 220, 227, 228
  City of God, 192
  Confessions, 219
  De Trinitate, 192
Aurelius, Marcus, xxii, 5, 167, 169, 207–9, 228
  Meditations, 208
Austrian Empire, 52, 92–3, 95–6

Badin, Donatella Abbate, xxi
  Thomas Kinsella (1996), xxi
Baggot Street, x, xii-iii, 52, 53, 186, 203
Ballylee, Thoor, 26
Ballymun, xiv, 170
bardic, 102, 112, 120–21, 123, 162
Barry, Kevin, xi
Basin Lane, ix, xii, 53, 88, 184
Battle of the Boyne, 146
Battle of Kinsale, 131
Beckett, Samuel, 92
Belief and Unbelief (2007), xxiii, 165, 169, 216–21
Bethge, Hans, 60, 63, 79
  Der Abschied des Freundes, 60, 79, 92
Bloody Sunday, xv
Bolcáin, Glen, 129,
  see '*A Selection of Verses attributed to Suibne Geilt*', Kinsella-translations
Book of Invasions, 37, 39, 45, 50, 70, 181, 184
Book of Kells, 62
Book of Leinster, 104
Bosch, Hieronymus, xii, 96
Boswell, James, xxiii, 168, 189, 194, 196–7
  The London Journal, 168, 195–7